Crystal Reports 9 For Dummies®

Standard Toolbar

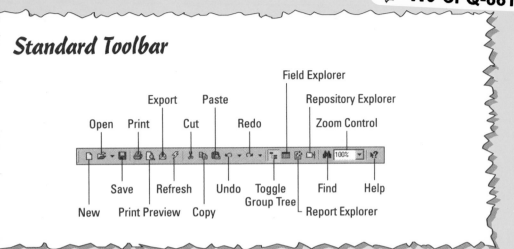

Open · Print · Export · Cut · Paste · Redo · Field Explorer · Repository Explorer · Zoom Control

New · Save · Print Preview · Refresh · Copy · Undo · Toggle Group Tree · Report Explorer · Find · Help

Formatting Toolbar

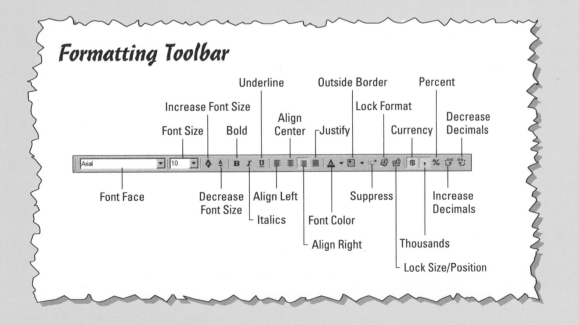

Increase Font Size · Underline · Outside Border · Percent

Font Size · Bold · Align Center · Justify · Lock Format · Currency · Decrease Decimals

Font Face · Decrease Font Size · Align Left · Italics · Font Color · Align Right · Suppress · Lock Size/Position · Thousands · Increase Decimals

For Dummies: Bestselling Book Series for Beginners

Crystal Reports 9 For Dummies®

Cheat Sheet

Expert Tools Toolbar

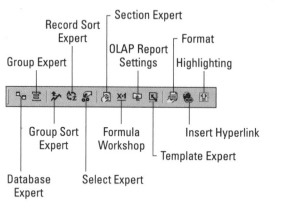

- Section Expert
- Record Sort Expert
- OLAP Report Settings
- Format Highlighting
- Group Expert
- Group Sort Expert
- Formula Workshop
- Insert Hyperlink
- Template Expert
- Database Expert
- Select Expert

Insert Tools Toolbar

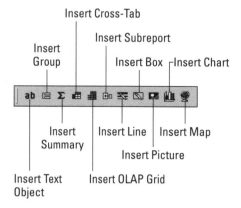

- Insert Cross-Tab
- Insert Subreport
- Insert Group
- Insert Box
- Insert Chart
- Insert Summary
- Insert Line
- Insert Map
- Insert Picture
- Insert Text Object
- Insert OLAP Grid

For Dummies: Bestselling Book Series for Beginners

Crystal Reports® 9

FOR

DUMMIES®

by Allen G. Taylor

Wiley Publishing, Inc.

Best-Selling Books • Digital Downloads • e-Books • Answer Networks • e-Newsletters • Branded Web Sites • e-Learning

Crystal Reports® 9 For Dummies®

Published by
Wiley Publishing, Inc.
909 Third Avenue
New York, NY 10022

www.wiley.com

Copyright © 2002 by Wiley Publishing, Inc., Indianapolis, Indiana

Published by Wiley Publishing, Inc., Indianapolis, Indiana

Published simultaneously in Canada

For general information on our other products and services or to obtain technical support, please contact our Customer Care Department within the U.S. at 800-762-2974, outside the U.S. at 317-572-3993, or fax 317-572-4002.

Wiley also publishes its books in a variety of electronic formats. Some content that appears in print may not be available in electronic books.

Library of Congress Cataloging-in-Publication Data:

Library of Congress Control Number: 2002108110

ISBN: 0-7645-1641-8

Manufactured in the United States of America

10 9 8 7 6 5 4

1B/RW/QY/QS/IN

Wiley Publishing, Inc. is a trademark of Wiley Publishing, Inc.

About the Author

Allen G. Taylor is a 30-year veteran of the computer industry and the author of 20 books, including *SQL For Dummies, Database Development For Dummies,* and *SQL Weekend Crash Course.* He lectures nationally on databases, innovation, and entrepreneurship. He also teaches database development internationally through a leading online education provider and teaches digital circuit design locally at Portland State University. For the latest news on Allen's activities, check out www.allengtaylor.com. You can also contact Allen at allen.taylor@ieee.org.

Dedication

This book is dedicated to my son, Sam Taylor, who frequently interrupted me during the writing of this book to discuss matters of the utmost importance. This did wonders for keeping my life in balance.

Author's Acknowledgments

Many people have contributed to the quality and content of this book. I would particularly like to recognize Kristina Kerr of Crystal Decisions for her helpfulness, to my acquisitions editor, Terri Varveris, for her overall management of the project, to my editor, Susan Pink, for keeping me honest, and to my technical editor, Allen Wyatt, whose input has made this a far better book than it otherwise would have been.

I also appreciate the unflagging support of my family and the interest of my friends and colleagues. It would not have been possible to complete a project of this magnitude without the support of those close to me.

Publisher's Acknowledgments

We're proud of this book; please send us your comments through our online registration form located at www.dummies.com/register/.

Some of the people who helped bring this book to market include the following:

Acquisitions, Editorial,
and Media Development

Project Editor: Susan Pink

Acquisitions Editor: Terri Varveris

Technical Editor: Allen Wyatt,
Discovery Computing, Inc.

Editorial Manager: Carol Sheehan

Media Development Supervisor:
Richard Graves

Editorial Assistant: Amanda Foxworth

Production

Project Coordinator: Dale White

Layout and Graphics: Laurie Petrone,
Heather Pope, Jacque Schneider,
Jeremey Unger, Erin Zeltner

Proofreaders: Susan Moritz, Carl Pierce,
TECHBOOKS Production Services

Indexer: TECHBOOKS Production Services

Publishing and Editorial for Technology Dummies

Richard Swadley, Vice President and Executive Group Publisher

Mary C. Corder, Editorial Director

Andy Cummings, Acquisitions Director

Publishing for Consumer Dummies

Diane Graves Steele, Vice President and Publisher

Joyce Pepple, Acquisitions Director

Composition Services

Gerry Fahey, Vice President of Production Services

Debbie Stailey, Director of Composition Services

Contents at a Glance

Cartoons at a Glance

By Rich Tennant

"I appreciate that your computer has 256 colors. I just don't think that they all had to be used in one book report."

page 303

"WELL, OBVIOUSLY ONE OF THE CELLS IN THE NAVIGATIONAL SPREADSHEET IS CORRUPT!"

page 291

"No, it's not a pie chart, it's just a corn chip that got scanned into the document."

page 7

Ever the innovator, Larry beta-tests the Personal Belt-Buckle Assistant/Wireless Fax.

Hold on a second, Stu, I'm getting a fax.

page 275

"This isn't a quantitative or a qualitative estimate of the job. This is a wish-upon-a-star estimate of the project."

page 61

"I did this report with the help of a satellite view atmospheric map from the National Weather Service, research text from the Jet Propulsion Laboratory, and a sound file from 'The Farting Lungworms' new CD."

page 157

Cartoon Information:
Fax: 978-546-7747
E-Mail: richtennant@the5thwave.com
World Wide Web: www.the5thwave.com

Table of Contents

Introduction

• •

Crystal Reports 9 is the latest in a long and celebrated series of report writers for personal computers. Crystal Reports is by far the best-selling report writer package in the world, although you may have never heard of it. In the past, it has been bundled with many of the most popular applications without being acknowledged by name. It's currently bundled into Microsoft's Visual Studio .NET as well as being sold as a standalone product. If you want to produce a top-quality report quickly, Crystal Reports is the top choice to do the job.

About This Book

Crystal Reports 9 For Dummies is an introductory level book that will get you using Crystal Reports quickly and effectively. It covers all the major capabilities of Crystal Reports but doesn't bog you down in intricate detail. The objective is to give you the information you need to produce the types of reports that most people need most of the time. I also get into some out-of-the-ordinary report types that you might be called upon to generate on occasion.

Use this book as a handy reference guide. Each chapter deals with an individual feature that you may need at one time or another. Pull out the book, read the chapter, and then do what you need to do. In many cases, step-by-step procedures are given for commonly needed operations. You might find it worthwhile to lay the book down beside your computer and perform the operations as you read about them.

Anyone who may be called upon to produce a report based on database data can profit from the information contained in this book. It is also valuable to managers who may never personally produce a report, but have oversight of people who do. This book will tell you what is possible, what you can do easily, and what takes a little more effort to accomplish. This will help you estimate how long it should take to produce reports of various types.

Conventions Used in This Book

When an instruction in the book says, for instance, File⇨Save, it means to click the left mouse button on File in the main menu, then click Save on the submenu that drops down from it. If a menu selection has an underlined character, that means the underlined character is a hot key. If you press and hold down the Alt key while simultaneously pressing the hot key, it's the same as clicking that menu item.

Anything you see that is printed in a monospaced font is code. `This is a monospaced font`. Crystal Reports executes code that you enter as formulas or SQL commands.

What You're Not to Read

You can read the book through from cover to cover, working through the examples, although you don't have to. Whether you read it all the way through or not, you can use it as a quick reference when you want to perform a particular operation that you have not used in a while.

Consider yourself exempted from the requirement to read anything preceded by a Technical Stuff icon. This material may be interesting to techies like me (there must be some of you out there) but generally is not necessary for a full understanding of how to use Crystal Reports.

Foolish Assumptions

I've never met you, but because we're going to be together for a while, I'll make a few assumptions about you and what you know. I assume that you know how to use a personal computer and that you're somewhat familiar with Microsoft Word. If you know how to navigate around Microsoft Word, you already know almost all there is to know about navigating around Crystal Reports. The user interfaces of the two products are similar.

I assume that you've seen directory trees before, such as those extensively used in Microsoft Windows. You know that if you see a plus sign to the left of a node represented by a folder or other icon, it means you can click the plus sign to expand that node, to see what the node contains. Crystal Reports treats trees in a similar way.

I assume you know how to perform a drag-and-drop operation with your mouse. In Crystal Reports, when you click an object and start dragging it, your progress is shown by a rectangular placement frame. When you release the mouse button to drop the item, the placement frame is replaced by a duplicate of the item that you dragged.

How This Book Is Organized

This book contains six major parts. Each part contains several chapters.

Part 1: Reporting Basics

Part I introduces you to Crystal Reports and the art of report creation. You find out what a report should accomplish and what should it look like. Then you fire up Crystal Reports and use it to create a simple report based on data held in a database.

Part 11: Moving Up to Professional-Quality Reports

You can do many things beyond the basics to make reports more focused, more readable, and easier on the eye. This part gives you the information to do all those things.

Part 111: Advanced Report Types and Features

Part III gets into serious report creation. With the information in this part, you'll be able to zero in on exactly the data you want and display it in the most understandable way. You'll be able to nest one report within another, pull report elements from multiple non-database sources, present multidimensional data in OLAP cubes, and illustrate points with charts and maps. With these tools, you can produce reports fit for the eyes of the organization's CEO.

Part IV: Publishing Your Reports

After you create a report, you'll want to make it available to the people who need it. Crystal Reports makes it easy for you to distribute your report for viewing by any of the most popular methods. You can print it; you can export it to a file; you can make it available for viewing on a local area network; you can fax it to people around the world; or you can upload it to the Web. After you complete report development, distribution is easy.

Part V: Programming with Crystal Reports

Although Crystal Reports does a great job when used all by itself, you can also incorporate it into applications written in a computer language. Crystal Reports' new SQL Commands facility gives you direct control over the data in a report's underlying database. Because Crystal Reports is included as an integral part of Microsoft's .NET application development environment, you can incorporate the power of Crystal Reports into applications you write in Visual Basic, Visual C++, Visual C#, or any language compatible with the .NET framework. This gives the applications you write the sophistication of the world's leading report writer.

Part VI: The Part of Tens

It's always good to remember short lists of best practices. That's what the Part of Tens is all about. Listed here are pointers that will help you produce outstanding reports with a minimum of effort and in the shortest possible time.

Icons Used in This Book

Tips save you a lot of time and keep you out of trouble.

Pay attention to the information marked by this icon — you may need it later.

Technical Stuff is detail that I find interesting and you may also. But if you don't, no big deal. It is not essential to gain an understanding of the topic being discussed. Skip it if you like.

Heeding the advice that this icon points to can save you from major grief. Ignore it at your peril.

Where to Go from Here

Now you're ready to start finding out about creating professional quality reports based on data stored in your databases, using Crystal Reports 9. Crystal Reports 9 is the latest version of the most popular report writer in the world. You can use it to quickly whip out simple reports, or you can take a little longer and generate a world-class executive report.

Part I
Reporting Basics

The 5th Wave   By Rich Tennant

"No, it's not a pie chart, it's just a corn chip that got scanned into the document."

In this part . . .

There's data in the database, where it's not doing anyone any good. Your manager wants coherent information, based on that data, on her desk by the close of business today. What should you do? Panic? Consider joining the Foreign Legion?

There's no need to do anything drastic. The chapters in this part quickly tell you how to crank out the report your boss so desperately needs. It won't have all the bells and whistles that you find out about in other parts of this book, but it will put the needed information on the boss's desk before the lights go out tonight. And you'll start to build your reputation as a person who can deliver the goods when the pressure is on.

Chapter 1

Transforming Raw Data into Meaningful Information

In This Chapter

▶ Outlining the major features of Crystal Reports 9

▶ Discussing the four editions

▶ Viewing an existing report

Computers can store and process enormous amounts of data, and with the relentless advance of technology, those capabilities will soon become even more mind-boggling. Even now, the major challenge of getting value from computer systems is not to make them more powerful but to harness the power they already have in a way that delivers useful information to people.

Megabytes or gigabytes of raw data are neither meaningful nor useful to people. Instead, we need organized information, distilled and focused on answering specific questions. In businesses and enterprises of all kinds, organizing and presenting information has traditionally been the job of documents called *reports*. These documents generally consist of multiple pages that can include text, numbers, charts, maps, and illustrations. The best reports convey the facts needed to make the best decisions, unobscured by the clutter of data that is irrelevant to the task at hand.

Crystal Reports has been a leading report-writing application package for more than a decade and is by far the most commonly used report writer in the world. Many people have been using Crystal Reports unknowingly for years because it has been integrated with other applications and not specifically identified by name.

Major Features of Crystal Reports 9

Crystal Reports 9 includes all the features that made Crystal Reports 8.5 a worldwide best-seller, plus exciting new features that will save you time and effort as you develop your reports. Crystal Reports 9 is tightly integrated, so all the individual components of the system work together seamlessly to support the creation, modification, distribution, and viewing of reports.

Data Explorer and Report Experts provide highly intuitive visual tools that step you through the process of creating a report. The new Crystal repository and report templates allow you to reuse components or entire reports. There is never any need to reinvent the wheel. If a component in the repository or a report template comes close to meeting your requirements but doesn't meet them exactly, you can make minor modifications a lot easier than creating an equivalent component or report from scratch.

Formatting a report

The primary job of a report writer such as Crystal Reports is to take data from a database and put it into a pleasing, logical, and understandable format for viewing by users. With Crystal Reports, you are well-equipped to give your reports the appearance you want — without having to become a formatting guru.

Crystal Reports offers both absolute and conditional formatting. With *absolute formatting* you can put text, titles, charts, maps, columns of figures, cross-tabs, and graphical images pretty much anywhere you want on the screen. You can handle preprinted forms. You can optimize for screen display or for printing on paper. This is close to the ultimate in freedom, but not quite. *Conditional formatting* takes you one step further toward the ultimate by giving you the power to change the format of the data you're displaying based on the content of the data itself. With conditional formatting, every time the data in a report changes, a formula that you include in the report can cause the appearance of the report to change too.

A new feature of Crystal Reports 9 is the report alert. Suppose that a value being displayed crosses a critical threshold that requires immediate action on the part of the report's target audience. When that threshold has been crossed, not only is its value displayed, but a report alert dialog box pops up that can't be ignored.

Another new feature is the Template Expert, which enables you to create and save a report template that you can then use to quickly format multiple reports with a common look. This could potentially save you lots of time and labor.

Enhancing a report with formulas and custom functions

In the preceding section, I mention that conditional formatting makes use of formulas to change the format of a report. You can use formulas for far more than that. A formula is like a little computer program that can make computations or other manipulations of the data before displaying the result. This makes Crystal Reports more than merely a report writer that takes your data and puts it into a nice format. You can use formulas to select specific records or groups of records to display. You can declare and use variables in formulas. All the common flow of control structures (If-Then-Else, Select Case, For, While Do, and Do While) are available.

After you create a useful formula that you might want to use again later, you can save it as a custom function. Custom functions are added to the standard functions that come with Crystal Reports, so if you ever want to reuse a formula that you have created and saved as a custom function, it will be available to you.

Getting visual with charts and maps

Crystal Reports has excellent capabilities when it comes to the graphical display of data. All the most commonly used chart types are available, so you can display your data graphically in the most meaningful way. If the data happens to be geographical, involving countries, regions, provinces, or cities, Crystal Reports can give you visual depictions of them with maps. A variety of methods are available to associate values with specific regions, including colors, symbols of various sorts, and even charts.

Displaying a report

Crystal Reports is designed for distribution in today's highly connected environment. You can build reports that are optimized for viewing by people at any computer attached to your organization's local area network. You can also put a report on the Web, for viewing by anyone who has a Web connection and a browser. Of course, you can also distribute your reports the old-fashioned way by printing them on paper and putting them on the target reader's desk.

Distributing a report

You can get your report into the hands of its intended recipients in many ways. As just mentioned, you can print it and deliver it by hand. You can fax the report directly from your computer to a fax machine anywhere in the world.

You can also export the report to a file. Crystal Reports supports many output file formats, including HTML for viewing over the Web. At least one of these formats is bound to be readable by the people in your audience. The one caveat here is that if you export a report to any format other than the Crystal Reports native format (.rpt), you may lose some of the report's formatting in the process. You can even export directly to an application, such as Microsoft Word or Lotus Domino. In such a case, Crystal Reports will launch the target application and open your report in it.

Supplying Crystal Reports with data

As important as the output formats of a report are, the inputs to the report are equally important. Crystal Reports shines in this area too. It accepts data from a wide variety of data sources, including both personal computer databases such as Microsoft Access and enterprise-wide client/server databases such as Oracle, IBM's DB2, and Microsoft's SQL Server. In fact, Crystal Reports can accept data from any ODBC-compliant database or any data source that complies with Microsoft's OLE DB standard. Essentially, if your data exists in a commonly used modern data source, Crystal Reports will be able to use it.

The Four Editions of Crystal Reports 9

Crystal Reports 9 comes in four editions that differ in their target audiences and their capabilities. The four editions are the Standard Edition, the Professional Edition, the Developer Edition, and the Advanced Edition.

The Standard Edition

The Standard Edition of Crystal Reports 9 is the least capable of the four, but that is not to say that it's deficient in any way. It is designed to be used by business professionals. The Standard Edition contains nearly all the functionality I cover in this book. Rather than try to enumerate the features that it contains, it's easier to describe the features that it lacks.

First, it lacks the tools for creating reports designed to be displayed on the Web. If you intend to develop reports for display on the Web, you need at least the Professional Edition.

Second, the Standard Edition lacks tools designed to integrate reports into application programs. Because the target audience for the Standard Edition consists of people who are not typically programmers, application integration tools would be more confusing than useful.

The Standard Edition doesn't support XML or OLAP (discussed in Chapter 15) and doesn't include the repository (covered in Chapter 9).

Finally, the Standard Edition lacks native drivers for client/server databases such as Oracle, DB2, Hyperion Essbase, and SQL Server. If you want to draw data from these databases, you need at least the Professional Edition.

The Professional Edition

The Professional Edition is aimed at IT and MIS professionals, such as database administrators, report developers, and systems analysts. It's the product you need to publish reports on the Web. It also gives you more flexibility in using SQL than the Standard Edition does. The Professional Edition also allows you to draw data from client/server databases. The repository is available in the Professional Edition and above.

The Developer Edition

The Developer Edition is for guru-class, heavy-duty application developers. It is designed to be used by programmers who want to incorporate reports in the applications they develop.

The Developer Edition has all the capability of the Standard and Professional Editions plus the tools you need to take full control of the underlying functions of Crystal Reports. The Developer Edition is what you would use to create enterprise-wide applications that incorporate reports.

The Advanced Edition

The Advanced Edition is targeted at people who want to develop Enterprise Web applications using either Java, COM, or .NET. It has essentially the same functionality as the Developer Edition, but it also has a license structure that accommodates the possibility of large numbers of simultaneous users. People who receive Crystal Reports .NET as a part of Visual Studio .NET may want to upgrade to the Advanced Edition of Crystal Reports 9 when they're ready to deploy their application on the Web.

Viewing a Crystal Report

The majority of this book deals with telling you how to create a new report, based on data that you have in a database file, using Crystal Reports. It also tells you how to modify a report to create a new report that is similar to, but distinct from, the existing report. These are concerns of the report developer. But what if you just want to view a report that has already been developed?

The world has many more people viewing reports that someone else has created than people creating such reports. You may be one of the former. Before I launch into telling you how to create reports using Crystal Reports in subsequent chapters of this book, I'll briefly describe the simple process of viewing reports.

Reading a printed report

Reading a Crystal report that has been printed on paper is the simplest but also the most limited method of getting the information you want. It doesn't take a lot of technical sophistication to read text and view charts and maps on a sheet of paper. People were doing so long before the invention of computers.

For some kinds of information, printed reports are not as valuable as those that you view online. Printed reports are not updated when the database from which they were derived is updated. They may contain obsolete, and thus misleading, information. This is a factor you must always bear in mind when basing decisions on printed reports.

Viewing a report with Crystal Reports

As you might expect, you can do more than just create or modify a report with Crystal Reports software — you can also view an existing report. This has some major advantages over reading a printed report, but only for those who have the Crystal Reports software installed on their computer.

The most obvious advantage of viewing a report this way is that the report's connection to the database that's the source of its information is still in place. If the data in the database has changed since the last time you viewed it, you can refresh the report before viewing it again by pulling current information from the database. Crystal Reports automatically checks the database to see whether it has been updated since the last time your report was run. If so, it asks you whether you want to refresh the report with the current data.

Another advantage of viewing the report online is that you will be able to use the drill-down capability of Crystal Reports to selectively view the detail underlying summary reports. This enables you to get an overview of the subject by viewing the summary, and then drill down into the specific parts that interest you for more detail. (For more on drill down, see Chapter 6.)

A third advantage of viewing a "live" report involves Crystal Reports use of hyperlinks. You can follow a hyperlink from one part of a report to another part, from one report to another report on the same computer, or from one report to a report on another computer on your network.

A fourth advantage is that you can view reports that include color graphics or text that uses font colors other than black. For the many people who don't have high-speed color printers, this provides a way to access the full richness of a report's contents.

To view an existing report on a computer that has Crystal Reports installed on it, follow these steps:

1. **Launch Crystal Reports from your computer's Start menu.**

   Crystal Reports appears, displaying the Welcome to Crystal Reports dialog box, as shown in Figure 1-1. You can choose to create a new report or open an existing report. The dialog box lists several of the existing reports that may be on your system or gives you the option of looking at more report files if you don't see the one you want in the list.

2. **Select the report that you want to view.**

   If you see the report, click it and then click OK. If you don't see the report, click More Files, click OK, and use the Open dialog box to select any report available on the system.

   Crystal Reports retrieves and displays the report, as shown in Figure 1-2.

   If the toolbars shown in Figure 1-2 don't appear, you can display them by choosing View⇨Toolbars. In the dialog box that appears, click to select the toolbars that you want to see.

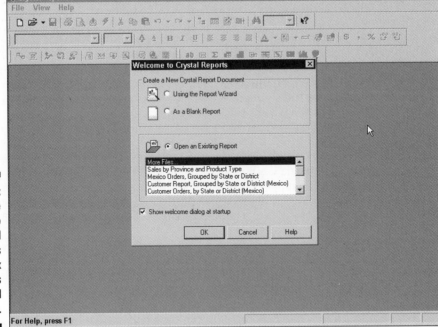

Figure 1-1:
The
Welcome to
Crystal
Reports
dialog box
offers
several
options.

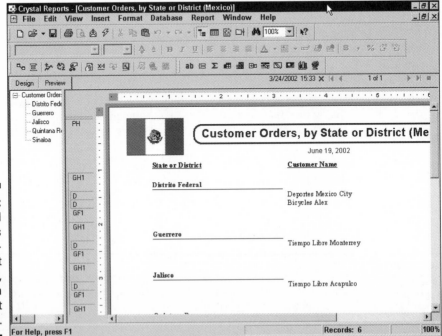

Figure 1-2:
Crystal
Reports
report-
development
environment,
with a
report
displayed.

3. **Move through the report.**

   Scroll around the report, and move back and forth among its pages. You can drill down into any summary report that supports drill-down. If the report contains hyperlinks, you can follow them to other locations in the report or in other reports

4. **When you are finished viewing the report, choose File⇨Close to close it.**

Viewing a report on your local area network or the Web

Crystal Reports has a companion product named Crystal Enterprise that enables users on client machines to view, schedule, and keep track of published reports. Whether on a local area network that's directly connected to the server that runs the administrative part of Crystal Enterprise, or on a remote connection via the Web, users can access reports using Crystal Enterprise's ePortfolio component. The user interface is a standard Web browser, such as Internet Explorer or Netscape.

Chapter 2

Build a Report Right Now!

*W*hen you start Crystal Reports, you generally want to do one of three things: create a report, modify a report, or run a report against the data in your database. Reports take data from a database, process it, format it, and then output it to a printer, a computer screen, or a Web site.

Crystal Reports comes with a sample database you can use for practice. It's a Microsoft Access database for a fictitious company named Xtreme Mountain Bikes Inc. You might be able to buy one of their fictitious bikes with fictitious money, if you ever find a fictitious bike shop — and the Treasury Department doesn't nab you first.

The xtreme.mdb database contains a number of database tables that are representative of the tables that a real bike manufacturer might maintain. The tables are filled with sample data that you can manipulate and display with Crystal Reports. You can use this sample data as the basis for your first report.

To create a report, you need to know a few things.

- ✔ Which tables in the database contain the data that you want

- ✔ Which data items you want in those tables

- ✔ What manipulations of the data must be performed to give you the information you want

- ✔ How you want your report to be formatted

- ✔ Whether the users of your report will retrieve it from a black-and-white printer, a color printer, a local computer screen, or a Web site

For this introduction, assume that you know all those things.

Starting Crystal Reports 9

You've probably chosen Crystal Reports because you have a database that contains information that's important to you. In all likelihood, the data in that database changes with time, and you want to be able to keep up with its current status. You *could* retrieve the information you want by making SQL queries, but that would be too much like work. It's far better to create a report with Crystal Reports, and then run the report whenever you want the latest status of the information of interest. You have to create the report only once, but you can run it many times, getting the latest results with each successive run. You don't have to learn SQL or any other method of pulling data out of databases. Reports created with Crystal Reports are easy to build, easy to read, and easy to understand. What could be better?

SQL is the international standard language for communicating with databases. It differs from most common computer languages in that it's non-procedural. It deals with data a set at a time rather than a record at a time. Database developers use SQL. If you're a database user rather than a developer, Crystal Reports may give you everything you need to get what you want out of your databases.

The first step to creating a report is to launch Crystal Reports from the Windows Start menu. When you do, the Crystal Reports main window appears and the dialog box shown in Figure 2-1 is displayed.

Figure 2-1:
Welcome
to Crystal
Reports!

Welcome to Crystal Reports

Create a New Crystal Report Document

○ Using the Report Expert

○ As a Blank Report

◉ Open an Existing Report

More Files...
E:\Program Files\...\USA
E:\Program Files\...\Custlist

☑ Show welcome dialog at startup

OK   Cancel   Help

You are invited to choose from three options. You can create a Crystal Reports document using Report Wizard or by starting with a blank report. Alternatively, as demonstrated in Chapter 1, you can open a report that already exists, either to change it or to run it.

In this chapter, you get right to the point and create a report. Furthermore, you do it your way. That means starting from a blank report rather than using Report Expert. Although Report Expert can save you time and labor, it does constrain the form of the report.

Creating a Report with the Blank Report Option

To create a report from scratch, starting with the blank report option, follow these steps:

1. **Start Crystal Reports.**

   The Welcome to Crystal Reports dialog box appears

2. **Select the As a Blank Report option, and then click OK.**

   The Database Expert dialog box appears, as shown in Figure 2-2.

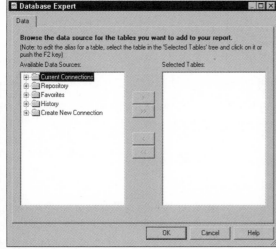

Figure 2-2:
Database
Expert
shows
where the
source of
your data
might be
found.

3. In the Available Data Sources pane, double-click the plus sign to the left of the Create New Connection folder to expand it.

This is the folder you choose whenever you're creating a report from scratch. Crystal Reports will remember where it is after you connect to the database.

4. Double-click the database type that matches your data source.

Crystal Reports recognizes a variety of different database types. You must select the right one. If you don't know which type is correct, ask someone familiar with the data source.

To follow along with the example, double-click Access/Excel (DAO). The Access/Excel (DAO) dialog box appears, as shown in Figure 2-3.

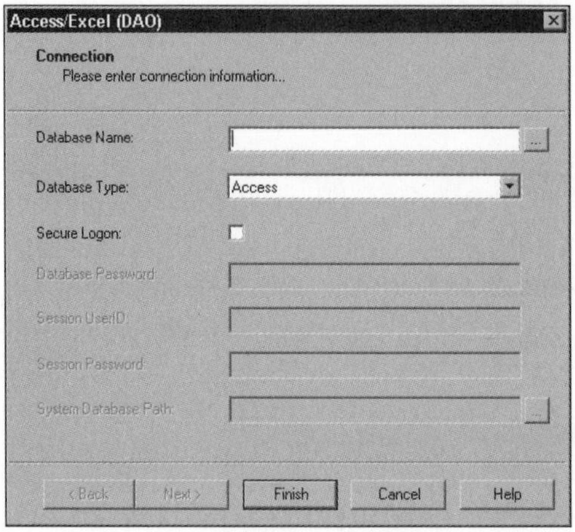

Figure 2-3: Connecting to your data source.

5. Click the ellipsis (...) to the right of the Database Name box.

The Access and Excel files on your system should appear, if they don't you will have to search for the folder that holds them. I selected an Access database file named xtreme. Mine was located at `E:\Program Files\Seagate Software\Crystal Reports\Samples\En\Databases\xtreme.mdb`.

6. Click the Finish button.

Database Expert reappears, as shown in Figure 2-4, with the xtreme database connected.

7. Expand the Tables node, and then double-click the table that you want to base your report upon.

The tree in the Available Data Sources pane consists of a number of nodes, some of which branch off from others. Every data source has four nodes: Add Command, Tables, Views, and Stored Procedures.

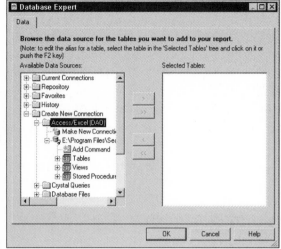

Figure 2-4:
The xtreme
database is
connected
to the
report.

To follow along with the example, expand the Tables node and then double-click Product. This copies the Product table from the Available Data Sources pane to the Selected Tables pane.

8. **Click OK to close Database Expert.**

A blank report fills the window, as shown in Figure 2-5.

Figure 2-5:
A blank
report.

The Design tab (on the left edge) shows five sections of the report:

- ✔ **Report Header section:** Appears only at the top of the report, the first thing that a viewer sees

- ✔ **Page Header section:** Appears below the report header and at the top of all the other pages in the report

- ✔ **Details section:** The actual content of the report

- ✔ **Report Footer section:** Appears after the last detailed information in the report

- ✔ **Page Footer section:** Appears at the bottom of every page of the report

Allocating more space to the layout

Depending on the resolution of your computer screen, the Crystal Reports window may not display the full width of your report. You can give yourself a little more width in the display by changing one of the display options. Follow these simple steps:

1. **Choose File⇨Options.**

   The Layout tab of the Options dialog box appears, as shown in Figure 2-6.

Figure 2-6: Control center for the appearance of your report.

2. **Select the Short Section Names option.**

   This reduces the section names on the left edge of the window to one- or two-letter abbreviations, freeing up a little horizontal real estate.

3. **Click OK.**

Giving the report a title

The Report Header area, which appears at the top of the first page of the report, is the ideal place to tell the reader exactly what the report contains. However, this forces you, right here at the beginning, to *decide* what the report will contain. You need to consider who your target audience is and what they want to know.

If you are Xtreme Mountain Bikes, the target audience for your Products report is potential customers. They surely will want to know what products you carry, including information on color and size, where appropriate. They probably also want to know price information. They should also know the stock number of an item, so that they can specify it properly when they decide to purchase a bike.

It also makes sense to put your company logo in the report header — Xtreme has an image of their company logo saved in a .bmp file — along with a title, such as *Product Price List*.

To add a logo to a report, do the following:

1. **Dismiss Field Explorer, if necessary, by clicking the X in its upper-right corner.**

2. **Click the Design tab.**

3. **On the Insert Tools toolbar, click the Insert Picture icon.**

   A dialog box appears, displaying the image files in the Databases folder. You can find out the names of the toolbar icons by hovering the cursor over them. After a few seconds, a tooltip appears, telling you the name of the tool you're looking at.

4. **Double-click the icon for the image that you want to add to the report, and then drag its outline to its new location on the report.**

   For the example, click the Xtreme image. This places the logo on the report, wherever the cursor happens to be pointing.

5. **Move the cursor to the upper-left corner of the Report Header section, and then click to place the logo there.**

   Figure 2-7 shows the result.

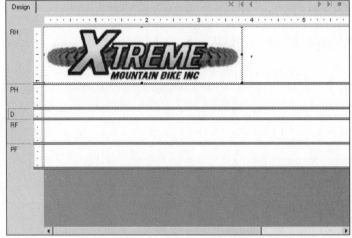

Figure 2-7:
A company
logo has
been placed
in the
report.

Next, you put a report title into the Report Header section as well. To do this, you will have to use several of the tools on the Insert Tools toolbar:

1. **Drag the dividing line between the Report Header section and the Page Header section down so that you can place the report title below the level of the logo.**

2. **On the Insert Tools toolbar, click the Insert Text Object icon.**

   A text object rectangle appears.

3. **Drag the rectangle into the Report Header section and drop it under the logo.**

   A text cursor starts to blink in the rectangle.

4. **At the blinking cursor's location, type the report title.**

   For the example, type **Product Price List**.

5. **Select the title you just typed, and then increase its size by clicking the Increase Font Size icon.**

6. **Make the title bold by clicking the Bold icon.**

7. **Move the left and right edges of the text object to the left and right edges of the report, respectively, and then click the Align Center icon to locate the title in the center of the page. Move the top and bottom edges of the text box to accommodate the expanded text.**

At this point, your report should look similar to Figure 2-8.

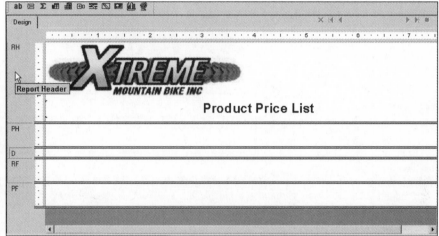

Figure 2-8:
The report title is now in the Report Header section.

Choosing the fields that will appear in your report

The next logical step is to place in the Details section the fields that you want the report to display. Simply follow these steps:

1. **If the Field Explorer is not currently visible at the left edge of the screen, display it by choosing View⇨Field Explorer on the main menu.**

2. **In Field Explorer, click the plus sign to the left of Database Fields, and then click the plus sign to the left of the Products table.**

(The Database Fields entry is the top node in Field Explorer.) When you click the plus sign to the left of the Database Fields icon, the icon for the Products table drops down. When you click the plus sign to the left of this icon, icons for all the fields in the Products table drop down, as shown in Figure 2-9.

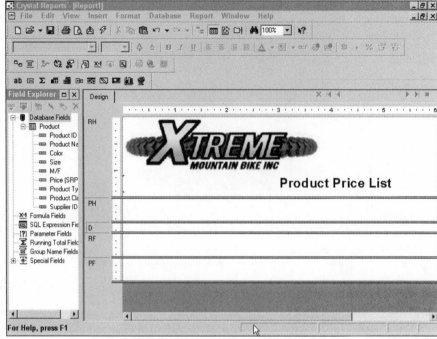

Figure 2-9:
Field
Explorer
displays the
fields in the
Product
table.

3. **Click the first field that you want to include in the report, and then drag it to the left edge of the Detail section.**

   When you drag the field, a rectangle appears.

   For the example, click the Product ID field. The field name appears in the rectangle in the Detail section and also above it in the Page Header section. Later, you may want to change the column titles in the Page Header section for cosmetic reasons. For now, just leave the default column titles.

4. **Repeat Step 3 for any other fields that you want to include in the report.**

   For the example, place the Product Name, Color, Size, and Price (SRP) fields in order in the Detail section, leaving just a little space between them.

   You may have to shrink some of the field sizes by grasping the handles on the left and right edges of the fields and moving them. You can move the fields back and forth until you arrive at a well-balanced appearance. At this point, your report layout should look similar to the one in Figure 2-10.

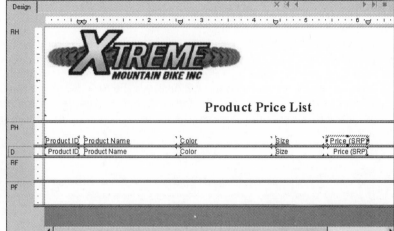

Figure 2-10:
All fields
have been
placed in
the Detail
section.

Improving the readability of page headers

Everything in the Page Header section will appear just below the Report Header on the first page of the report and at the top of all following pages. By default, the field names in the Page Header section are displayed in a normal font and underlined. I think they'd look better in a bold font and not underlined, so I select the Bold attribute for each of them and deselect the Underline attribute. I'll wait to see what the report looks like before deciding whether I want to change the font size as well. Figure 2-11 shows the layout with the enhanced column headings.

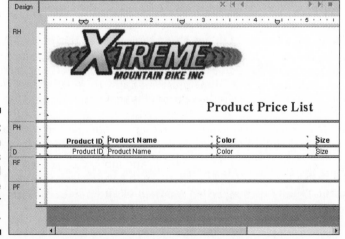

Figure 2-11:
The column
headings
are modified
to improve
their
appearance.

Previewing the report

So far, you've been able to see the layout of your report only in the sectioned structure of Design mode. To get a better idea of what the final report will look like, you can switch to Preview mode. To do so, click the Print Preview icon on the Standard toolbar. This displays the Preview tab in the upper-left corner of the work area and displays the report, complete with data pulled from the Products table. Figure 2-12 shows as much of the report as the screen will hold.

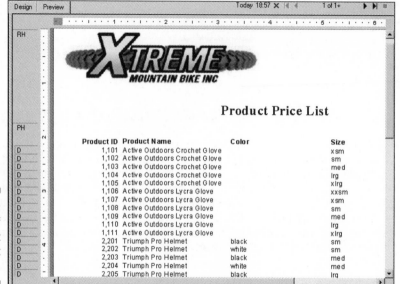

Figure 2-12:
A preview of
the Product
Price List
report.

You can notice a couple of things about the report at this point. First, Crystal Reports apparently automatically inserts commas between groups of three digits in number fields such as the Product ID field. This is not what you want. Second, the color attribute must not apply to gloves, because no color information is shown for the glove products that you can see.

The fact that gloves have no color is not a problem, but the comma in the middle of the Product ID is a problem. You can correct this as follows:

1. **Click the Design tab to return to Design mode.**

2. **In the Details section, select the field whose number format you want to change.**

   For the example, select the Product ID field.

3. **On the main menu, choose Format⇨Format Field.**

   Format Editor appears.

4. **Select the numeric format that you want, and then click OK.**

   For the example, you want the format with no commas, as shown in Figure 2-13. This changes the format of the Product ID field to eliminate the unwanted commas.

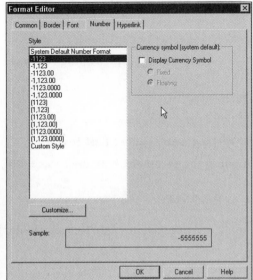

Figure 2-13: Selecting a different numeric format.

You can verify the change by returning to Preview mode and noting that the commas are gone. By moving the sliders at the right and bottom edges of the report window, you can verify that all the columns and rows are as they should be.

Page footers carry useful information

At the bottom of each page, you might want to display some useful information, such as the page number. If you ever drop a stack of reports off your desk, page footers can be a valuable aid to putting them back together again in the proper order.

For the Product Price List, the page number, date printed, and report title are valuable additions to the page footer. (Prices tend to change frequently in a fast-moving industry such as the mountain bike business, so the date of a price list is very important.) Follow these steps to create a page footer for your report that includes all three of these items:

1. **Make sure that you're in Design mode.**

2. **On the Insert Tools toolbar, click the Insert Text Object icon.**

   You click this icon because all the items you want to place in the page footer are text items.

3. **Drag the text object rectangle to the Page Footer section.**

4. **Drag the handles on the left and right sides of the rectangle until it spans the full width of the page.**

5. **Click the Align Center icon.**

   There isn't any text there yet, but there will be.

6. **Right-click the text rectangle and choose Edit Text.**

7. **At the blinking cursor in the rectangle, type the report title, followed by a comma.**

   For the example, type **Product Price List**.

Next, place the current date and page number into the page footer by following these steps:

1. **In Field Explorer, scroll down to Special Fields and expand it.**

   Remember, you expand a node by clicking the plus sign to its left.

2. **Click the Print Date icon or the Print Date name next to it, and drag it to the Page Footer area, right after the comma.**

3. **After the Print Date field is in position, type a comma after it, and then type** Page **followed by a hyphen.**

4. **Click the Page Number icon or the name next to it, and drag it to right after the hyphen.**

   This gives you an arrangement that looks much like Figure 2-14.

5. **Click the Preview tab at the top of the screen to switch to Preview mode.**

   You can see that the field names are replaced by actual values, as shown in Figure 2-15.

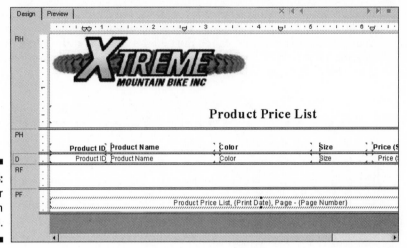

Figure 2-14:
Page footer
in Design
mode.

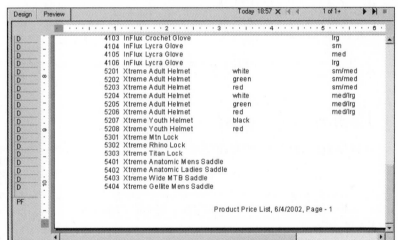

Figure 2-15:
Page footer
in Preview
mode.

Wrap things up with a report footer

For some types of reports, it's appropriate to have a final item to close out
the report. This would appear after the last of the data on the last page. Items
such as this go into the Report Footer section in Design mode. Remember,
the report footer comes immediately after the last line of detail information
and before the final page footer.

To illustrate this feature of Crystal Reports, put a company slogan at the bottom of the Product Price List. Place the slogan *"Xtreme Mountain Bikes Take You to the Limit"* into the Report Footer section in the same way that you put the report title into the Page Footer section. The result, in Preview mode, looks like Figure 2-16.

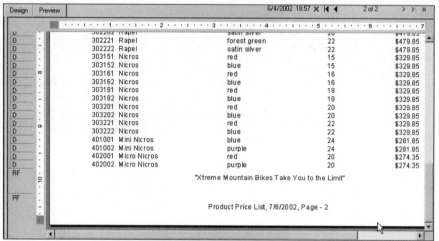

Figure 2-16:
The company slogan as a report footer.

Recording helpful information about your report

Now that the Product Price List report is essentially complete, you may want to generate some descriptive information about the report that's associated with the report but not normally printed or displayed. To do this, follow these steps:

1. **Choose File⇨Summary Info.**

   The Document Properties dialog box appears.

2. **Fill in the boxes with whatever information you want to associate with your report.**

   I added the information shown in Figure 2-17.

3. **Click OK.**

   The document properties you entered are stored along with the report and can be retrieved whenever anyone views the report with Crystal Reports.

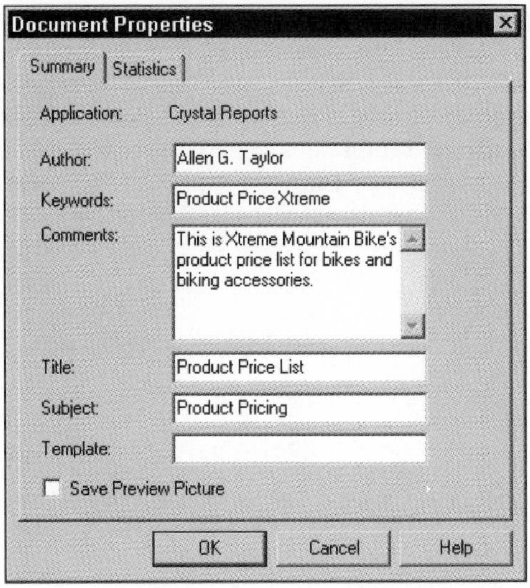

Figure 2-17:
Pertinent
information
about the
Product
Price List
report.

Troubleshooting a Report That Doesn't Look Quite Right

Sometimes the vision you have in your mind is not adequately reflected in the report you produce. There are various reasons why this might be true. Perhaps your vision is not something that can be built in the real world. You can't do much about that. But you can do something about other reasons, such as not using Crystal Reports properly or not being aware of all its capabilities.

Crystal Reports gives you tremendous freedom in how you lay out your report. It also gives you great latitude in what you include in the report. In addition to text and columns of numbers, you can include graphical images, charts, graphs, and maps. You could even crank out a full-length science fiction novel with Crystal Reports if you wanted to, although other tools are better suited to that task.

The bottom line is this: If you feel sure that a report ought to be able to include something, you can almost certainly do it with Crystal Reports. This book tells you about many of the most powerful and useful features of Crystal Reports. If I don't mention a feature or capability that you'd like to use, it may nonetheless be available. Check the *Crystal Reports User's Guide* and online help for additional information on advanced features.

Printing a Report

Printing a report from Crystal Reports is really easy. Open the report in the Crystal Reports environment, and then click the Print icon or choose File⇨ Print⇨Printer. Then select print options for the report in the same way you select print options for any document in a Microsoft Windows environment.

Chapter 3

Report Design Guidelines

● ●

In This Chapter

▶ Defining the purpose of the report

▶ Deciding what the report should include

▶ Linking the report to a database

▶ Laying out the report

▶ Conveying the right message

● ●

*N*o book can tell you in a step-by-step manner exactly how to build the report that you want. However, this book tells you about general principles of good report design and gives you examples of several common types of reports. From those general principles and examples, you'll be able to decide how best to design reports that meet the needs of your organization.

A report design depends on many things. It depends on the data that the report draws from the database. It depends on the way the database is structured. It depends on the level of detail that the users of the report require. It depends also on the purpose of the report. It depends on the capabilities of the computer that will be displaying or printing the report. Most of all, it depends on an understanding of what the users of the report really need.

Audience

Every report should have a definite audience. A key question to ask at the beginning of any report development effort is, "Who will be reading this report?"

Some potential audience members may be familiar with the information that the report will contain and the nomenclature used in the database. These people may prefer a streamlined presentation of the data. Other audience members might be unfamiliar with the report content, so you may have to translate terms, use graphical devices such as charts, and include explanatory text. If you have two such divergent audiences, you may need to produce two reports. Both would contain the same information, but presented in different ways.

Another question to ask is, "What information does the audience need and in what form should it be delivered?" If they need several unrelated things, you may serve them better by creating several reports, each one focused on one specific purpose.

Although it's best when a report is written with one audience in mind, sometimes a report must be designed for multiple audiences, each of which has its own needs. The challenge is to give each audience the information they need in a form they can easily understand, without handicapping the members of other audiences by subjecting them to irrelevant material. The key is to organize the information so that each audience can quickly and easily find and understand the information that is of interest to them.

Purpose

In addition to having a specific audience, the report should be restricted to one specific purpose and should accomplish that purpose by providing thorough, accurate, and timely information to the target audience. This information, more often than not, is the basis for important decisions that the readers of the report will make.

Restricting a report to serving a single purpose is important. Reports that cover multiple topics generally do not do justice to any one of them and are confusing to readers. A good report covers a single topic and conveys a message that the reader can easily comprehend and act upon.

Knowing how important the report is to its audience may affect the amount of time and effort you should put into creating it. Is the report something on which "bet the business" decisions will be based? Perhaps it merely makes visible some facts that are nice to know but aren't all that important.

Another consideration is how often the report will be run. Some reports are one-shot affairs that are run against the database once, and then never run again. Other reports are run repeatedly, perhaps on a weekly, monthly, quarterly, or annual basis. Each time they're run, they contain the latest information in the database. Reports that are run multiple times, by multiple people, deserve more attention to detail than reports run only once.

Content

After you know who the report is for, and the kinds of decisions they want to make based on the information in the report, it's time to decide exactly what information should be in the report. It's just as important to leave out distracting, irrelevant material as it is to include material of interest.

Reports should be succinct and to the point. They should give readers the information they want quickly and easily and not be cluttered with information they don't care about. Also keep in mind, based on the audience and the purpose of the report, the level of formality or informality that is most appropriate.

As mentioned, a report often has to meet the needs of several audiences. You should determine which audience is the most critical, and then determine which information is the most important to that audience. This information should be displayed most prominently in the report. Other, less important information for that same critical audience should be located in a nearby but subordinate position. Information for other audiences should also be clustered in such a way that those reading the report will be likely to find all the information they're interested in within a single area of the report.

Interfacing the Report to a Database

Your clients have told you what they want the report to deliver. Hopefully the raw material for that report exists in the database the report will draw from. Your job as the report developer is to make the connection to the database so the needed data can flow into your report, where it will be massaged, formatted, combined, graphed, or otherwise processed to produce a finished report.

The first step in that process is connecting your report to the database that will be supplying it with data. Crystal Reports has built-in interfaces to a wide variety of data sources. You can get some idea of the breadth of choices you have for data sources when you start a report design in Design view.

Connecting to Microsoft Access

Suppose you want to create a report based on data in a Microsoft Access database. Follow these steps:

1. **Start Crystal Reports.**

   You are greeted by the Welcome to Crystal Reports dialog box.

2. **Select the As a Blank Report option.**

   Database Expert is displayed, as shown in Figure 3-1. As you can see, a number of different data sources are available.

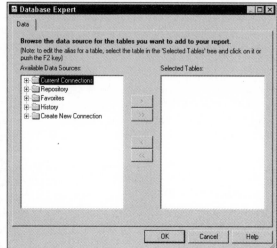

Figure 3-1: Places where the database you want might be located.

3. **Connect to the appropriate database and display its tables in the Available Data Sources pane of Database Expert, as shown in Figure 3-2.**

   For more information on this process, see Chapter 2. To follow along with an example, connect to the xtreme database.

4. **Select the tables in the database that contain the data that you want to include in the report.**

   For the example, double-click the Customer and Orders tables in the Available Data Sources pane to add them to the Selected Tables pane, and then click OK to close Database Expert.

5. **Click OK.**

   The Link view appears, showing how the selected tables relate to each other.

6. **Click OK to exit Database Expert.**

   You're now connected to the database of choice and have selected from it the tables that contain the data that will be included in your report.

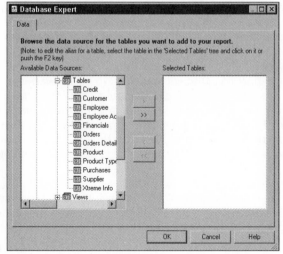

Figure 3-2:
Tables in the
xtreme.mdb
database
are listed.

So, how do you connect your report to the Access database? You don't have to. It's all transparent. Crystal Reports has made the connection behind the scenes, without any help from you, beyond specifying the name of the database, finding it on your system, and choosing which tables to use from the database.

Connecting to other data sources

Access is a desktop database and usually resides on the same physical computer that you are sitting in front of while you're working with it. It also might be on another computer on a small local area network. Access is not designed to handle large databases or large numbers of simultaneous users. For those larger applications, a client/server relational database is the preferred solution. In such a system, the DBMS, along with the data, resides on the server computer, while users sit in front of multiple client machines. Because the bulk of the processing takes place on the same machine that holds the data (the server), the amount of data that must be sent over the network is minimized and good performance can scale to very large systems.

To connect a report to a client/server relational database, you must log on to the database. The connection is mediated by a database driver, of which there are several kinds. A *direct database driver* is specifically designed and optimized to connect to a specific DBMS, such as Microsoft SQL Server, Oracle, or IBM's DB2. Crystal Reports includes direct database drivers for the most popular DBMS products, including these. In addition, Crystal Reports includes drivers for data sources that are not relational databases, such as Excel spreadsheets, Outlook folders, and Lotus Notes databases.

ODBC is a second type of database connection. Unlike a dedicated direct database driver, a report can connect via ODBC to a wide variety of data sources, many more than those that are available via direct database driver. In fact, you can connect to the Access xtreme.mdb database via ODBC as well as by the direct route. Crystal Reports' support of ODBC means that you should be able to create a report based on the data in any data source that is ODBC-compliant, and ODBC compliance is practically universal today.

OLE DB (pronounced "o-lay-dee-bee)" is a newer interfacing technique similar to but more flexible than ODBC. OLE DB allows a report to pull data from multiple sources, some of which may be relational databases and others may be non-relational. I cover specific data access techniques in Part IV.

What Should the Report Look Like?

Information can be presented in a report in many different ways. One way is with narrative text. Another way is with tables of numbers. In between those two extremes are a variety of different presentation methods, each effective in its own way for certain kinds of information display.

Having determined your audience and what the report needs to contain, the next decision to make is how to present that information to that audience. If you were producing a report on video game sales figures, you would present the information in one format for game industry executives and in an entirely different format for teen-aged video game enthusiasts. The information in those two reports might be identical, but to be effective, the presentation of the data should be vastly different.

Making a good first impression

I've heard that when you meet someone for the first time, within the first 30 seconds they form a judgment of you. They decide whether they like you or not, whether they trust you or not, whether they respect you or not. That snap judgment, based on 30 seconds of input will affect how they deal with you from then on.

Salespeople have known this truth about first impressions for a long time, which is why they dress for success when making a sales call. They want to make a good first impression so their prospect will be predisposed to like them, trust them, respect them, and buy from them. For all the same reasons, you want all the reports that you create to make a good first impression. You want your report's readers to "buy" what you are selling, which is the information in your report.

One important way to make a good first impression is to make sure that the appearance of your report is appropriate for the audience and for the occasion. Know who your audience is and what they are expecting from this particular report. Make sure that their expectations are met when they look at the first page of your report for the first time. They should see a clear indication of what the report is, and an engaging presentation of the information that they are most interested in seeing.

It would be a mistake to bury the most important information somewhere in the back pages of the report. For some reports, it may be appropriate to state the conclusions that can be drawn from the data, right up front. This can encourage readers to dig deeper and digest the data pulled from the database that backs up your conclusions.

Deciding how best to present the information

The Report Creation Wizard gives you the option of formatting your report with either a columnar, tabular, or justified layout, in either a portrait or landscape orientation. This gives you six different ways of formatting your report. For reports that don't have to impress anybody or for quick-and-dirty reports that you intend to run only once, one of these six options is probably fine. However, for most applications, you probably want to create the report from the ground up, using Design view.

With Design view, you have complete freedom as to how to arrange the various report elements on the page. You also are able to use many more different kinds of report elements than the Report Creation Wizard allows, and to add considerable functionality beyond mere displaying of data taken from the database. Throughout the remainder of this book, I will show you progressively more sophisticated ways to give your report's readers the information they want, in the most effective way.

Deciding whether to include graphs, charts, or pictures

There is an old saying that a picture is worth a thousand words. There is a lot of truth to that. It's also true that a graph is worth more than a large table of numbers. Graphs and charts are valuable parts of any report that needs to show relationships between data items or trends in data. Some types of reports, such as those displaying sales figures for a product or family of products, have much more impact if they include graphs of the data along with the figures that back up the graphs. Other types of reports, such as membership lists for organizations, would not benefit from having graphs or charts.

Pictures such as photographs, illustrations, or line drawings can greatly increase the value of some types of report by presenting the information in an alternative way. Generally, the more pathways into the brains of the readers that you use, the likelier it is that they will fully receive and appreciate the message you are trying to convey.

When you are designing a report, ask yourself this question, "Would a graph, chart, or other illustration improve the understanding and acceptance of the content of this report?" If the answer is "Yes," consider adding such an illustration. If you can't justify adding an illustration on the basis of improved understanding and acceptance, it's probably better not to include one. In such a case, it may be no more than a distraction from the message the report is supposed to convey.

Considering how style communicates meaning

The words, numbers and graphs in a report embody the data, but the way these report elements are put together, and the judicious use of fonts, color, layout, and white space, can also make an impression on the reader. You want that impression to be a favorable one. Give some thought to how to use all of these style elements together to create the desired effect.

You want to communicate with the reader on an emotional level as well as merely on an intellectual level. If, for instance, your report is designed to inform potential investors about the benefits of investing in your company, the report should convey an aura of professionalism, but at the same time be consistent with the business you are in. The prospectus for an investment banking firm should have a very different style from the prospectus for a cutting-edge video game company. Both should convey the idea that the company understands the business it is in, but differences in the two industries dictate that company information should be presented differently. Reports should convey a style that readers would expect to see from the top organization in its field. This, on an emotional level, adds credibility to the facts being presented.

Conveying the message

Some reports just need to present some facts in a straightforward way. Membership lists, price lists, and inventory lists fall into this category. There is another category of reports that must do more if it is to be effective. These reports are not just trying to give the reader information. They are trying to change the reader's thinking. To influence a reader, the sum of what is in the report should convey a uniform and unmistakable message. To make sure that point gets across, you may want to state it explicitly at the end of the report. The report footer that Crystal Reports provides for when you are using Design view is the ideal place for any such summarizing text. If appropriate, it might also include a call to action.

Chapter 4

Reporting Overview

• •

In This Chapter

▶ Using Standard Report Creation Wizard

▶ Building a report from scratch

▶ Getting the data

• •

You can start a report in several ways. In Chapter 2, you look at creating a report from scratch, starting with a blank report. Another way to create reports is to use Report Wizard, which makes some assumptions and does much of the work for you. The last way is to use an existing report as a template for a new report that is different but bears some structural similarity to the existing report.

In this chapter, I walk you step by step through report building with Report Wizard. You give up some of the freedom and flexibility of the from-scratch approach in exchange for having the wizard do much of the work for you.

Creating a Report with Report Creation Wizard

Generally, you use Report Wizard when you want to create a report that's conceptually simple and doesn't require unusual formatting or a custom appearance. Report Wizard can produce reports using a few standard layouts. When you first launch Crystal Reports, it assumes, reasonably enough, that you want to create a report and displays the Welcome to Crystal Reports dialog box. If you select either Using the Report Wizard or As a Blank Report, and then click OK, the Crystal Reports Gallery appears, as shown in Figure 4-1.

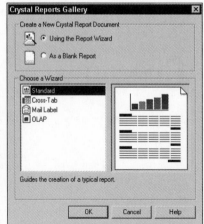

Figure 4-1:
Crystal
Reports
Gallery asks
what kind of
report you
want to
create.

The default assumption is that you want to use Report Wizard; the various styles of reports that Report Wizard can produce are listed in the pane on the left. The pane on the right displays a sample layout for the currently selected report.

Creating a standard report

You start your investigation with a standard report, which is the one most people will need most of the time. The example is from the fictitious Xtreme Mountain Bikes Inc., a business that sells mountain bikes and associated accessories. However, its information needs are much the same as the needs of any business that buys products from suppliers and sells them to customers. Thus, the kinds of standard reports that Xtreme needs are representative of the reports that many retail businesses would find useful.

Suppose that Xtreme's sales manager would like a detailed report of all orders placed in December 1996. She would like the report to include the customer's name, the order date, the order number, the salesperson's name, the items ordered, the quantities ordered, and the extended price of the items ordered. To build this report, data must be extracted from multiple tables.

Follow these steps:

1. **Start Crystal Reports.**

   The Welcome to Crystal Reports dialog box appears.

2. **Make sure that the Using the Report Wizard option is selected, and then click OK.**

   The Crystal Reports Gallery dialog box appears.

3. **At the top of the screen, select the Using the Report Wizard option.**

4. **In the Choose a Wizard area, select the Standard option, and then click OK.**

   The Standard Report Creation Wizard dialog box appears, as shown in Figure 4-2.

5. **Use the procedures outlined in Chapter 2 and used again in Chapter 3 to find the database, and click the plus sign to its left. Then click the plus sign to the left of the Tables item.**

   To follow along with the example, click the plus sign to the left of the Xtreme Mountain Bikes Inc. sample database, xtreme.mdb, and then click the plus sign to the left of the Tables icon. You see the names of the tables in the database.

6. **Select the tables that contain data that will be used by the report, moving them to the Selected Tables pane.**

   To follow along with the example, double-click the Customer table in the Available Data Sources pane and move it to the Selected Tables pane. Do the same for the Orders, Employee, Orders Detail, and Product tables.

7. **Click Next.**

   Standard Report Creation Wizard displays the Link view.

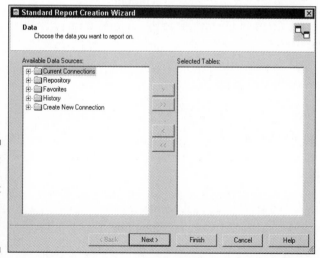

Figure 4-2:
Standard
Report
Creation
Wizard
dialog box.

In the main pane of the Link view, the tables are shown, with links to the tables to which they are connected by common columns. Figure 4-3 shows what the Link view looks like at this point. The pane isn't large enough to show all the tables, but you can use the scroll bars to see that they're all there and are all linked by common columns.

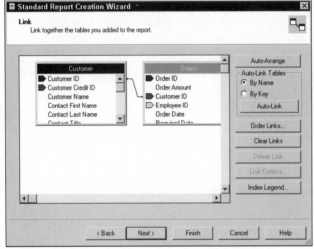

Figure 4-3:
You can
see the
connection
between the
selected
tables.

Standard Report Creation Wizard has inferred that columns with the same name in different tables refer to the same objects. This is a valid assumption in this case, although it may not always be true. If any of the links that the wizard has assumed are incorrect, you can change them manually by clicking them to remove them and by dragging the pointer from one table to another to add new links.

After the tables and links are arranged to your satisfaction, do the following to continue with the example:

1. **Click Next.**

    The Fields view appears.

2. **From the tables selected previously, select the fields you want for the report.**

    To follow along with the example, select Customer ID and Customer Name from the Customer table; Last Name and First Name from the Employee table; Order ID, Order Amount, and Order Date from the Orders table;

Product ID, Unit Price, and Quantity from the Orders Detail table; and Product Name from the Product table. At this point, Standard Report Creation Wizard looks like Figure 4-4.

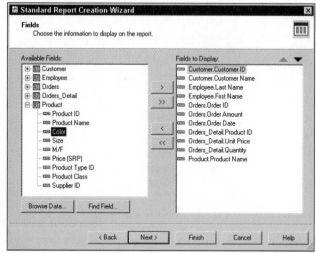

Figure 4-4:
The fields
for the
report have
been
specified.

3. **Click Next.**

   The Grouping view appears.

4. **Because you don't want to do any grouping in this report, click Next.**

   The Record Selection view appears.

5. **Double-click the field that you want to filter on to move it to the Filter Fields pane.**

   For the example, you want to filter out all orders that were not placed during December 1996, so double-click the Orders.Order Date field.

6. **Pull down the list below the Filter Fields pane and select the method for filtering. Then make any secondary filtering selections, if necessary.**

   For the example, select is between. In the sublist, select the dates of the first and last orders that were placed during December 1996. Figure 4-5 shows this. If you want, you may select a different month, such as December 2000.

7. **Click the Finish button.**

   The finished report is displayed, using the Preview tab in Crystal Reports, as shown in Figure 4-6.

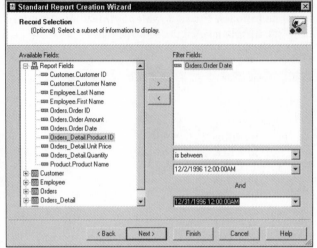

Figure 4-5:
The order date has been specified for filtering.

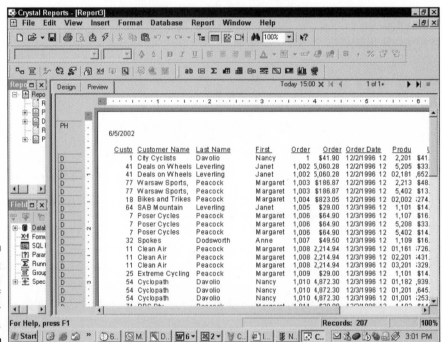

Figure 4-6:
A standard report of December 1996 orders.

To fit everything on an 8½-x-11-inch sheet, the columns have been squeezed together and some of the information in some columns does not appear. An easy remedy to this situation is to choose File➪Printer Setup and change the orientation from Portrait to Landscape mode. This provides some additional room.

After a little rearranging with the Design tab active, the report might look like Figure 4-7.

This isn't bad, but you probably want to make it clear what this report is about by adding a report header. You can also change column headings in the Page Header section if you want to. In general, you can use Standard Report Creation Wizard to do the bulk of the layout of a fairly standard report, and then fine-tune the result using the tools available on the Design tab.

To quickly produce a report that is close to one of the templates used by Standard Report Creation Wizard, use the wizard to produce the basic layout and then refine the report using the Design tab. In many cases, this is quicker and easier than designing the report from scratch.

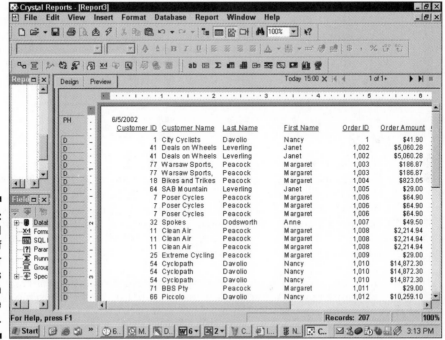

Figure 4-7:
Standard
report of
December
1996 orders
shown in
Landscape
mode.

When you're satisfied with your report, save it by choosing File⇨Save on the main menu. When you run the report in the future, it will reflect the state of the database at the time it was run. This is probably not important when you're reporting on historical data such as in the example report, but it's valuable for reporting on data that changes on an ongoing basis.

The rest of the Report Creation wizards

The Standard Report Creation Wizard gives you a good idea of how Report Creation wizards work. The other Report Creation wizards have a lot in common with the Standard Report Creation Wizard, as follows:

- ✔ **Cross-Tab Report Creation Wizard** builds a report that displays data as a cross-tab object. I cover cross-tab reports thoroughly in Chapter 16.

- ✔ **Mailing Labels Report Creation Wizard** automates the task of laying out a report formatted to print mailing labels. It's already set up to print standard commercial label formats, but you can also design a custom label format.

- ✔ **OLAP Report Creation Wizard** displays OLAP data as a grid object. OLAP reports are similar to cross-tab reports but have different data sources. OLAP data is structured differently than data used by the other types of reports. This causes the OLAP reports based on that data to be different too. For more information on when you would use OLAP and how to report on OLAP data, see Chapter 15.

Starting with a Blank Report

Although Crystal Reports Gallery makes the default assumption that you want to use Report Wizard, starting with a blank report is the best choice in many cases. To make report development quick and easy, Report Wizard makes some default assumptions about the look of your report. If what you want is not consistent with what one of the several different versions of Report Wizard can produce, you're probably better off starting with a blank report.

In some cases, it may make sense to use Report Wizard to generate the basic structure of your report, and then switch to the Design tab to modify the report into the final product.

Leveraging work in an existing report

Few things are more frustrating than having to redo work. It's not uncommon for a report developer to be asked to develop a report that's similar to a report that already exists. One way to save time and effort is to start with the existing report, save it under a new name, and then modify it to serve a new purpose. This is worthwhile if the effort you put into modifications is less than what it would take to build the new report from scratch.

If you foresee that a report that you've been asked to write could be the first of several similar reports, you can make the job of creating those follow-up reports even easier. Save a version of the first report that contains only those elements that you believe will be common to all the follow-on reports. This will serve as a template for those reports and will give you a valuable head start in producing them. After the template is safely stored on disk, you can proceed to add the elements to the original report that set it apart from all the others that might follow.

In Chapter 2, I lead you on a step-by-step journey through the development of a report, starting with a blank report. There's little benefit in redoing that here. In the following chapters, you have plenty of opportunities to design and build a variety of reports, all starting from a blank report. When you read those chapters, I assume that you've already mastered the basics of report design from scratch and are ready for some advanced material.

Connecting Your Report to Its Data Source

Crystal Reports can accept data from a variety of data sources, using several methods. The breadth of Crystal Reports' data compatibility makes it a versatile tool that you can apply in a number of ways beyond merely creating reports based on the data in relational databases.

Crystal Reports can accept data from five kinds of sources: direct access database files, ODBC data sources, OLE DB, Crystal SQL Designer files, and Crystal Dictionary files. Each of these types of files is accessed in a different way, but you don't need to know the details of how those connections are made.

Accessing database files directly

The fastest way to pull data out of a database and include it in a report is through a direct access interface. This makes sense. The less stuff you have between the database and the report, the shorter the transit time for data going from one to the other. Another advantage of direct data access is the simplicity of the connection. As a report developer, you don't have to know a whole lot about types of connections and middle-tier dynamic link libraries (DLLs). All you need to know is the name of the data source you want to tap for data.

However, as you know, There Ain't No Such Thing As A Free Lunch (TANSTAAFL). The price you pay for the speed and simplicity of a direct connection is the fact that a different, highly customized driver must be used for every different data source. Crystal Reports offers a wide variety of such drivers, so in many cases this is not a handicap. The one area where this becomes a problem is for reports that draw data from two or more different data sources. In such a case, you can't use direct access because you'd have to talk to each data source in its own "language," and Crystal Reports doesn't support using multiple such languages in a single report.

Crystal Reports has direct access drivers for most of the popular PC database formats, including Microsoft Access, the dBase/FoxPro/Clipper triad, and Paradox. In addition, it supports Microsoft DAO/OLE, Btrieve, ACT!, Microsoft Exchange, and Microsoft Outlook. Crystal Reports has direct access drivers for the following client-server SQL databases: Oracle, Microsoft SQL Server, Sybase System 10/11, Informix Online Server, and IBM's DB2 Server. Crystal Reports also talks directly to IBM's Lotus Domino, your computer's local file system, the Windows NT, 2000, or XP Event Log, the Microsoft IIS or Microsoft Proxy log file, Web or IIS log files, SAP database files, and BAAN database files. If it holds data, is fairly widely used, and runs on a Windows box, Crystal Reports probably has a direct access interface for it.

Linking to ODBC data sources

ODBC (Open Database Connectivity) is a standard method of connecting to a wide variety of data sources. It places a layer between applications such as Crystal Reports and databases that translates the ODBC standard requests from the application into the specific form that each different data source requires. Practically all data sources in widespread use today offer an ODBC interface. The ODBC driver connects to the database through this interface. All the application needs to know is that it is communicating with an ODBC-compliant data source.

An ODBC database connection may suffer a performance disadvantage relative to a direct access connection because information must pass through an extra layer of processing. This may or may not be significant, depending on the implementation and the needs of the application. On the plus side, an application that communicates to its data sources through ODBC may pull data from multiple different data sources. It puts out its request in the same ODBC format regardless of which data source it is talking to. Each such source has its own ODBC driver that translates the common ODBC commands into data source-specific commands that the data source can understand and obey.

Data sources for which Crystal Reports has a direct access connection are also reachable through ODBC. For example, you can connect to Microsoft Access either through the direct connection or through ODBC. Performance through the direct connection may be better. As long as your report requires only data from Access, the direct connection may be the better choice. However, if you want to also include data from an Excel spreadsheet, you must use ODBC for both Access and Excel. Excel is an example of a data source for which Crystal Reports does not supply a direct access connection.

Retrieving data from Crystal SQL Designer files

Crystal Reports Designer is a tool you can use to create SQL queries of ODBC data sources. The query runs on a server and returns a result set to your computer in the form of a Crystal SQL Designer file. This off-loading of query processing frees up your computer to concentrate on other tasks, possibly improving performance. The performance improvement is the primary advantage of using Crystal SQL Designer. A second advantage is that you have the full power of SQL to retrieve exactly the data you want.

A potential disadvantage of using Crystal SQL Designer is that you must be fluent in SQL to use it. Gaining that fluency requires some effort, but may be well worth the time you put into it. Start by reading my *SQL For Dummies*, 4th Edition (published by Wiley Publishing, Inc.). It gives you a painless introduction to SQL, while providing a thorough description of all the major features of the language.

Another thing to be aware of is that when you run a Crystal SQL Designer query, it returns a result to your computer in the form of a .QRY file. This file is a snapshot of the data at the time the query was run. If the data in the database is updated later, you have to rerun the query to capture the changes.

Reporting on data in OLE DB data sources

OLE DB is a connectivity methodology similar to ODBC. Both OLE DB and ODBC were developed by Microsoft. OLE DB adds some flexibility in the types of data sources that it can communicate with, such as multidimensional OLAP sources and Web servers. ODBC is designed to communicate with relational databases that use SQL. OLE DB addresses data sources that do not fall into that category, although it works well with relational databases, too. Crystal Reports supports OLE DB data sources, which are called OLE DB providers.

Creating customized data access with Crystal dictionaries

Dictionaries are filters that tailor the appearance of data for specific groups of users or even individual users. Typically set up by Information Systems (IS) managers, a dictionary can give customized access to multiple data sources. Only the database tables or other sources in the dictionary are accessible. Table and source names may be changed to make more sense to the target users. A dictionary can also manipulate the data pulled from the sources without the user being aware that such manipulation is taking place. Users don't need to know as much to use the system effectively, and there is less opportunity for them to make errors.

Which interface should you use?

Which interface to use? It depends. You knew I was going to say that, didn't you? You can, however, draw a few conclusions from the information in this chapter.

- ✔ If your report draws data from only one source and there is a direct access driver for that source, using a direct access driver will probably give you your best performance.

- ✔ If your report draws data from two or more different sources, direct access is not an option.

- ✔ If you're drawing data from multiple relational databases, ODBC is designed to give you what you need.

✔ If one or more of your multiple data sources is not compatible with ODBC, but all your data sources support an OLE DB interface, OLE DB should be your connectivity choice.

✔ SQL programmers prefer Crystal SQL Designer when they want to make a complex retrieval and the bandwidth of the connection between client and server is limited. Keep in mind, however, that the result set returned by a Crystal SQL Designer query is a snapshot of the state of the data sources at the instant in time when the query was run. It does not necessarily reflect the current state of the data.

✔ IS managers can keep their users out of trouble, protect sensitive data, and make the data sources easier to understand by building dictionaries that give users what they need in an understandable form but do not expose parts of the data sources that are not relevant to the users' jobs.

Part II

Moving Up to Professional-Quality Reports

The 5th Wave   By Rich Tennant

"This isn't a quantitative or a qualitative estimate of the job. This is a wish-upon-a-star estimate of the project."

In this part . . .

After you know how to create a report based on database data, it's time to move up to the next level. In the chapters in this part, you discover how to tease out of the database the exact data you want, unobscured by the irrelevant data that surrounds it. You find out how to arrange data in the report to maximize comprehension. You start to master the art of formatting a report so as to draw the reader's attention to the most important information. Finally, you preserve the valuable features that you worked so hard on, so that you can reuse them again and again in reports that you're called on to produce in the coming weeks, months, and years.

Chapter 5

Pulling Specific Data from a Database

*I*f your reports had to only display all the data in your data sources, report creation would be easy. Organizations would not need people as smart and well educated as you to design their reports. Luckily for the job security of people like you and me, report creation is not that simple. Most reports that are of value to people gain that value by extracting from the mass of data in the database only specific information. This usually requires filtering out unwanted records, leaving behind irrelevant fields, combining data, and presenting it in a meaningful way. Database report designers add significant value to any organization that depends on timely access to the information buried in its databases. In this chapter, I introduce you to some of the most useful data retrieval tools in Crystal Reports.

Get Data Quickly with Select Expert

Select Expert is an interactive tool for defining which data items to extract from a database and display in a report. Probably the best way to describe Select Expert is to give examples that show it in action.

Suppose Albert Hellstern, the business manager of Xtreme Mountain Bikes Inc., would like to know the current inventory status and how it compares to the minimum inventory levels that the company likes to maintain for all its products. A query into the relevant tables using Select Expert will retrieve the needed information, and the Report Wizard will format it into a report. Great! This sounds like just what Albert needs.

Follow along to generate this report:

1. **Choose File⇨New.**

   The Crystal Reports Gallery appears.

2. **Select the Using the Report Wizard option. In the Choose a Wizard area, select the Standard Wizard. Click OK.**

   Standard Report Creation Wizard appears.

3. **Find and connect to the xtreme.mdb database.**

   For more information on this process, see Chapters 2 and 3.

4. **Add the tables needed to determine the inventory status.**

   Select the Product, Product Type, and Purchases tables.

5. **Click Next.**

   The Link view of Standard Report Creation Wizard appears, as shown in Figure 5-1. You can see the links that Crystal Reports has inferred to exist between the selected tables. In this case, the inferred links are correct, so there is no need adjust them. The icons to the left of some fields indicate that those fields are indexed. Indexing is a technique used to increase the speed of retrievals. I say more about indexing a little later in the chapter.

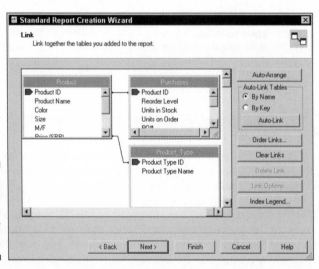

Figure 5-1:
Selected
tables
and their
relationships.

6. **Click Next to move to the Fields view.**

   The tree in the Available Fields pane displays the fields that are available in the tables you have chosen.

7. **Select the fields that you want in the report, and then click the Add button to transfer them to the Fields to Display pane.**

   Figure 5-2 shows how the screen looks after the selection. I selected five fields from the Product table, one from the Product Type table, and two from the Purchases table.

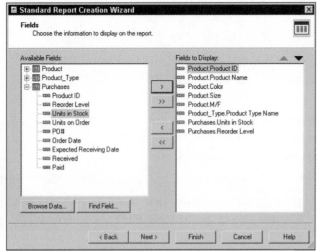

Figure 5-2: The selected fields.

8. **Click Next to move to the Grouping view, and then click Next again to move to the Record Selection view.**

   Albert is primarily concerned with how the Units in Stock field in the Purchases table compares with the Reorder Level in that same table. Grouping is not appropriate.

9. **Select the Reorder Level field and the Units in Stock field from the tree in the left pane, and add them to the right pane.**

   The screen should look like Figure 5-3. Notice that when you add a field to the Filter Fields pane, a pull-down list appears below the pane. The list displays a number of comparison operators that allow you to compare the contents of the selected field to values that appear in that field in the table in the database. This feature, by itself, does not give Albert what he wants. He wants to compare the In Stock status of each product against the specific Reorder Level for that product, not against some fixed number. By continuing, Albert can arrive at the solution he wants.

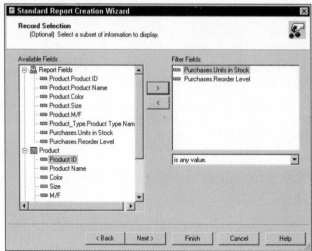

10. **For the present example, leave the default choice of** is any value, **and then click Next to display the Template view.**

   Several templates are available.

11. **Select the No Template option, and then click the Finish button.**

   Many of the templates are fancy or colorful, but Albert doesn't care about being fancy, so he sticks with the No Template option. The report is on the Preview tab, as shown in Figure 5-4.

The report shows the information you expect, but the formatting could be improved. Some columns, such as Color and Product Type Name, are wider than necessary to fully display the data they contain. Other columns are too narrow to fully display their headings. Switch to the Design tab and make manual adjustments to these layout features. Figure 5-5 shows one result.

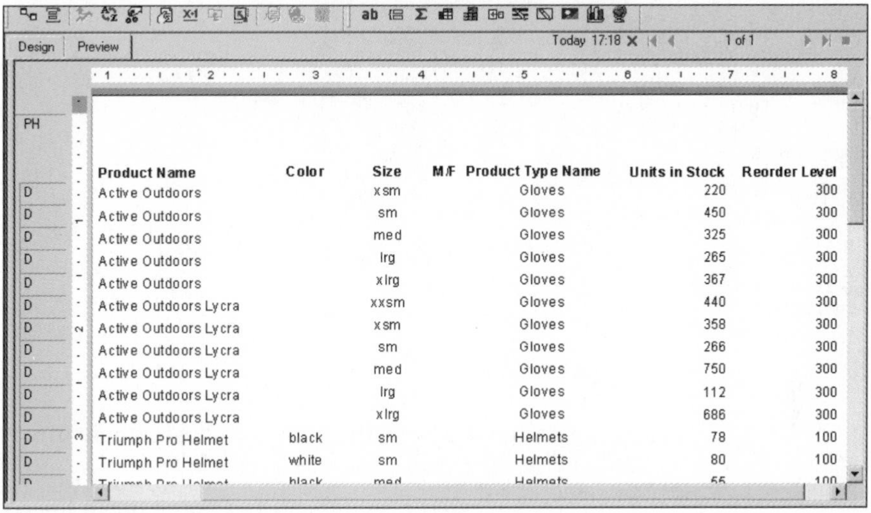

Product Name	Color	Size	M/F	Product Type Name	Units in Stock	Reorder Level
Active Outdoors		xsm		Gloves	220	300
Active Outdoors		sm		Gloves	450	300
Active Outdoors		med		Gloves	325	300
Active Outdoors		lrg		Gloves	265	300
Active Outdoors		xlrg		Gloves	367	300
Active Outdoors Lycra		xxsm		Gloves	440	300
Active Outdoors Lycra		xsm		Gloves	358	300
Active Outdoors Lycra		sm		Gloves	266	300
Active Outdoors Lycra		med		Gloves	750	300
Active Outdoors Lycra		lrg		Gloves	112	300
Active Outdoors Lycra		xlrg		Gloves	686	300
Triumph Pro Helmet	black	sm		Helmets	78	100
Triumph Pro Helmet	white	sm		Helmets	80	100

Figure 5-5: Reformatted inventory level report.

This is pretty good. It displays all the products and shows their inventory levels compared to their reorder levels. However, the report doesn't emphasize the products in critically short supply. What Albert would really like to see is a report that lists only those products whose inventory level is at or below their reorder level. To get that, you have to go beyond what a straightforward use of Crystal Reports can provide.

Suppose an emergency crops up before you can figure out how to get the report that Albert wants. A worker comes in from the warehouse and tells him that some of the helmets are in short supply. It's difficult to keep a full line of helmets in stock because they come in several different sizes and colors. Albert knows that the reorder level for helmets is 100 units, so he asks you to modify the report you have just created to show only items where fewer than 100 units are in stock.

Your job now is to quickly give Albert the information he needs:

1. **With the inventory report open, choose Report⇨Select Expert.**

   The Choose Field dialog box appears.

2. In the Purchases table, select Purchases.Units in Stock. Make sure that you select the field from the Report Fields category, not from the actual tables.

Your screen should appear as shown in Figure 5-6.

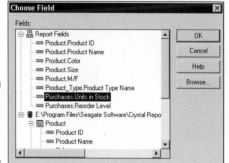

Figure 5-6:
Selecting the Units in Stock field.

3. Click OK.

Select Expert appears, with the pull-down list that you can use to specify a condition for the Purchases.Units in Stock field.

4. Select is less than or equal to **and enter** 100 **in the comparison field, as shown in Figure 5-7.**

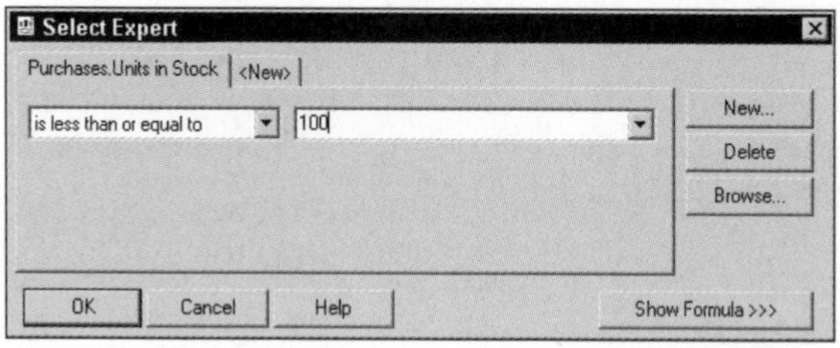

Figure 5-7:
Selecting a condition.

5. Click OK.

A dialog box appears, asking whether you want to use data that was saved earlier or refresh the data by querying the database again.

This question has major performance implications. For a large database with many records, refreshing the data could take a significant amount of time. On the other hand, saved data is available instantly. If you have reason to believe that the database has not changed since it was saved, you can speed up your task by using saved data. In Albert's case, that's not a good idea because someone may have just bought a lot of helmets.

6. **Albert wants to know what the inventory status is right now, so click the Refresh Data button.**

   Figure 5-8 shows the report that appears.

Figure 5-8:
Inventory
report
showing
only
products
where the
stock is
less than
or equal
to 100.

Product Name	Color	Size	M/F	Product Type Name	Units in Stock	Reorder Level
Triumph Pro Helmet	black	sm		Helmets	78	100
Triumph Pro Helmet	white	sm		Helmets	80	100
Triumph Pro Helmet	black	med		Helmets	55	100
Triumph Vertigo	black	sm		Helmets	89	100
Triumph Vertigo	red	med		Helmets	92	100
Triumph Vertigo	white	lrg		Helmets	69	100
Guardian "U" Lock				Locks	22	75
Guardian ATB Lock				Locks	56	75
Guardian Mini Lock				Locks	87	75
Roadster Jr BMX			youth	Saddles	75	50
Vesper Comfort ATB			mens	Saddles	41	50
Vesper Comfort Ladies			ladies	Saddles	69	50
Vesper Gelflex ATB			mens	Saddles	88	50
Vesper Gelflex Ladies			ladies	Saddles	97	50

The report shows all products where quantities in stock are less than or equal to 100. This includes some helmets, some locks, and some saddles. All listed helmets are below their reorder quantities and should be ordered immediately. Some of the locks and saddles are below their reorder quantities and some are above, due to the fact that locks and saddles have lower reorder quantities than helmets. Albert can quickly tell from this report which helmets he needs to order. However, it would be better if the report was not cluttered with lock and saddle information, which are not his present concerns. To have that level of specificity, you have to use a formula.

When your comparison is on a numeric field, such as Units in Stock, the available comparison operators, such as *is less than or equal to*, are appropriate for making numeric comparisons. Likewise, for date type data, comparison operators appropriate for dates are available. The types of comparisons you can do depend on the type of data you're looking at.

Using Formulas to Retrieve Data

In Chapter 12, I give formulas extensive coverage. For now, you'll see whether you can help Albert by finding out a little bit about formulas. Suppose he decides that it *is* helpful to know about products other than helmets that are also below their reorder levels, but without the confounding data presented by the rows for those products that are not below their reorder levels. You can help.

You'll manually replace the selection criterion that Units in Stock be less than or equal to 100 with a new, more complex selection criterion that Units in Stock be less than or equal to Reorder Level. In the original selection, you're comparing against a fixed quantity (100). In the new selection, you're comparing against a quantity that varies, depending on the type of product you are examining.

Follow these steps:

1. **Choose Report⇨ Selection Formulas⇨Record.**

    Formula Workshop's Record Selection Formula Editor window appears, as shown in Figure 5-9. It displays the formula that governs the current selection that resulted in the report shown in Figure 5-8. The formula is

    ```
    {Purchases.Units in Stock} <= 100
    ```

    This is the formula that Select Expert created in response to the choices you made.

2. **Create a new formula, replacing the 100 to the right of the <= sign with** `{Purchases.Reorder Level}`.

    To do so, select the 100 and delete it, and then double-click Purchases. Reorder Level in the Report Fields tree (the tree in the upper-left corner of the Record Selection Formula Editor window). Figure 5-10 shows the result.

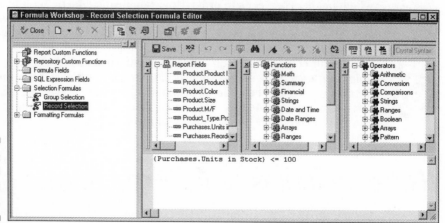

Figure 5-9: The original selection formula.

3. **Click the Close icon in the upper-left corner of the Record Selection Formula Editor.**

   Formula Workshop disappears.

4. **When asked whether you want to save the revised formula, click Yes.**

5. **When asked whether you want to refresh or use saved data, select Refresh Data.**

   The modified report appears, as shown in Figure 5-11. This report displays inventory items where the quantity in stock is less than or equal to the reorder level for that item. This gives Albert a good idea of what he needs to order.

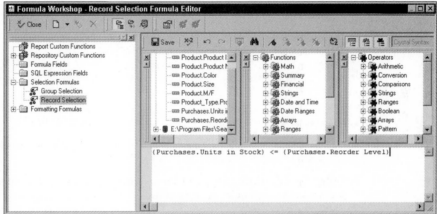

Figure 5-10:
New selection criterion restricts retrieval to items whose stock level is below the reorder level.

Figure 5-11:
The inventory report showing items that are below reorder level.

Product Name	Color	Size	M/F	Product Type Name	Units in Stock	Reorder Level
Active Outdoors		x sm		Gloves	220	300
Active Outdoors		lrg		Gloves	265	300
Active Outdoors Lycra		sm		Gloves	266	300
Active Outdoors Lycra		lrg		Gloves	112	300
Triumph Pro Helmet	black	sm		Helmets	78	100
Triumph Pro Helmet	white	sm		Helmets	80	100
Triumph Pro Helmet	black	med		Helmets	55	100
Triumph Vertigo	black	sm		Helmets	89	100
Triumph Vertigo	red	med		Helmets	92	100
Triumph Vertigo	white	lrg		Helmets	69	100
Guardian "U" Lock				Locks	22	75
Guardian ATB Lock				Locks	56	75
InFlux Crochet Glove		med		Gloves	198	300
InFlux Crochet Glove		lrg		Gloves	220	300

Using Parameter Fields to Retrieve Data at Runtime

To show one of the many things that you can do with parameter fields, let's suppose that Xtreme's Vice President of Sales, Andrew Fuller, would like to have a report that he can run from time to time that will show major purchases and who has made them. To help focus the company's sales efforts, he wants to identify customers who have placed large orders, but wants to also specify what constitutes a large order at the time he runs the report.

The first step in this process is to create a report that lists customers and the orders they have made. The next step is to place a condition on the report that restricts the rows displayed to orders that have a higher dollar value than the value that Andrew enters at runtime. This requires a parameter field rather than a fixed value or a database table field value.

To create the first version of the report that Andrew needs, follow these steps:

1. **Choose File⇨New to display the Crystal Reports Gallery.**

2. **Use the Report Wizard, and select the Standard Wizard option. Click OK.**

3. **When Standard Report Creation Wizard appears, make sure that the xtreme.mdb database is connected.**

   For more information on this process, see Chapters 2 and 3.

4. **Drag Customer and Orders to the Selected Tables pane.**

5. **Click Next.**

   The Link view displays a graphical representation of the tables and the links between them, as shown in Figure 5-12.

6. **Click Next to display the Fields view.**

7. **Select the following fields to display on the report: Customer ID, Customer Name, Contact First Name, Contact Last Name, and Phone from the Customer table and Order Amount from the Orders table.**

   Figure 5-13 shows the Fields view after you make these selections.

8. **Move all the way to the Template view by clicking Next three times, because you're not going to do anything with the Grouping or Record Selection view at this time.**

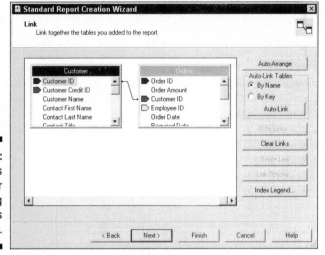

Figure 5-12:
Tables
needed for
the Big
Orders
report.

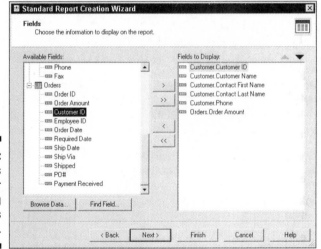

Figure 5-13:
Fields
needed for
the Big
Orders
report.

9. **In the Template view, retain the No Template option, and then click the Finish button.**

   The report looks like Figure 5-14.

   The spacing of the columns is not the greatest, but you can adjust them manually, and do some other formatting, resulting in the report shown in Figure 5-15.

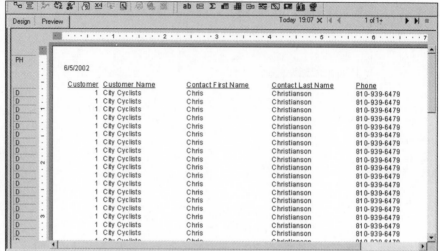

Figure 5-14: First version of the Big Orders report.

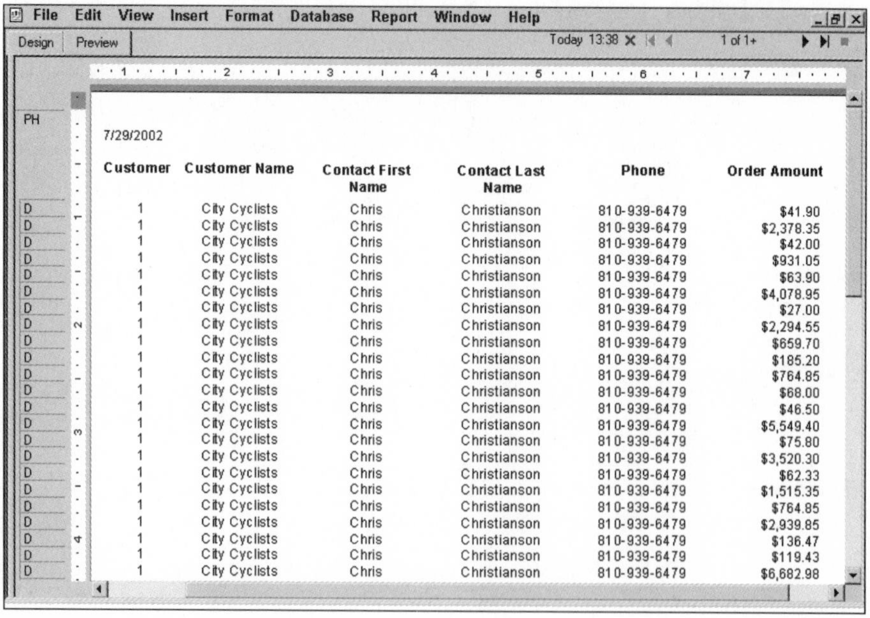

Figure 5-15: Second version of the Big Orders report.

Speed retrievals with indexes

Remember those icons in Figure 5-1? The ones that look like overturned Monopoly© houses? They indicate which fields in the tables are associated with indexes. Records in a database table are generally not arranged in any useful order. Usually, they're in the order in which they were first entered into the table.

To make a selective retrieval such as the one Andrew made to find all orders that exceed $5000, every single record must be examined. If the records had been sorted by Order Amount in descending order, however, only the records that equaled or exceeded $5000 would need to be checked. This could represent a big savings in retrieval time for a large table in which relatively few orders had values of more than $5000.

A lot of overhead is associated with maintaining a data table in sorted order. In addition, sorting it on one field will unsort it on any other field that you might want to use as a retrieval key. The answer is to create indexes for fields that you'll be using as retrieval keys. The icons in Figure 5-1 show which fields are indexed. As you can see, Order Amount is not one of them. If the Orders table grows to hundreds of thousands of rows, and if people are going to be making frequent retrievals based on Order Amount, Andrew might want to ask Xtreme's database administrator to create an index field for Order Amount in the Orders table of the company's database.

The report has almost 2200 records, each of which represents a single order by one of Xtreme's customers. The next step is to create a parameter field to allow Andrew to enter the dollar amount that represents the minimum value of the records he wants to see in this report:

1. **If you can't see Field Explorer on the left edge of the screen, choose View⇨Field Explorer.**

   Field Explorer appears.

2. **In the Field Explorer tree, right-click the Parameter Fields option and choose the New command.**

   The Create Parameter Field dialog box appears.

3. **Enter a name for the parameter field, the prompting text that will tell the user what to enter, and the data type of the entry you expect the user to make.**

   For the example, name the parameter field *Lower Limit*. Use *Lower limit for a big order:* as the prompting text. And select the Currency data type in the pull-down list. Figure 5-16 shows the Create Parameter Field dialog box after you make these entries. The choices in the Options area are left at their default values: Multiple values are not allowed and the value entered must be discrete.

4. **Click OK.**

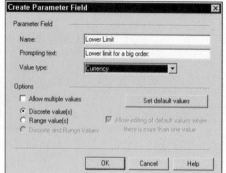

Figure 5-16:
The lower limit parameter field.

Now that you have a parameter field, you need to add it to the Big Orders report as the selection criterion for which of the couple of thousand records in the Orders table will be retrieved. Select Expert is the tool that will enable you to do that:

1. **On the toolbar, click the Select Expert icon.**

   The Choose Field dialog box appears.

2. **Select the field you want to compare against, and then click OK.**

   For the example, select the Order Amount field in the Orders table. Crystal Reports displays the Orders.Order Amount tab of Select Expert.

3. **In the pull-down list, select** is greater than or equal to.

   A data entry field with a pull-down control appears to the right of the list.

4. **Pull down the list and select** {?Lower Limit}.

   Crystal Reports denotes a parameter field by enclosing it in curly braces and prepending the parameter field name with a question mark.

5. **Click OK.**

   The Enter Parameter Values dialog box appears, with the cursor blinking in the Discrete Value text entry box.

6. **Enter** 5000 **as an initial value, and then click OK.**

   The by-now familiar Change in Record Selection Formula Detected dialog box appears, asking whether you want to use saved data or refreshed data.

7. **If there's any possibility that the data has changed since the last time it was saved, select Refresh Data.**

   Figure 5-17 shows the result. The report looks much as it did in Figure 5-15, except there are only a few hundred records instead of thousands and every one of them has an Order Amount of at least $5000.

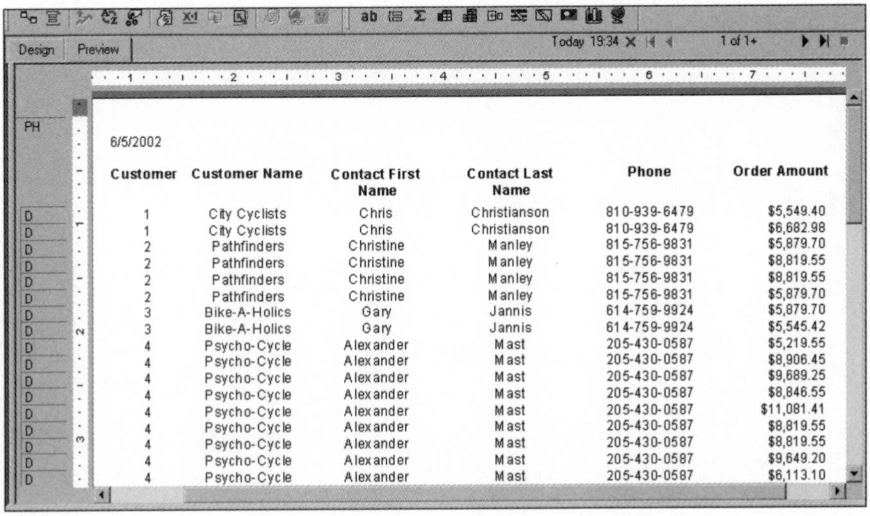

6/5/2002

Customer	Customer Name	Contact First Name	Contact Last Name	Phone	Order Amount
1	City Cyclists	Chris	Christianson	810-939-6479	$5,549.40
1	City Cyclists	Chris	Christianson	810-939-6479	$6,682.98
2	Pathfinders	Christine	Manley	815-756-9831	$5,879.70
2	Pathfinders	Christine	Manley	815-756-9831	$8,819.55
2	Pathfinders	Christine	Manley	815-756-9831	$8,819.55
2	Pathfinders	Christine	Manley	815-756-9831	$5,879.70
3	Bike-A-Holics	Gary	Jannis	614-759-9924	$5,879.70
3	Bike-A-Holics	Gary	Jannis	614-759-9924	$5,545.42
4	Psycho-Cycle	Alexander	Mast	205-430-0587	$5,219.55
4	Psycho-Cycle	Alexander	Mast	205-430-0587	$8,906.45
4	Psycho-Cycle	Alexander	Mast	205-430-0587	$9,689.25
4	Psycho-Cycle	Alexander	Mast	205-430-0587	$8,846.55
4	Psycho-Cycle	Alexander	Mast	205-430-0587	$11,081.41
4	Psycho-Cycle	Alexander	Mast	205-430-0587	$8,819.55
4	Psycho-Cycle	Alexander	Mast	205-430-0587	$8,819.55
4	Psycho-Cycle	Alexander	Mast	205-430-0587	$9,649.20
4	Psycho-Cycle	Alexander	Mast	205-430-0587	$6,113.10

Figure 5-17: Big Orders report run with a $5000 lower limit.

Andrew can now see at a glance which customers make a large number of orders valued at over $5000 as well as which ones occasionally make orders that large. He can now formulate sales promotions targeted at these customers.

Suppose now, after seeing the hundreds of entries in the report in Figure 5-17, Andrew wants to see a list containing only customers who have made *really* big orders, those that exceed $9000. All you have to do is rerun the report:

1. **Save the report.**

   Choose File➪Save As, and name it Big Orders.

2. **On the toolbar, click the Refresh icon to rerun the report.**

   The Refresh Report Data dialog box appears, asking whether you want to use the current parameter values or prompt for new parameter values.

3. **Select the Prompt for New Parameter Values option, and then click OK.**

   The Enter Parameter Values dialog box appears.

4. **Enter** 9000 **in the Discrete Value field, and then click OK.**

   Now the report contains only 43 records. Only orders of at least $9000 are included in this version of the Big Orders report.

You can rerun the report as many times as you want, changing the Lower Limit parameter each time, to get a precise idea of which customers make large buys, regardless of how you want to define a large buy.

Troubleshooting Tips

Three basic problems might arise when you try to retrieve specific data from a database:

- ✔ You don't retrieve all the data that you want.
- ✔ You retrieve data that you don't want.
- ✔ You retrieve all the data that you want and none of the data that you don't want, but the retrieval takes an unacceptably long time.

One possible reason for not retrieving all the data you want is failing to specify all the tables that you need. Some of these tables may not contain a single field that you will display, but they are needed anyway to provide a link between the tables that contain fields that do get displayed.

A second possible reason for not retrieving all the data you want is failing to specify all the fields you need from the tables that you have selected. Make sure you understand exactly how the tables relate to each other and to the information you're asking for. If what you need depends on multiple fields in multiple tables, all of those fields must all be selected.

A third possible reason for not retrieving all the data you want is specifying your selection condition incorrectly with Select Expert. You must choose from a number of comparison operators and must apply the operator to the correct constant value, field value, or parameter value. You can verify that you're comparing against the correct constant value or field value when you create the report. However, if the user enters an incorrect parameter value at runtime, it could cause incorrect results that might slip by undetected.

Retrieving data that you don't want is another possible consequence of not specifying the right tables, or the right fields within those tables, or the right comparison conditions with Select Expert. All the comments just expressed for not retrieving all the information you want apply equally well to the problem of retrieving data that you don't want.

Slow retrievals, which can cause problems when dealing with large data sets, can often be speeded up tremendously by careful analysis followed by indexing the fields upon which retrieval criteria are based. This is a job for the database administrator, not the report designer.

Chapter 6

Sorting, Grouping, and Totaling Result Sets

In This Chapter

▶ Putting report data in a logical order by sorting

▶ Clustering similar data items with grouping

▶ Figuring out percentages

▶ Adding drill-down functionality

▶ Adding things with running totals

▶ Solving sorting, grouping, and totaling problems

*T*he primary goal in creating a report is to put database data into a meaningful and easily understandable form. To achieve this goal, you must extract only the data you want, from the specific rows and columns of the relevant tables. However, if you don't present the information in the report in a logical manner, meaning and understanding can suffer.

You can greatly enhance the value of a report by arranging the retrieved data in a way that clearly conveys what it means and emphasizes its important features. Sort the records, and group related records in such a way that the significant information is emphasized. Crystal Reports has powerful tools to help you sort report data in a variety of ways, group related data together, and summarize data within groups.

Sorting Report Data

In most cases, the original order of the data in a database is not the most helpful order, so you must reorder the data to have the most useful report. The sort function in Crystal Reports will do this for you.

The way that data is sorted depends on how you specify the sort and on the type of data that you want to sort. You can sort data in ascending order or descending order. In general, *ascending* means lowest to highest and *descending* means highest to lowest. What ascending and descending mean for any given sort, however, depends on the type of data you are sorting.

The types of data you might want to sort include the following:

- ✔ Single-character string fields
- ✔ Multiple-character string fields
- ✔ Currency fields
- ✔ Number fields
- ✔ Date fields
- ✔ Date-time fields
- ✔ Time fields
- ✔ Boolean fields

Assuming an ascending sort order, Table 6-1 shows how things will be sorted. For descending order, just reverse the sequence.

Table 6-1	Ascending Sort Order for Various Data Types
Field Type	*Sort Order*
Single-character string field	Blank
	Punctuation mark
	Numeral
	Uppercase letter
	Lowercase letter
Multiple-character string field	First character, then second, then third, and so on; for example: *mm* comes before *mmm* and ALLEN comes before Abe
Currency field	Numeric order
Number field	Numeric order
Date field	Chronological order

Field Type	Sort Order
Date-time field	Chronological order, first by date and then by time
Time field	Chronological order
Boolean field	False, then true

If a sort is based on a field that contains null values, the null values are sorted before non-null values. A field is said to have a *null value* when it has nothing in it. In contrast, zero is not a null value; it's a definite value. A blank space is not a null value; it's also a definite value.

Sorting based on multiple fields

When you sort data items based on the value of one field, the outcome is straightforward. If the sort is ascending, it proceeds according to the rules shown in Table 6-1. If the sort is descending, the sorted order is the reverse of an ascending sort. Sometimes, however, you want to sort data based on the contents of more than one field.

Consider for example, the Customer table in the Xtreme database. Xtreme's Sales Manager might want a list of customers sorted first by country, then by region within a country, and finally by customer name within a region. Crystal Reports can perform such a nested sort. In fact, it can do so for as many levels of nesting as you want. To build such a report, follow these steps.

1. **In Crystal Reports Gallery, select the Using the Report Wizard option. Under Choose a Wizard, select Standard. Click OK.**

2. **Add the Customer table from the xtreme.mdb database to the Selected Tables pane.**

3. **Click Next (in Standard Report Creation Wizard) to display the Fields view.**

4. **Add the Customer ID, Customer Name, Region, and Country fields to the Fields to Display pane.**

5. **Click Next three times to display the Template view.**

   At this point, you don't want to group records or select specific records, so you skip those pages.

6. **Retain the No Template option, and then click the Finish button.**

   This produces the report shown in Figure 6-1.

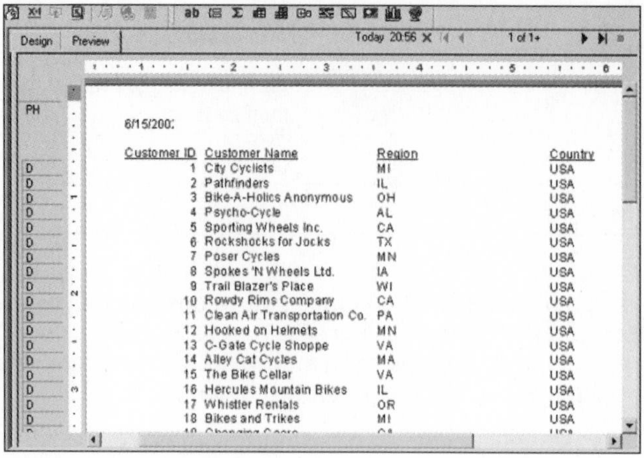

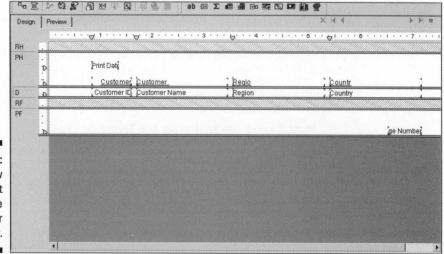

Figure 6-1:
First draft
of the
Customer
report,
sorted by
Customer
ID.

At this point, the report has the data you want, but it's sorted by Customer ID because that's the first field you specified in the Fields view. Furthermore, the columns are not centered, and the report needs a title. To correct these problems, do the following:

1. **Switch to Design view.**

   The report appears like that shown in Figure 6-2.

2. **Click each field in both the Page Header and Data sections to select them, and then click the Align Center icon in the Formatting toolbar to center the field's contents.**

   Changing the justification of all fields to center balances the appearance of the report.

Figure 6-2:
Design view
of the first
draft of the
Customer
report.

3. **Right-click in the area to the left of the Report Header section and choose Don't Suppress.**

4. **Pull down the border between the Report Header section and the Page Header section to make room for the report title in the Report Header.**

5. **On the Insert Tools toolbar, click the Insert Text Object icon, and then drag the text box that appears into the Report Header.**

6. **In the text box, type** Customer List, Sorted by Country and Region.

    This is the report title.

7. **Expand the text box to the left and right so that it spans the entire width of the report. Expand it vertically so that it can accommodate a large font.**

8. **Center the report title in the text box, make it Bold, and increase its font size by clicking the Increase Font Size icon.**

    Figure 6-3 shows what Design view looks like after you have made these modifications.

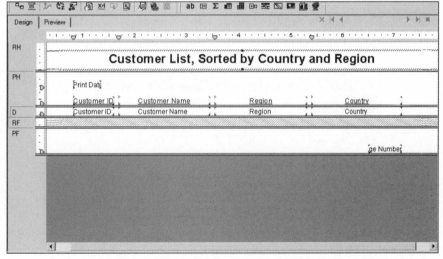

Figure 6-3: Design view of the modified Customer report, still sorted by customer ID.

This design produces the report preview shown in Figure 6-4.

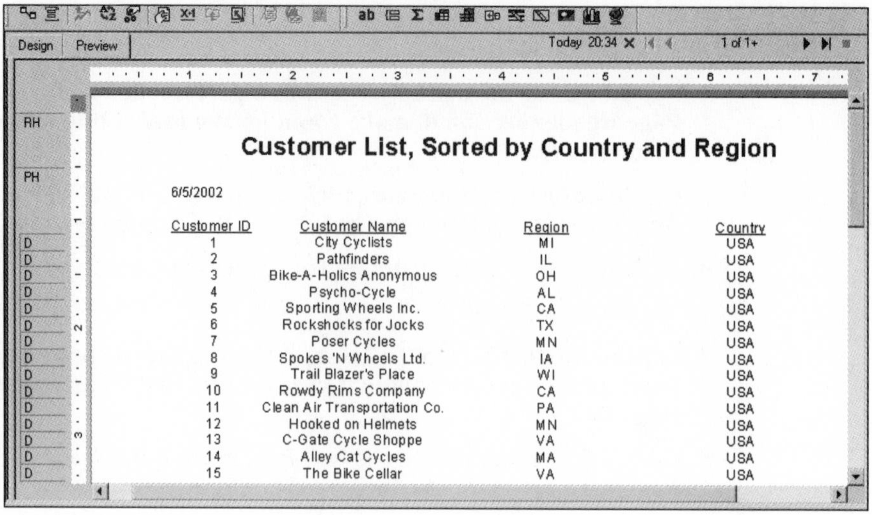

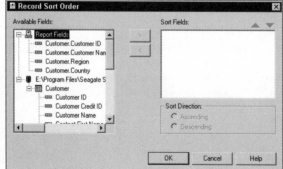

Figure 6-4:
Preview of
the modified
Customer
report,
sorted by
country and
region.

The report looks nice, but it is not sorted by country and region. To remedy
that problem, follow these steps:

1. **Choose Report⇨ Record Sort Expert.**

    The Record Sort Order dialog box appears, as shown in Figure 6-5.

Figure 6-5:
Specify how
the report
will be
sorted.

2. **In the Report Fields area of the Available Fields pane, select
   Customer.Country, and then click the > button. Do the same for
   Customer.Region and then for Customer.Customer Name.**

3. **Make sure that the Sort Direction is Ascending (A) for all three fields, and then click OK.**

   The records of the report are sorted first by country, then by region within a country, and finally by customer name within a region. Figure 6-6 shows the properly sorted report.

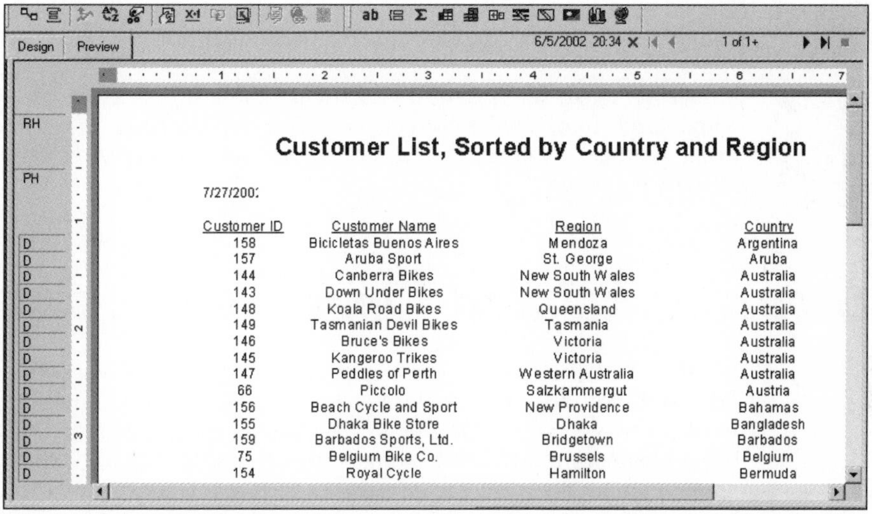

Customer List, Sorted by Country and Region

7/27/200:

Customer ID	Customer Name	Region	Country
158	Bicicletas Buenos Aires	Mendoza	Argentina
157	Aruba Sport	St. George	Aruba
144	Canberra Bikes	New South Wales	Australia
143	Down Under Bikes	New South Wales	Australia
148	Koala Road Bikes	Queensland	Australia
149	Tasmanian Devil Bikes	Tasmania	Australia
146	Bruce's Bikes	Victoria	Australia
145	Kangeroo Trikes	Victoria	Australia
147	Peddles of Perth	Western Australia	Australia
66	Piccolo	Salzkammergut	Austria
156	Beach Cycle and Sport	New Providence	Bahamas
155	Dhaka Bike Store	Dhaka	Bangladesh
159	Barbados Sports, Ltd.	Bridgetown	Barbados
75	Belgium Bike Co.	Brussels	Belgium
154	Royal Cycle	Hamilton	Bermuda

Figure 6-6: Customer report, sorted by country, region, and customer name.

Notice that the first record is for a customer in Argentina and the second is for a customer in Aruba. The first sort key is Country. Notice also that within Australia, New South Wales comes before Queensland, which precedes Tasmania and Victoria. The second sort key is Region. Finally, note that within Victoria, Bruce's Bikes comes before Kangaroo Trikes. The third sort key is Customer Name. The report meets the objectives of the development effort in terms of both information content and ease of understanding.

Sorting and performance

The time it takes Crystal Reports to produce a report can depend, to a large measure, on the sorting that the report requires. For databases with tables consisting of many records, sort times can be a major portion of the total times it takes to produce a report.

Sort time is affected by the fields that you sort on. In most cases, you can sort a large table on a field that has been indexed orders of magnitude faster than you can sort the same table on a nonindexed field. The lesson here is to sort on indexed fields whenever possible. If you regularly run reports that include sorts on nonindexed fields, consider talking to your database administrator (DBA) about adding indexes to those fields. A performance penalty is associated with maintaining an index, but if you don't update the data table often and run reports frequently, the updating overhead may be insignificant compared to the speedup in report generation.

It does *not* make sense to index a field in a table with few records or in a table with a large number of records if the index field can take on only one of a small number of values. The cost of maintaining the index exceeds the benefit to be gained from it.

Grouping Related Items

A simple sort, such as the one in the preceding section, works fine when all you want to do is put a list of items in some order. Often, however, you want to do more with your data, such as displaying subtotals, counts, averages, or other summary information along with each group. Crystal Reports offers great flexibility in specifying groups, as well as a wide variety of summarization facilities. Taken together, these grouping and summarization capabilities are among the most advanced of any reporting tool.

To demonstrate a small fraction of the power of Crystal Reports' grouping facilities, take another look at the Xtreme Mountain Bikes database. Suppose that the Vice President of Sales wants to get a better idea of where customer orders are coming from. Focusing on Mexico, he wants a report that shows order totals grouped by state and sorted by customer name within each state. Follow these steps to build that report for him:

1. **In Crystal Reports Gallery, select the Using the Report Wizard option. Under Choose a Wizard, select Standard. Click OK.**

2. **In the Available Data Sources pane, add the Customer and the Orders tables to the Selected Tables pane.**

3. **Click Next.**

   This displays the Link view, as shown in Figure 6-7.

4. **Click Next.**

   The Fields view is displayed.

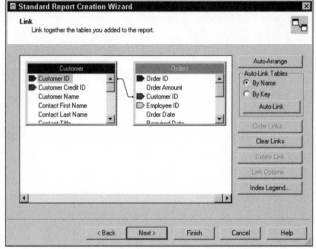

Figure 6-7:
The
Customer
and Orders
tables,
connected
by Customer
ID.

5. **Select the Customer Name and Region fields from the Customer table and the Order Amount field from the Orders table.**

6. **Click Next.**

   The Grouping view is the next to appear.

7. **To meet the Vice President's needs, group by Region.**

   To do so, move Customer.Region to the Group By pane.

8. **The default sort order (ascending) is fine, so click Next.**

   The Summaries view appears. Crystal Reports has assumed that the field you want to summarize is the Order Amount field, because it's the only numeric field in the report. This is a good assumption, as is the assumption that the type of summary you want is a sum rather than an average or some other kind of summary.

   Although the default summary type of Sum is the one you want for this report, a number of other options are available. Average gives you the average value for the group; maximum displays the maximum value for the group, and minimum displays the minimum value. Statistical functions and a simple count of the number of records in the group are available as well.

9. **Click Next three times.**

   You don't need to change anything on the Group Sorting view, and you don't want a Chart, so you skip these views.

10. **In the Record Selection view, include in the report the records for customers only in Mexico.**

    In the Available Fields pane, select Country and add it to the Filter Fields pane. In the pull-down list below the Filter Fields pane, select `is equal to`, and from the pull-down list that pops up below it, select `Mexico`.

11. **Click Next.**

    The Template view appears.

12. **Retain the No Template option, and then click the Finish button.**

    This displays the report shown in Figure 6-8.

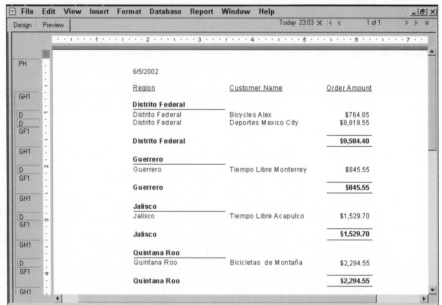

Figure 6-8: Customer report, grouped by region.

As with most reports created by Standard Report Creation Wizard, this one could use some fine-tuning. The customer regions appear too often, and the report could use a bold, centered title. Switch to the Design tab and make the adjustments that will correct these problems. After the adjustments, the Design view appears as shown in Figure 6-9 and the Preview view appears as shown in Figure 6-10.

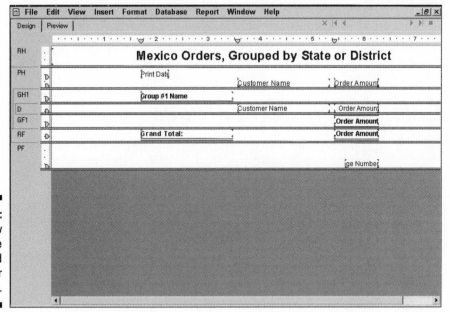

Figure 6-9:
Design view
of the
reformatted
Customer
report.

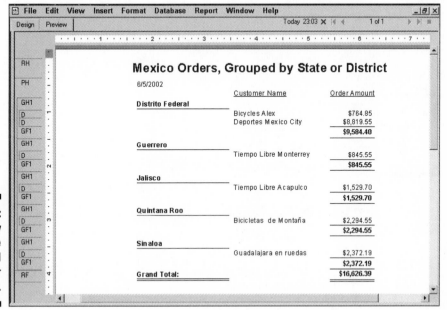

Figure 6-10:
Preview
of the
reformatted
Customer
report.

It's now easy for the Vice President of Sales to see which states in Mexico are producing orders, and which customers in those states are placing orders. Thanks to the group subtotals and a Grand Total at the bottom of the report, he can also see the total value of orders in each state and in the entire country.

Calculating Percentages

Suppose Xtreme's Vice President of Sales feels it would be more instructive to know the percentage rather than the dollar value of Mexico's order total coming from each state. Simply modify the existing report to include percentage summary fields instead of the sum field:

1. **In Design view, right-click the Order Amount field in the GF1 section and choose Edit Summary.**

   The Edit Summary dialog box appears, as shown in Figure 6-11.

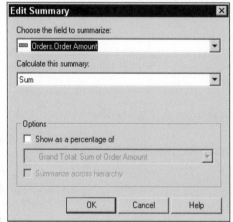

Figure 6-11: The Order Amount field.

2. **Select the Show as a Percentage of option.**

   This activates the drop-down list that shows the default choice, Grand Total: Sum of Order Amount.

3. **You want to display the group totals as percentages of the Grand Total, so click OK.**

4. **Switch to the Preview tab.**

   The report looks like Figure 6-12.

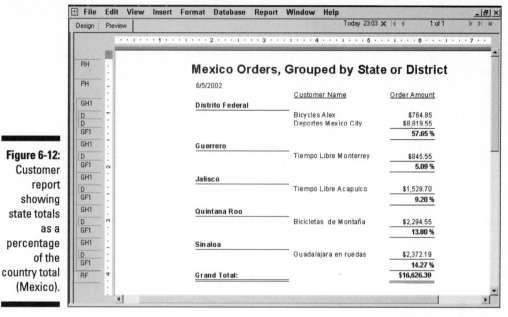

Figure 6-12:
Customer
report
showing
state totals
as a
percentage
of the
country total
(Mexico).

This report makes it immediately obvious that more than half of Mexico's orders are coming from Distrito Federal. This information could cause the company to change its marketing strategy to encourage orders in other parts of the country.

Drilling Down for Detail

In the report you just prepared for Xtreme's Vice President of Sales, it's easy to see which states most sales are coming from because there aren't that many customers in Mexico. The same report might not be so informative if it were run for the U.S., where many more customers are located. In fact, the first page of the same report for the U.S would look like Figure 6-13.

To change the Mexico report to a report on U.S orders instead, follow these steps:

1. **Choose Report⇨Select Expert.**

   The Select Expert dialog box appears.

2. **Select Customer.Country is equal to USA in place of the existing Customer.Country is equal to Mexico.**

3. **Click OK.**

Figure 6-13:
Customer
report
showing
state totals
as a
percentage
of country
total (USA).

4. **Click Refresh Data.**

5. **Save this report as Customer Orders, Grouped by State or District (USA).**

This report is not too helpful. It tells us that Psycho-Cycle, Benny—The Spokes Person, and The Great Bike Shop in Alabama have made a lot of orders, but that's about it — unless you're willing to riffle through a lot a pages. You can hide specific customer information to present a more general picture of orders. If a report viewer then wants the specific information about any particular state, he or she can drill down by double-clicking that item. When the user hovers the cursor over the group header of interest, it changes to a magnifying glass icon. At that point, double-clicking displays the hidden detail data about individual orders.

To add drill-down functionality to this report, do the following:

1. **Switch to Design view.**

2. **Right-click the D designator to the left of the Detail section and choose Select Hide (Drill-Down OK).**

   The Detail section appears dimmed.

3. **Switch back to Preview mode, and you see the display in Figure 6-14.**

This information is much more helpful for strategic decision making. It's easy to see which states are contributing to Xtreme's bottom line and which are not. If report viewers want to see the detail for a specific state, they can double-click the group header or group footer for that state. Figure 6-15 shows what this looks like.

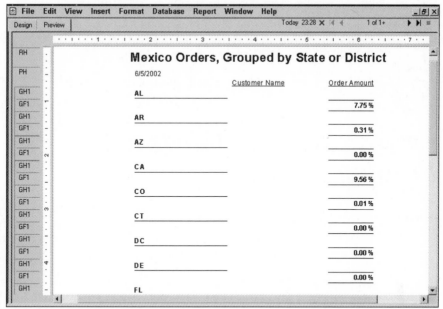

Figure 6-14:
Customer report with the details hidden.

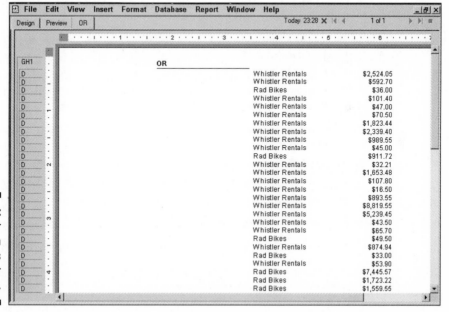

Figure 6-15:
Customer report with details shown for Oregon.

The drill-down capability of Crystal Reports provides tremendous flexibility to online report viewers. Different viewers can see different levels of detail, even though they're all viewing the same report. Save this report before moving on to the next section.

To return from a drilldown, simply click the Preview tab.

Keeping Track of Things with Running Totals

Reports with summarized group totals, like those in the preceding section, are valuable for many purposes, but don't satisfy all needs. Sometimes it's helpful to see how the status of an item changes with time. Crystal Reports' running total facility gives that kind of information.

To see how that might work, construct a variant of the Order report for Mexico where the total value of all orders is tracked as a function of order date:

1. **Select Standard Report Creation Wizard and the xtreme.mdb database.**

2. **Select the Customer and Orders tables and make sure they're linked by the Customer ID field.**

3. **Add the Customer Name field from the Customer table and the Order Amount and Order Date fields from the Orders table to the Fields to Display pane in Standard Report Creation Wizard.**

4. **For this report, skip the Grouping view and move to the Record Selection view.**

5. **Add the Customer table's Country field to the Filter Fields pane. In the pull-down lists that appear, select** is equal to **and** Mexico.

   This means the report will display results only for Mexico.

6. **Retain the No Template option, and then click the Finish button.**

   You're not really finished, as one look at the report preview (Figure 6-16) will tell you.

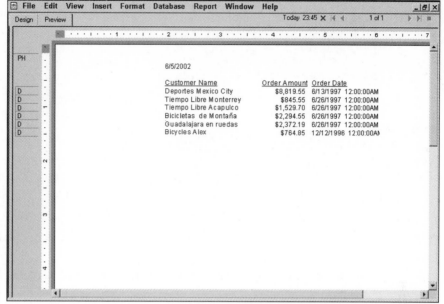

Figure 6-16:
Customer
report with
an
incomplete
running
total.

As yet, the running total column is not on the report, the Order Date column shows times, and the report title is missing. Switch to the Design tab to put the report into final form. You can add the title — Mexico Orders, with Running Totals — in much the same way that you did for the previous examples. You can change the format of the Order Date field to eliminate the time information. Just right-click the Order Date field and choose Format Field. When the Format Editor appears, use it to change the date format.

For the running total, you want to place a fourth column to the right of the Order Date column. To do that, follow these steps:

1. **Make sure that the Design tab is displayed.**

2. **If the Field Explorer is not currently displayed, choose View⇨Field Explorer.**

3. **Select the Running Total Fields option.**

4. **Click the New icon at the top of Field Explorer.**

   The Create Running Total Field dialog box appears, as shown in Figure 6-17.

5. **In the Running Total Name box, replace the default name with** Order Total.

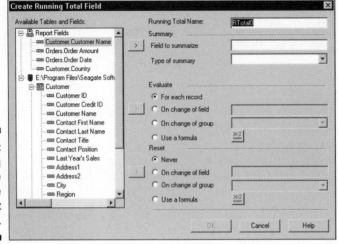

Figure 6-17:
The Running
Total Name
is the
default
name.

6. **In the Report Fields area of the Available Tables and Fields pane, select Order Amount. Then click the arrowhead pointing to the Field to Summarize box.**

   The default *sum* appears in the Type of Summary pull-down list. This is what you want, so proceed to the next step.

7. **From the Orders table in the Available Tables and Fields pane, select Orders.Order ID. In the Evaluate area, select the On Change of Field option, and then click the arrowhead pointing to the Evaluate area.**

   The report will be displaying all the orders for Mexico, so you want the running total to be updated for each order (each time the Order ID changes).

8. **Because you want the running total to be cumulative for the entire report, leave the Reset option set to Never, and then click OK.**

   The Create Running Total Field dialog box disappears, once again showing Field Explorer.

9. **Drag the running total field (Order Total) from Field Explorer to your report, just to the right of the Order Date field.**

   Your Design view should look similar to Figure 6-18.

10. **Switch to Preview mode, and you see a display similar to the one in Figure 6-19.**

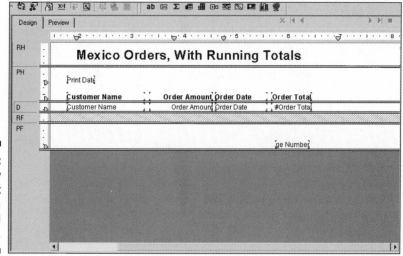

Figure 6-18:
Design view
of the report
with a
running total
column.

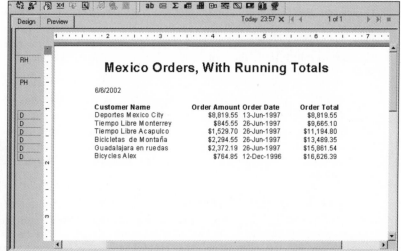

Figure 6-19:
Preview of
the report
with a
running total
column.

The report is now nicely laid out and balanced, but it's not sorted in chronological order. To remedy that situation, follow these steps:

1. On the Expert Tools toolbar, click the Record Sort Expert icon.

The Record Sort Order dialog box appears.

2. **Add Orders.Order Date to the Sort Fields pane.**

3. **Leave the Sort Direction at Ascending, and then click OK.**

4. **Switch to Preview mode, if necessary.**

   You can see that the report is sorted in chronological order.

Troubleshooting Sorting, Grouping, and Totaling Problems

What can go wrong when you try to include sorting, grouping, or totaling in a report? In this section, I take each case in turn.

Sorting problems and how to solve them

Crystal Reports gives you many options for sorting, so many things can go wrong. Crystal Reports will always do exactly what you tell it to do. The problem is that it's not always clear what you should tell it. You can sort on one field or on multiple fields. You can sort an entire report or within each group in the report.

The main solution to any sorting problem is to have a clear idea of how you want the report to be sorted. Decide which fields you want to sort on and which should be specified first. For a field with multiple sort keys, the second sort key comes into play only when multiple records have the same value for the first sort key. Decide whether you want the sort to be ascending or descending.

After you decide exactly how you want your information to be sorted, choose Report➪Record Sort Expert or click the Record Sort Expert icon to display the Record Sort Order dialog box. The left pane shows all the fields you might want to sort by; the right pane (Sort Fields) is waiting for you to add them.

You must add the fields to the Sort Fields pane in the correct order. First add the field that you want as your primary sort key; next add the field that you want as the secondary sort key, and so on. After you select the appropriate sort direction (ascending or descending) for each sort key, click OK to execute the sort. In the Sort Fields pane, a field that will be sorted in ascending order is preceded by the letter *A*. Similarly, a field that will be sorted in descending order is preceded by the letter *D*. A field with multiple sort keys might be sorted in an ascending direction for one key and a descending direction for another.

Unusual grouping options

Separating report records into groups of related items is not difficult, but the rich array of options that Crystal Reports gives you for grouping might be confusing. For example, you can sort not only individual records but also groups. You can sort them in ascending order, descending order, the original order in which they appear in the database, or in some other specified order. To place a new level of grouping into an existing report, choose Insert⇨Group and specify the options you want in the Insert Group dialog box that appears.

You can choose to include some groups in the report and exclude others. Select Expert is the tool you use to do that job. With Select Expert, select the groups to display by specifying a field to select on or by specifying a formula that determines which groups to include.

If you've created groups in a report but now decide that the grouping you've created is not the best, you can change it. Choose Report⇨Group Expert. This displays the Group Expert dialog box, as shown in Figure 6-20.

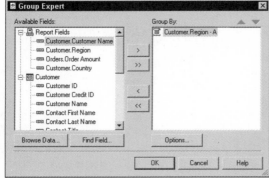

Figure 6-20:
You can change the grouping in a report.

You can change the field that the group is sorted by, the sort order, and the name of the group. You can specify whether or not you want to keep the group together after the change, and whether to repeat the group header at the top of each page.

Getting the right totals

Crystal Reports enables you to print subtotals in group footers as well as a grand total at the end of the report. You can print running totals also. With all these possibilities, you might specify your subtotals incorrectly. It's a good idea to run your report with a few records of sample data, where you know what the correct subtotals should be. If what you get isn't what you expect, check how you specified the subtotals to be computed. If you find an error in the way you've specified a subtotal, you can delete the erroneous total and replace it with the correct one.

Chapter 7

Mastering Report Sections

● ●

In This Chapter

▶ Resizing sections

▶ Controlling group placement

▶ Creating summary and drill-down reports

▶ Generating mailing labels

▶ Troubleshooting problems with layout

● ●

As you might have seen in other chapters, Crystal Reports divides a report document into sections, including the Report Header section, the Page Header section, the Details section, the Report Footer section, and the Page Footer section. What you perhaps have not seen yet is the tremendous flexibility this architecture provides. A report can have multiple copies of each section, each one serving a different purpose.

You also have a lot of leeway in how you format a section. You can vary the height, the color, and even the number of columns in each section. By using Crystal Reports tools creatively, you can give your report the appearance you want.

Changing the Size of a Section

The width of a section is the same as the width of the report that the section is in. You determine this value when you set your margins.

The height of a section begins at some default value. If that value agrees with the appearance that you want, you can leave it the way it is. If you want a different height for a section, it's easy to change, as shown next.

Vertical spacing between lines

Consider the vertical spacing between the lines of a variant of the Mexico Orders, with Running Totals report that you create in Chapter 6. This version of the report has a box around the fields and vertical lines between the columns. You can add this effect to your reports using the Insert Box and Insert Line icons on the Insert Tools toolbar.

As you can see from Figure 7-1, the horizontal lines are quite close. This arrangement allows the maximum number of lines to be displayed on each page.

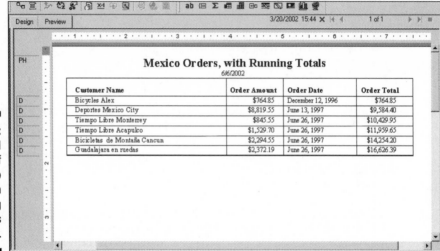

Figure 7-1: Enhanced version of the Mexico Orders, with Running Totals report.

Because this report has only a few lines, placing the lines close together has no real advantage. To make it easier to read the report, it would be better to give each line a little more room. This is an easy adjustment to make:

1. **Switch to the Design tab.**

2. **Move the cursor to the bottom of the Details section.**

   The cursor changes shape, as shown in Figure 7-2. When the cursor takes on the appearance of the sizing cursor, you can use it to drag the section boundary up or down to give you the amount of vertical height you want for the section in question.

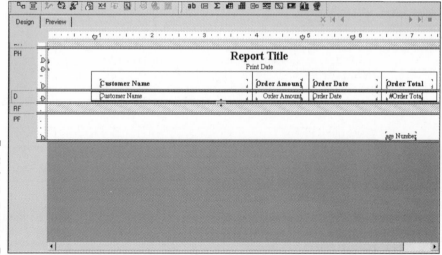

3. **Drag the Details section boundary down, as shown in Figure 7-3.**

   Note that the borderline below the Detail fields has not moved.

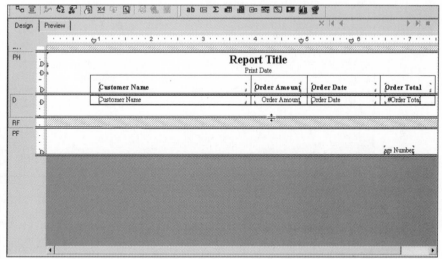

4. **To maintain an appearance similar to the original report, click the borderline to select it.**

   This highlights the border box and displays drag handles at the corners and the middle of the box.

5. Grab the center-bottom handle and drag the bottom borderline down to the section boundary, leaving it as shown in Figure 7-4.

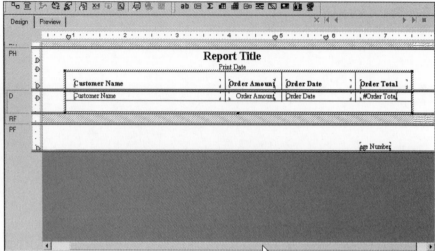

Figure 7-4: The bottom borderline is now on top of the bottom boundary of the Details section.

6. Switch to the Preview tab.

The report now looks like the one in Figure 7-5.

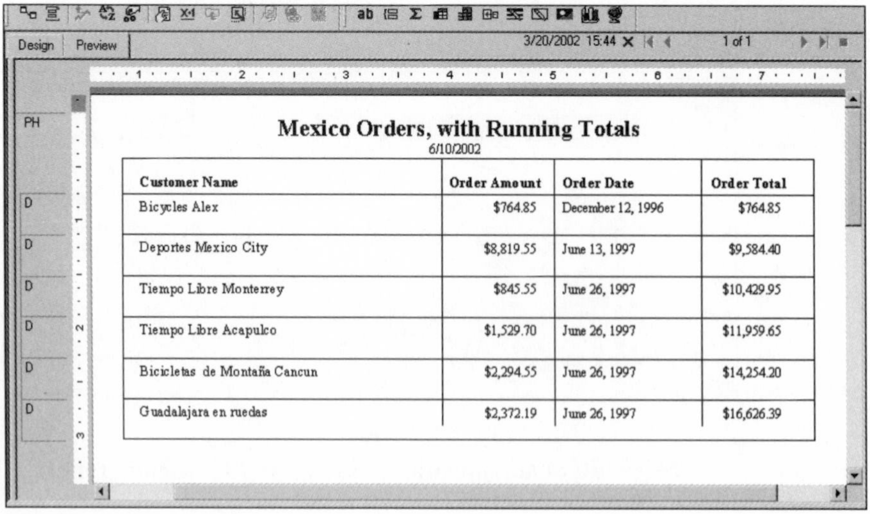

Figure 7-5: A preview of the report.

The report is more readable, but it has a few small problems. First, the report would look better if the detail lines were centered vertically within each box. Second, the vertical lines between boxes do not extend all the way down to the bottom borderline below the last record. Both these problems are easy to correct.

To center the records within their boxes:

1. **Switch back to the Design tab.**

   Notice that the left margin has a little triangle-shaped thing pointing towards the lower edge of the fields in the Details section. This is a horizontal guideline indicator used to align fields on a single horizontal line.

2. **Use the mouse to grab the triangle (the horizontal guideline indicator), and drag it down to just below the center of the section.**

   The fields move down with it.

The horizontal line that used to be located at the bottom of the fields must now be moved down also:

1. **Hover the cursor over the line until the Drawing Object tooltip appears.**

2. **Click the line.**

   Grab handles appear on either end. The mouse cursor changes to the object-moving cursor shape, as shown in Figure 7-6.

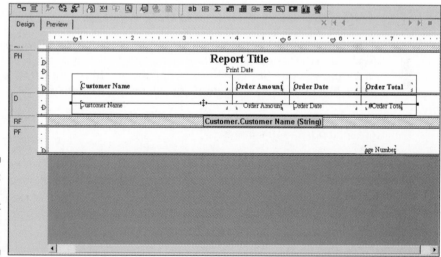

Figure 7-6:
The line object has been selected.

3. Move the line down to coincide with the bottom border of the Details section.

4. Repeat Steps 1 through 3 for the three vertical lines that divide the fields.

This completes the modification of the report, as shown in Figure 7-7.

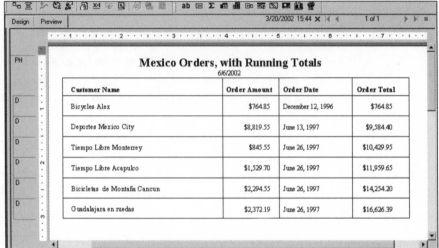

Figure 7-7:
The
formatted
report.

The Section Formatting menu

To create a summary report in Chapter 6, you use the Hide (Drill-Down OK) function in the Section Formatting menu. Right-clicking in the area to the left of a report section displays the shortcut menu. This menu contains other useful functions in addition to the Hide function, as shown in Figure 7-8.

Figure 7-8 is the menu for the Details section. Following is a brief description of each option in this menu:

- Hide (Drill-Down OK): Doesn't display this section of the report but allows the user to drill down to view it.

- Suppress (No Drill-Down): Doesn't display this section of the report, and doesn't allow the user to view it by drilling down.

✔ Section Expert: Displays Section Expert.

✔ Show Long Section Names: Toggles between long and short section names.

✔ Insert Line: Adds an additional horizontal guideline to the section. If there's not enough room for an additional line, the section is automatically expanded to accommodate the additional guideline.

✔ Delete Last Line: Deletes the bottom guideline from the section and raises the bottom of the section up to just below the next higher guideline.

✔ Arrange Lines: Arranges guidelines vertically so that they're evenly spaced. Adds more guidelines if there aren't enough.

✔ Fit Section: Brings the bottom of the section up to the bottom of the lowest object, removing any guidelines that are lower.

✔ Insert Section Below: Adds another section of the same type as the current section, just below it.

✔ Select All Section Objects: Selects all objects in the section.

✔ Cancel Menu: Removes the menu from the screen.

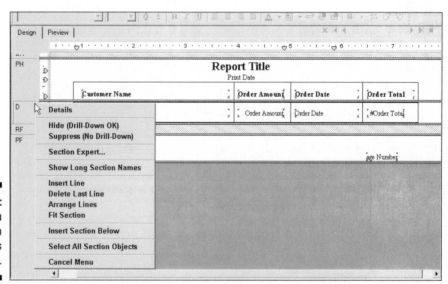

Figure 7-8:
Things you
can do in
the Details
section.

The options on the Section Formatting menu provide a convenient way to make basic formatting changes to a section.

Common tab of Section Expert

Section Expert is the primary tool for changing the formatting of a section. With it, you can set a number of options to determine what gets displayed, how it gets displayed, and what color the display will be. Section Expert has two tabs: the Common tab and the Color tab.

Figure 7-9 shows the default settings for the Report Header section of the Common tab. (Each section has different default settings.)

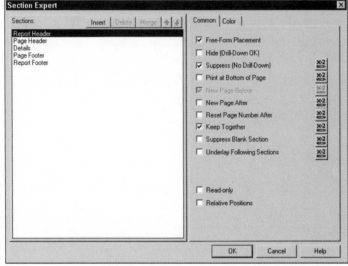

Figure 7-9:
The
Common tab
for the
Report
Header
section.

The Free-Form Placement setting, if checked, allows you to place objects anywhere in the section without snapping to horizontal guidelines. If unchecked, horizontal guidelines are functional.

The Hide (Drill-Down OK) setting, as noted previously, hides the section. However, drilling down displays the section's contents.

The Suppress (No Drill-Down) setting hides the section, and drill-down does not override the suppression.

Print at Bottom of Page prints the section at the bottom of the page. This option doesn't make much sense for a Details section but is useful when applied to a Report Footer that otherwise would be printed near the top of the last page of a report.

New Page Before prints the section at the top of a new page, rather than immediately following the previous section. You would probably not use this for a Details section, but it could come in handy for a Group Header section.

New Page After prints the next section after the current one at the top of a new page. This is similar to the New Page Before option but is more appropriate in a Group Footer section.

Reset Page Number After resets page numbering to the beginning of the sequence. If you apply this setting to a Group Footer, the first page of the next group is numbered 1 rather than the last page number of the current group being incremented.

Keep Together prevents a page break in the middle of a section. This is useful if a section contains a small number of detail lines that should be viewed together, regardless of where they happen to fall on a page.

Suppress Blank Section closes the gap between the preceding and the following sections if a section is blank. If this option is not checked, the empty space assigned to the section will be on the report.

Underlay Following Sections prints the section and then prints all following sections right on top of this one. The function is often used to apply a faint watermark on the text on a page. It can be used also to overlay two different kinds of content, such as text and a chart.

The Read-only option locks the format and position of all objects in the section. In the process, it disables all the foregoing options, as well as those that are normally available on the toolbars and in the shortcut menus.

The Relative Positions option freezes the relative positioning of objects in a section. If one object moves, its spacing relative to an adjacent object is retained.

The X+2 icon to the right of most of the options on the Common tab displays Format Formula Editor. With this editor, you can write a formula that tests a condition. For true/false conditions, if the condition is satisfied (true), the chosen formatting option is applied; if false, it is not applied. For multivalued conditions, an If-Then-Else structure is used, which defines which one of several formatting options to apply. For more on formulas, see Chapter 12.

Color tab of Section Expert

With the Color tab, you can specify a background color for a report section. You can give each section a different background color if you like, or you can have multiple colors within a section, using Format Formula Editor to write a formula that specifies which lines within a section will have a specific background color. Figure 7-10 shows the Section Editor's Color tab.

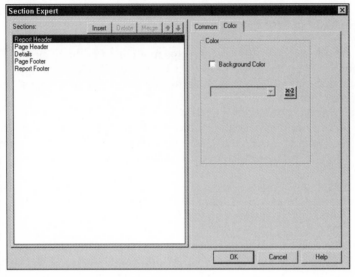

Figure 7-10:
You can change the background color of a report section.

If you don't check the Background Color option, Crystal Reports will not give the background any color. If you do select the option, the pull-down list becomes active, as shown in Figure 7-11.

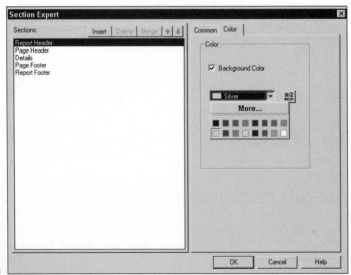

Figure 7-11:
These are the standard colors.

Quite a few colors are available. If none of the standard choices meet your needs, however, you can select the More option, which displays the Color menu. As shown in Figure 7-12, you can define thousands of colors from the Color menu.

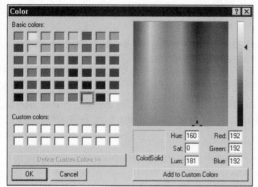

Using different colors for different sections

Using the Color tab of Section Expert, you can specify a background color for each section of the report. Depending on the effect you want the report to convey, you might leave all section backgrounds uncolored or create a rainbow effect, with each section a different color. A more conservative approach is to use colored backgrounds sparingly but tastefully.

Be aware of how your users will view your report. If the report will be printed on a black-and-white printer, it's not a good idea to go overboard with color. However, if your users will be viewing the report on computer screens or as the output of a color printer, take advantage of the expanded possibilities that color gives you.

Giving reports a classic banded look

Back in the early days of computing (the 1950s and 1960s), computers printed reports on wide paper that was sprocket-fed through electro-mechanical line printers. The paper had sprocket holes on the left and right edges and alternating green and white horizontal bands. Each band was high enough to hold two printed lines. The bands helped you focus on a single line.

You, too, can simulate that classic banded look in your reports. Doing so requires the use of a conditional formula. To demonstrate this, you add silver bands in the background of the single-month Orders report you built and saved in Chapter 4, as follows:

1. **Open the report and switch to the Design tab.**

2. **Right-click the margin to the left of the Details section and choose Section Expert.**

   Section Expert appears.

3. **Switch to the Color tab.**

4. **Select the Background Color option.**

5. **In the pull-down list, select a color and then click the Formula icon.**

   For the example, select Silver. Formula Workshop appears in Format Formula Editor: Background Color mode.

6. **In the text area in the bottom half of the editor, enter the following formula, replacing *color* with the color you selected:**

   ```
   If Remainder (RecordNumber, 4) In [1,2] Then color Else NoColor
   ```

   If you follow along with the example, the formula should be the same as the one shown in Figure 7-13.

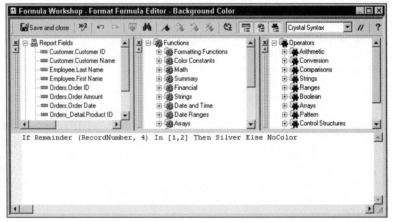

Figure 7-13:
The color banding formula has been added.

7. **Click the Save and close icon.**

8. **In Section Expert, click OK.**

9. **Switch to the Preview tab.**

   You can see the effect of this change on the single-month Orders report, as shown in Figure 7-14.

This report brings back memories of the good old days and makes it easy to correlate the Order Amount on the right with the Customer Name on the left.

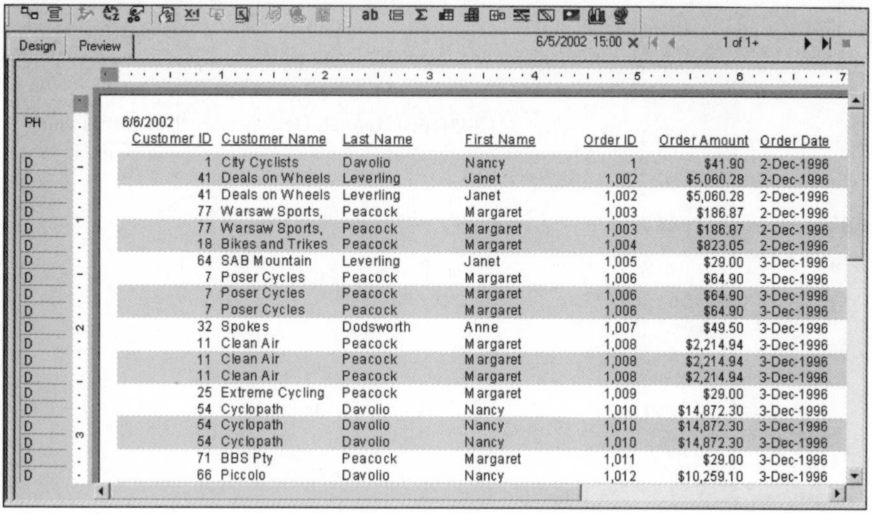

Figure 7-14: The report on simulated banded paper.

Placing Groups Where You Want Them

Depending on the type of report you're creating, you might want to depart from the default position of groups in the Details section or of an entire section. You can do so in several ways, as shown next.

Starting each group at the top of its own page

Suppose that you have a number of groups, and each group includes a large number of detail lines. Each group will end at some random place in the middle of a page, with the next group following immediately. For large groups, you might want to start each group at the top of a new page, to provide a proper separation between groups.

Figure 7-15 shows one page of Xtreme's Customer Report for the U.S. It has the last few records for Iowa, followed by the Idaho group.

For branch managers responsible for a single state, it makes sense to have each state's records start on a new page. This makes it easier to distribute the appropriate information to the appropriate person, while not revealing what is happening in another state.

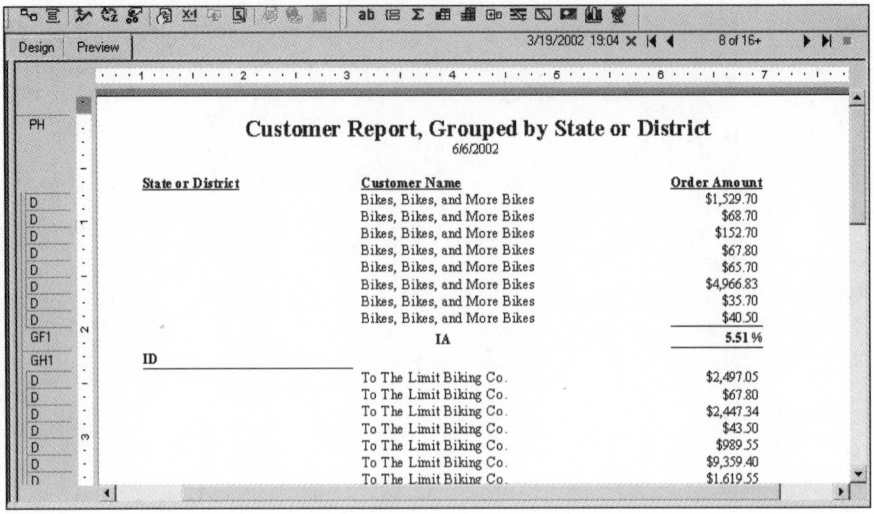

Figure 7-15:
The
Customer
Report page
showing
Iowa and
Idaho
records.

To make each group start on a new page, follow these steps:

1. **Right-click the GH1 area to the left of the first group header on the report and choose Section Expert.**

   Section Expert appears.

2. **On the Common tab, select the New Page Before option.**

On this report, that's all you need to do because there's no report header. On a report that does have a report header, checking this option will cause a page feed after the report header is printed on the first page, and the first group will appear at the top of the second page. To avoid this problem, when you check the New Page Before option, also click its Formula Editor button to display the Format Formula Editor. In the formula entry area, type `Not OnFirstRecord`. This ensures that the first group always prints on the first page of the report.

Printing totals at the bottom of a page

For a multipage report with subtotals for each group and a grand total at the end, you might want to print the grand total at the bottom of the last page. This is not the default format in Crystal Reports, which puts the grand total immediately after the subtotal for the last group, as shown in Figure 7-16.

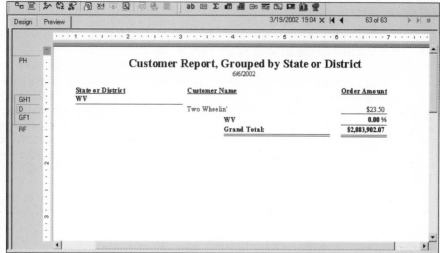

Figure 7-16:
The grand
total is near
the top of
the last
page of this
report.

Xtreme did not get a lot of sales out of West Virginia, so the grand total prints near the top of the last page. Printing the total at the bottom of the page is another job for Section Expert:

1. **Right-click in the area to the left of the Report Footer section and choose Section Expert.**

2. **On the Common tab, select the Print at Bottom of Page option.**

   This puts the grand total at the bottom of the page, where it's traditionally located.

Giving each group its own page numbers

If you're starting each group on a new page and the group extends for multiple pages, it might make sense to restart the page numbering every time you start a new group. This would cause less confusion to people who receive a distribution consisting of only one group. To restart page numbering at the beginning of each new group, access Section Expert from the Group Footer, and select the Reset Page Number After option in the Common tab.

Hiding Details with Summary and Drill-down Reports

In Chapter 6, you take a brief look at summary reports and drilling down into them to see the hidden detail they contain. By making a simple selection from the Section Formatting menu, you can choose to either display or hide a report's detail information. You can print a detailed report for one client, and then print a summary that hides the detail but shows the summary information in the group footer for another client.

For example, aside from the full detailed report that you might give to the branch manager responsible for a single state and the drill-downable summary report that you might produce for the national sales manager, you can also produce a summary report for which drill-down is not possible. All three types of reports can be produced from the same basic report. To create the drill-downable report, use the Hide (Drill-Down OK) option from the Section Formatting menu. To create a similar summary report for which drill-down is not enabled, use the Suppress (No Drill-Down) option instead. With one report, you can satisfy the needs of three different classes of users.

Creating Mailing Labels

You'll use multicolumn reports in a variety of situations. One example is a report for printing three or four columns of mailing labels on 8-1/2 by 11-inch label stock. Crystal Reports recognizes that people frequently want to print mailing labels, so it provides a wizard for that specific task.

To create a report that prints mailing labels in multiple columns, follow these steps:

1. **In the Crystal Reports Gallery, select Mail Label, and then click OK.**

   Mailing Labels Report Creation Wizard appears.

2. **Connect to the xtreme.mdb database, and add the Customer table to the Selected Tables pane.**

   For more information on this process, see Chapter 2.

3. **Click Next to display the Fields view.**

4. **Add the following from the Available Fields pane to the Fields to Display pane: Contact First Name, Contact Last Name, Customer Name, Address 1, Address 2, City, Region, and Postal Code.**

5. **Click Next to display the Label view.**

   The Label view enables you to select a standard label type or specify the dimensions and margins of nonstandard labels. You can also specify the direction in which they will be printed: across the page and then down, or down and then across.

The standard labels include not only labels that you might put on envelopes, but also disk labels, audiocassette labels, and videotape labels.

6. **Select a standard label type.**

   For this example, choose Avery 5160.

7. **Click Next to display the Record Selection view.**

8. **Specify which records you're printing labels for.**

   For this example, suppose you want to write to customers only in the United States. You can restrict the label printing to those customers by specifying that the Country field from the Customer table is equal to USA.

9. **Click the Finish button.**

   If you followed along with the example, you get the report shown in Figure 7-17.

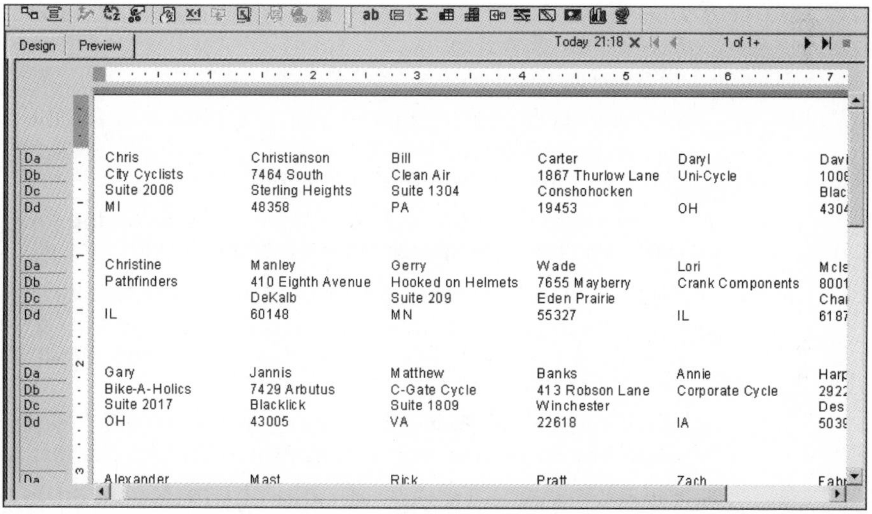

Figure 7-17:
Mailing labels produced by Mailing Label Expert.

The three columns of labels are not quite laid out in the most readable way. To correct that, follow these steps:

1. **Switch to the Design tab to move things around a little.**

   Figure 7-18 shows the Design tab view of the report.

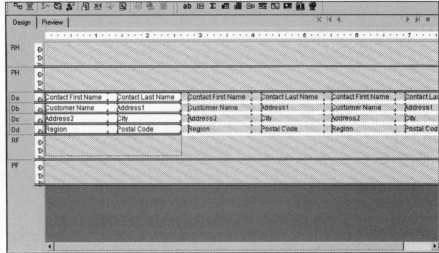

Figure 7-18:
Design view
of the
mailing
labels.

2. **Concatenate the Contact First Name field and the Contact Last Name field on the first line.**

   To do so, move the fields into the Page Header temporarily. Next, click the Insert Text Object icon and drag a text box down to the Da section. Now drag the Contact First Name and Contact Last Name fields into the text box, with one blank space separating them.

3. **Concatenate the Address1 and Address2 fields on the third line, putting a couple of spaces between them.**

   To do so, move Address2 and City out of the way temporarily. Next, click the Insert Text Object icon and drag a text box into the Dc section. Now drag the Address2 field into the text box. Insert the cursor between the two fields, and press the space bar twice.

4. **Move Region and Postal Code out of the Dd section, and then drag a text box down into that section. Move City into the text box in Dd.**

5. **Type a comma and a space after the City field, then move the Region field after that. Follow Region with a space, and then drag Postal Code into the text box after the space.**

   The result should look similar to Figure 7-19.

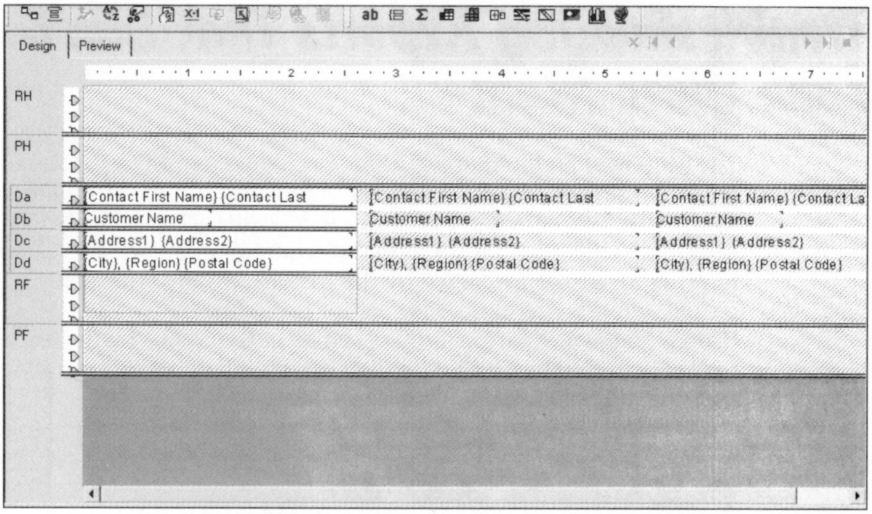

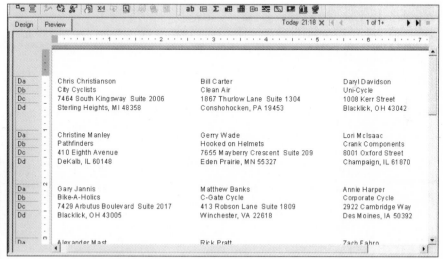

Figure 7-19: Design view of the modified mailing labels.

6. **Switch to the Preview tab.**

The screen should look similar to Figure 7-20. These labels look great and will fit nicely on the Avery label stock you chose previously.

Figure 7-20: Preview of the modified mailing labels.

Troubleshooting Reports That Don't Look Quite Right

The sectioned architecture of a report created using Crystal Reports is a great timesaver and a great tool for organizing the report logically. However, sometimes items are inserted into the report that would be better left out or they're not placed exactly where you want them. On other occasions, as we have seen, reports produced by the wizards require tweaking.

Usually, anomalies in appearance can be corrected using the feature-rich toolset provided by Crystal Reports. In this section, you look at a few common problems and how to deal with them.

Problems in drill-down reports

When you're producing reports with different levels of summarization using drill-down, odd things can happen to your headings. For example, look at Figure 7-21, which was generated by Standard Report Creation Wizard. It's the report in Chapter 6 that shows Xtreme's orders from Mexico.

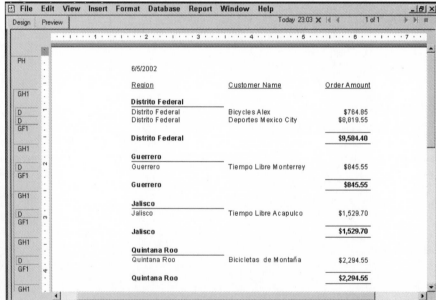

Figure 7-21: Customer Orders report generated by Report Expert.

Several elements about this report are less than the best:

- ✔ There's no report title.

- ✔ The region name is repeated in the group headers, each detail line, and the group footers.

- ✔ The column headings in the Page Header section should be emphasized more by using a bold font and eliminating the underlines.

These problems can be solved as they were in Chapter 6, with some manual intervention in Design view. You can add a title, delete redundant report elements, and spruce up the column headings.

Saving money on postage by doing a Zip sort

Earlier in the chapter, you looked at using Crystal Reports to produce mailing labels. Figure 7-20 showed an example of the way the addresses would print on label stock. The labels look great but are in the order that they were entered into the database, which means no particular order at all. The United States Postal Service gives a postage discount on mass mailings of first class letters if the letters are sorted by Zip code when you bring them to the post office.

It's a lot easier to apply the labels to envelopes in Zip-sorted order if the labels are in Zip-sorted order in the first place. Start with the report in Figure 7-20, and follow these steps:

1. **In Design mode, click the Record Sort Expert icon.**

   The Record Sort Order dialog box appears.

2. **Add Customer.PostalCode to the Sort Order pane.**

3. **Leave the sort direction as Ascending, and then click OK.**

4. **Switch to Preview mode.**

   The report shown in Figure 7-22 appears. The labels are now sorted in Zip code order.

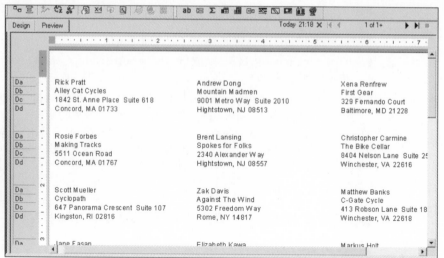

Figure 7-22:
Mailing
labels,
sorted by
Zip code.

Your first attempt at any given report will probably be less than perfect. This is not a cause for concern. Crystal Reports has the power and flexibility to produce the report that you want — it just takes a little back-and-forth to achieve it.

Chapter 8

Formatting Your Reports

- -

In This Chapter

▶ Exploring the differences between absolute and conditional formatting

▶ Enhancing readability with Highlighting Expert

▶ Inserting a picture into a report

▶ Working with preprinted forms

▶ Importing text-based objects from a file

▶ Using the Formatting Options dialog box

▶ Adding special fields to a report

▶ Emphasizing important information with report alerts

▶ Speeding development with report templates

- -

*F*ormatting is the primary reason for the existence of Crystal Reports — or any report writer for that matter. Any DBMS can retrieve results from a database and display or print them. The primary purpose of a DBMS, however, is to maintain data. DBMS vendors do not concentrate on putting retrieved results in the most understandable form.

Crystal Reports excels at taking the raw data retrieved from a DBMS and transforming it into a report that communicates. To achieve that communication, Crystal Reports provides tools you can use to shape the appearance of any report you generate to create the desired impression for your readers.

Absolute Formatting and Conditional Formatting

Absolute formatting is the regular kind of formatting that you can apply to text and fields with Crystal Reports to present data in the best way. After you format something with absolute formatting, the format is fixed, regardless of the values of the data that constitute the content of the report. With *conditional formatting,* you can vary the appearance (or even the presence or absence) of a field, depending on the value that the field contains.

Absolute formatting overview

Before you get involved with the intricacies of conditional formatting, take a look at the power and versatility of absolute formatting. In this section, you have some fun with the Mexico Orders, Grouped by State or District report (one of the reports in Chapter 6). The report is shown in Figure 8-1.

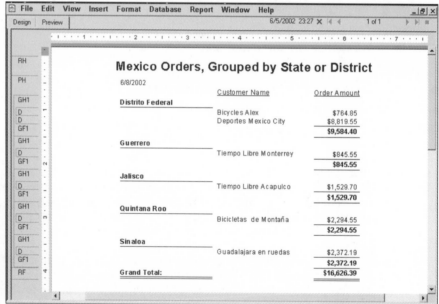

Figure 8-1:
The Mexico
Orders
report from
Chapter 6.

This isn't bad, but you might want to give the report more visual appeal by changing the fonts of various report elements. To alter the report title, follow these steps:

1. **In Design view, click the report title.**

2. **On the Formatting toolbar, select one or more of the fonts available on your machine to give the report title a different look.**

Make sure that whatever font you select is also available on all the computers and printers that will be used by people who will be viewing the report.

3. Select the style, size, and color of the font.

In the present case, the style and size are fine, but you might want to experiment with font color to get the look you want.

I chose the Times New Roman font face for the report title. It's a distinctive font and is available on virtually all Windows machines. I also chose to make the report title, date, grand total in the report footer, and group headers blue. The color change adds some contrast to the report and grabs more of the reader's attention. Figure 8-2 shows the report at this point.

Centering the date would be a good idea. You might also want to change the date format. Crystal Reports gave you the default format, but there are many others. Figure 8-3 shows the Date tab of Format Editor with a longer date format selected.

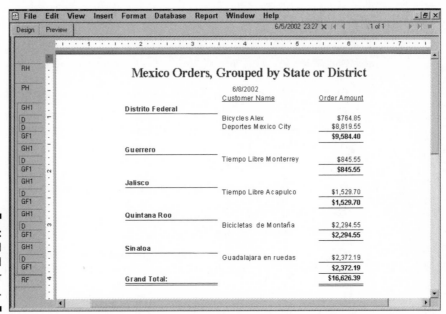

Figure 8-2:
Selected
font and
color
changes.

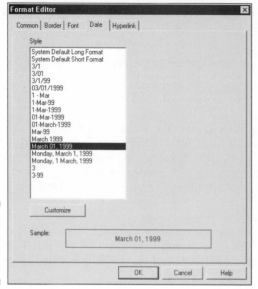

Figure 8-3:
Month, day,
and year are
selected.

Another technique that you can use to improve the visual appeal of your reports is to add graphical elements such as lines and boxes. For example, you can set the report title off from the rest of the report by enclosing it in a box. Follow these steps, and see how the visual impact of the report changes:

1. **Give the title some more vertical space, to make room for the box.**

   To do this, you have to expand Report Page Header section. In Design view, drag down the lower border of the Report Header section about ¼ inch. Center the report title vertically.

2. **Switch to Preview mode.**

3. **On the Insert Tools toolbar, click the Insert Box icon.**

   The cursor changes to a pencil.

4. **Draw a box around the title.**

   To do so, click one corner, drag to the diagonally opposite corner, and then release the mouse button. After you draw the box, you can format it.

5. **Click the box to select it, and then right-click it and choose Format Box.**

   Format Editor appears, as shown in Figure 8-4. The Box tab allows you to select a line thickness and a color, among other options.

6. **Select a line thickness and color.**

   To follow along with the example, select a medium thick line and blue color.

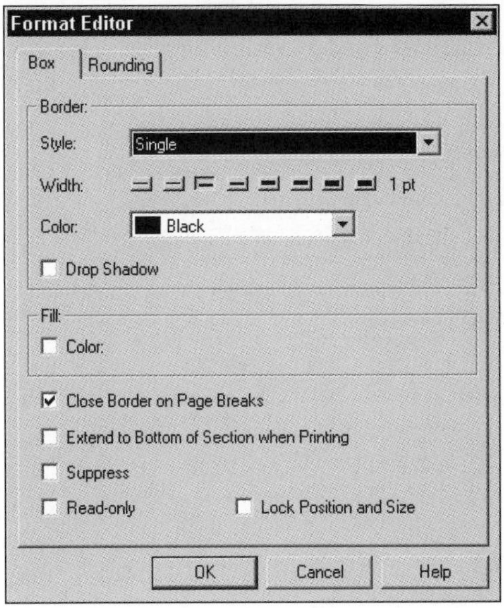

Format Editor
Box
Rounding
Border:
Style:
Single
Width:
1 pt
Color:
Black
Drop Shadow
Fill:
Color:
Close Border on Page Breaks
Extend to Bottom of Section when Printing
Suppress
Read-only
Lock Position and Size
OK
Cancel
Help

Figure 8-4: Select a style for the box.

7. **Click the Rounding tab, and then select the amount of rounding.**

   The Rounding tab enables you to round the corners to whatever extent you like, all the way from a rectangle to a circle. I selected a little bit of rounding (4%), as shown in Figure 8-5.

Format Editor
Box
Rounding
Rounding:
4
%
OK
Cancel
Help

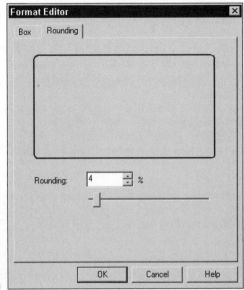

Figure 8-5: You can change the appearance of the box.

The result is the report shown in Figure 8-6. It's a substantial improvement over the first version, which was created automatically by Report Wizard.

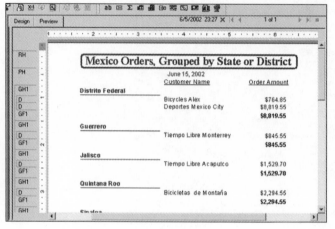

Figure 8-6:
The Mexico
Orders
report, with
a boxed
title.

After you set a format with absolute formatting, the format is fixed unless you change it with the Design tab or Format Editor. Every time you run the report, the formatting is the same. Sometimes, however, you want different formatting, depending on the data that you're displaying. For that, you use the extensive conditional formatting capabilities of Crystals Reports.

Conditional formatting

In contrast to absolute formatting, which is fixed after you complete a report's design, conditional formatting allows the appearance of a report to change each time it's run, depending on the data it contains.

For example, Xtreme might want to draw attention to underperforming regions by coloring group totals red for all states or districts that have cumulative orders below $2000. A state might qualify for a red group total one month but, through additional sales, earn the right to a black group total the following month.

To demonstrate how to add conditional formatting to a report, use the Mexico Orders report from the preceding section and add the condition that group totals less than $2000 should be red rather than black:

1. **Switch to Design view.**

2. **In the Group Footer section, right-click the Sum of Orders.Order Amount field and choose Format Field.**

Format Editor appears.

3. **Click the Font tab.**

   The default color is Black, which is the color you want most of the time but not this time.

4. **To add a condition for low order totals, click the Format Formula Editor button to the right of the Color menu.**

   The Format Formula Editor dialog box appears, as shown in Figure 8-7.

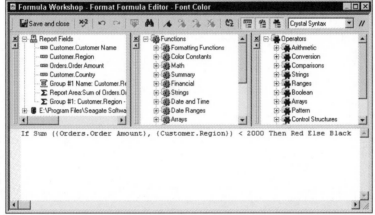

Figure 8-7:
This formula will cause totals less than $2000 to be printed in red.

5. **Build the formula shown in Figure 8-7.**

   To do so, type the keyword If. Then double-click the Σ Group #1 line in the Report Fields window (in the upper-left of the screen). Complete the formula by typing) < 2000 Then Red Else Black. The final formula should look like this:

   ```
   If Sum ({Orders.Order Amount}, {Customer.Region}) < 2000 Then Red Else Black
   ```

6. **Click the Save and close icon in Format Formula Editor.**

7. **Click OK in Format Editor.**

8. **Preview mode now displays the report in Figure 8-8.**

   State totals less than $2000 are displayed in red, and all totals greater than $2000 are black.

Format Formula Editor is a powerful tool for creating complex conditions that govern what's printed on a report and how it's printed. However, you do need to know Crystal formula language syntax (the default) or BASIC language syntax. You can type the formula by hand, or you can build it up by selecting fields, functions, and operators from the windows in the top half of the Editor. An easier way to get some of the features of Format Formula Editor — without learning formula syntax — is to use Highlighting Expert, coming up next.

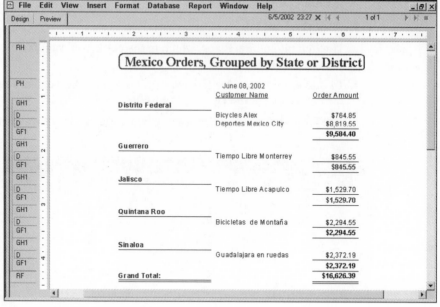

Figure 8-8:
The Mexico
Orders
report, with
group totals
less than
$2000
displayed
in red.

Highlighting Expert Creates Emphasis

Highlighting Expert is one of the easiest-to-use formatting tools in the Crystal Reports repertoire. Compared to Format Formula Expert, Highlighting Expert has limited flexibility, but you could have used it instead of a formula to get the same red group total that you developed in the preceding section. Highlighting Expert operates only on number and currency fields; Format Formula Editor works on any type of field.

To see Highlighting Expert in action, follow these steps:

1. **Return to the Mexico Orders report shown in Figure 8-8.**

2. **In the Group Footer section of the Design tab, right-click the Sum of Orders.Order Amount field and choose Highlighting Expert.**

   The Highlighting Expert dialog box appears, as shown in Figure 8-9. You can change the font color, the background color, or the border of the selected item. For this example, you'll put a single-line box around all state or district order totals that are equal to or greater than $5000.

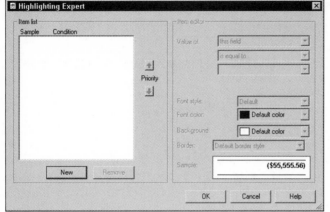

Figure 8-9:
Change the
color and
border of
the item.

3. **Click the New button.**

4. **In the Value of this Field box, select** greater than or equal to. **In the text box below Value is, enter** 5000.

5. **In the Border box, select Single box.**

   The Highlighting Expert dialog box now appears as shown in Figure 8-10.

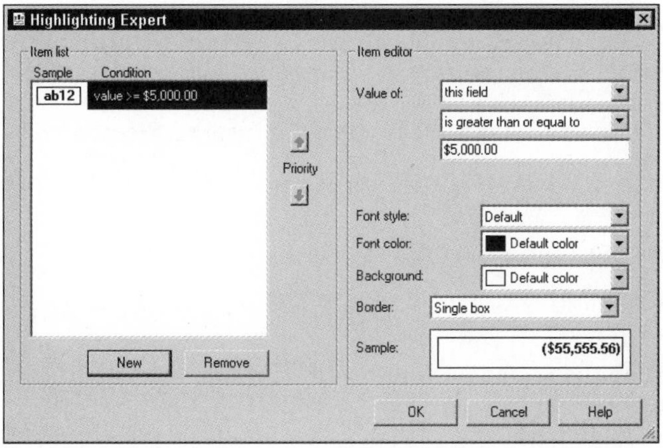

Figure 8-10:
A formatting
condition
has been
added.

6. **Click OK.**

   These settings produce the report shown in Figure 8-11. The total for Distrito Federal is enclosed in a box because its value is greater than $5000. The other group totals are unchanged.

Figure 8-11:
The
modified
report after
highlighting.

Adding Pictures to a Report

You can add bitmapped graphic images to a report to further enhance its visual appeal. To add a picture to your report, follow these steps:

1. **On the Insert Tools toolbar, click the Insert a Picture from a File icon.**

   A dialog box appears, from which you can select the image file that you want to add to the report.

2. **Select the appropriate file.**

   On the report, a rectangle appears that you can move around with the mouse.

3. **Position the rectangle where you want the image to be located, and then click.**

   The image appears on the report. Figure 8-12 shows the result of placing two instances of the Mexican flag on the report.

4. **Save the report as Customer Orders, by State or District (Mexico).**

   You now have a report fit for the eyes of a Vice President of Sales!

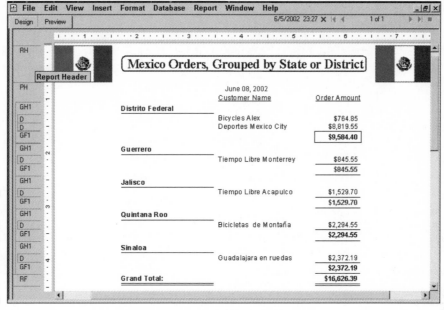

Figure 8-12:
The report
includes
bitmapped
graphic
images.

A Trick for Aligning Preprinted Forms

Preprinted forms are designed to be filled out by hand or run through a sprocket-fed line printer. With a laser printer or inkjet printer, it is devilishly hard to line up text with the lines and boxes on the form that are supposed to hold that text. Because most people today are more likely to have a laser printer or an inkjet printer than a sprocket-fed printer, this can be a problem.

Crystal Reports offers a clever solution to aligning text to preprinted forms. Because a report can have both text and graphical elements, and one can overlay the other, you can perfectly align text to a preprinted form by following a few simple steps. This trick requires that you have a scanner. Here's what you do:

1. **Scan the preprinted form and save it as a bitmapped file.**

2. **Place the scanned form in the Page Header section of the report as a bitmap.**

3. **Select the Underlay Following Sections property on Section Expert's Common tab.**

4. **Add text fields in the appropriate places of the Details section to line up with the form.**

   Both the form and the data will print in one operation.

Adding Text from a File

Crystal Reports is primarily designed to take data from a database, process it, format it, and then display it to the user. In addition, though, it can also display blocks of text stored in document files.

To insert a block of text into a report, follow these steps:

1. **Create a text object and insert it into the report at the location where you want the text to appear.**

2. **Right-click the object and choose Insert from File.**

   An Open dialog box appears, listing files in whatever directory was accessed last.

3. **Change to the directory that has the file you want to insert (if necessary), and then specify the file in the File Name box.**

4. **Click the Open button.**

   The text file is transferred to the text object.

Formatting Options

Report developers can customize the development environment by choosing File➪Options. The Options dialog box appears, as shown in Figure 8-13.

Figure 8-13:
Decide what will be displayed.

The Options dialog box has eight tabs, with the Layout tab on top by default. As you can see in Figure 8-13, you can change many options. They all have to do with what gets displayed and how it gets displayed. Most options are self-explanatory. Following is a quick rundown of each tab:

✔ The Layout tab enables you to select what will be displayed on the work surface in both Design and Preview modes.

✔ The Database tab, which is a little more interesting, can be used to view the system's tables and any synonyms or stored procedures that the database may have. You can look for approximate matches in table names, and decide how tables and fields are listed. The default values of the Advanced Options, shown in Figure 8-14, are better left as they are unless you have a compelling reason to change them.

✔ With the Editors tab, you can customize the formatting options for the text you create with any of the editors, such as the Formula Editor.

✔ The Data Source Defaults tab enables you to specify where to look for databases and how to recognize them.

✔ The Reporting tab gives you the opportunity to set a number of miscellaneous options.

✔ The Smart Tag tab enables you to define the Web server and viewing page that you want to use when selecting Office XP smart tags for Crystal report objects.

✔ The Fonts tab allows you to set default fonts for fields and text objects.

✔ With the Fields tab, you can customize the formats of the various field types.

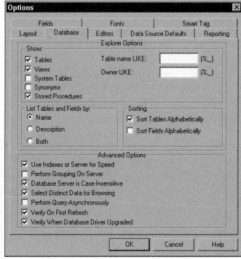

Figure 8-14: You can select which database objects are displayed and how they're accessed.

Crystal Reports' broad array of formatting options gives report developers a lot of latitude in the way their reports present information. Those options make the developer's job of communicating much easier. However, Crystal Reports offers other modes of communication that are just as effective. One of the most powerful is Crystal Reports' charting capability, which is the subject of Chapter 16.

Special Fields Contain Report Metadata

Metadata is data about data. Report metadata is descriptive data about a report. Crystal Reports enables you to include report metadata in the report that the metadata is describing.

For many kinds of reports, you might want to include certain metadata items in the report itself. For example, readers might want to know the date that the data in the report was last refreshed. They might want to know the name of the author of the report. These are the kinds of things that you can display in your reports as special fields.

You can access special fields in the Special Fields list in Field Explorer. Well over a dozen special fields holding pertinent information about the report are available in Field Explorer. You can drag them onto your report and drop them wherever you like.

Raising a Red Flag with Report Alerts

Sometimes, the data in a report indicates a condition that requires urgent attention on the part of the report reader. The urgency may not be immediately obvious just from perusing the report. To make sure that the message gets across, Crystal Reports provides the Report Alerts facility.

Report alerts are custom messages that appear when certain conditions are met by data in the report. A report alert may merely inform the reader of the condition, or it may specify a course of action to take.

You can create a report alert by entering a formula, as described in Chapter 12, using Formula Workshop. The formula evaluates conditions that you specify. If the overall condition evaluates to True, the alert is triggered and its message is displayed. The message may be a text string or a text string combined with one or more report fields.

For example, suppose that Xtreme's sales manager wants to be alerted whenever a customer in Mexico orders more than $5000 worth of merchandise. A report alert added to the Customer Orders, by State or District (Mexico) report will do the job. Here's how to add it:

1. **With the target report active, choose Report➪Alerts➪Create or Modify Alerts.**

   The Create Alerts dialog box appears, as shown in Figure 8-15.

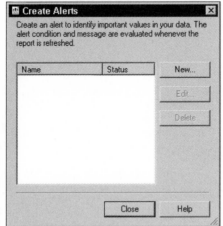

2. **Click the New button.**

   The Create Alert dialog box (which is different than the Create Alerts dialog box) appears.

3. **In the Name box, type** BonusTime.

4. **Click the Formula (x+2) icon to the right of the Message field.**

   The Alert Message Formula Editor version of Formula Workshop appears. Next, you build a formula to create the message that will be displayed.

5. **Drag Customer.Customer Name from the Report Fields pane down to the upper-left corner of the formula area that fills the lower half of Workshop.**

6. **To the right of the Customer.Customer Name field in the formula area, type a space, a plus sign, and then another space.**

7. **To the right of the plus sign and space, type the text string, "** has made a BIG order!"

   Be sure to include the double quotes in the string that you type. The formula should appear as shown in Figure 8-16.

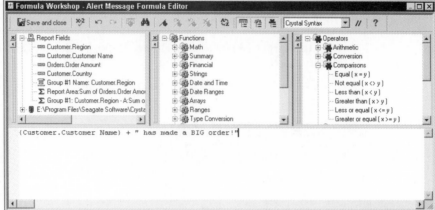

8. **Click the Save and close icon to return to the Create Alert dialog box.**

9. **Click the Condition button.**

   The Alert Condition Formula Editor version of Formula Workshop appears. Now you must specify the condition that must occur to trigger the display of this report alert.

10. **Drag the Orders.Order Amount field from the Report Fields pane down to the upper-left corner of the formula area.**

11. **In the Operators pane, expand the Comparisons node. Drag the Greater than operator down, just to the right of the Orders.Order Amount field.**

12. **To the right of the Greater than symbol, type** 5000.

    This produces the formula shown in Figure 8-17.

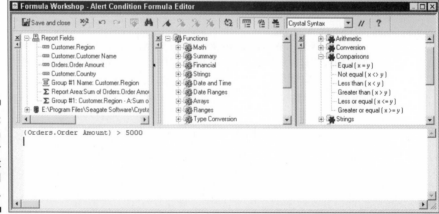

13. **Click the Save and close icon to once again return to the Create Alert dialog box.**

14. **Make sure that the Enabled condition is selected, and then click OK.**

    This puts your new report alert into the Create Alerts dialog box, as shown in Figure 8-18.

15. **Click the Close button to return to your report.**

    That's how you create a report alert.

To see your Report Alert in action, just click the Refresh icon on the Standard toolbar. If any customers have orders that exceed $5000, a report alert pops up to let you know. Figure 8-19 shows what a report alert looks like. You can click the View Records button if you want to see exactly how big the customer's order total is.

Report Templates Save Time and Effort

Crystal Reports makes the task of report creation much easier than it would be without such a powerful tool. However, it still takes considerable thought and work to come up with reports that are well proportioned and with an attractive choice of fonts, drawing elements, colors, and layout.

If you make that investment in time for one report, it would be nice if you could recycle the work on another, similar report. Such recycling of the general features of the first report would not only save you time and effort but also create a consistency from one report to the next that conveys a feeling of professionalism. You can achieve that consistency and save that time and effort by using templates.

What's a template?

A *template* is an existing report, complete with formatting, that you can use as a starting point for a new report that you create. You don't have to create the new report from scratch; you have to only change the things that are different between the template report and the new report you're creating. Sometimes you don't have to change anything.

Apply the template as the last step in your report creation process and you're finished, with a polished, professional report in a fraction of the time that it would normally take to create one.

How do you use a template in a report?

You can apply a template to a report in several ways, as follows:

- ✔ In the process of creating your report, select a template from the Template view in Standard Report Creation Wizard.
- ✔ After you create your report, select a template using Template Expert.
- ✔ Use an existing report as a template for your new report. After you use a report as a template, it's added to the list of available templates for possible use in the future.
- ✔ Create a report specifically for use as a template. It can serve as a formatted skeleton for a variety of reports that you build in the future.

Applying a template to an existing report

Applying a template to an existing report is easy. To see just how easy, look again at the Big Orders report, which you create in Chapter 5. It's shown in Figure 5-17 and again here in Figure 8-20.

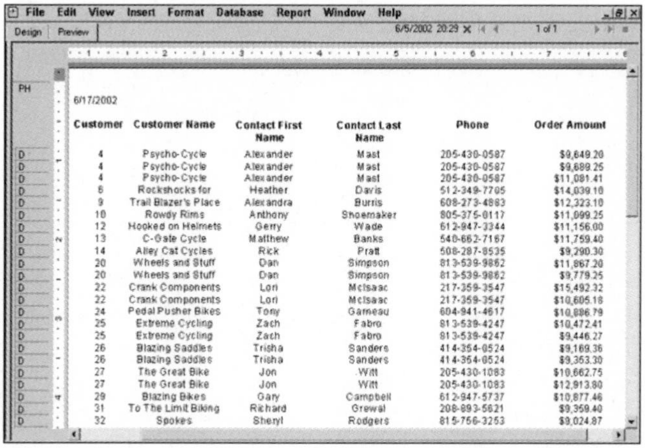

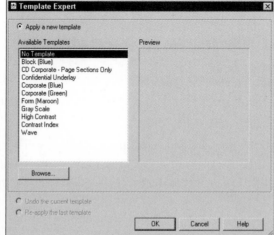

Figure 8-20: Big Orders report, run with a $5000 lower limit.

It looks pretty plain. You can spruce it up with one of Crystal Reports' standard templates. Here's how:

1. **On the Expert Tools toolbar, click the Template Expert icon.**

   This launches Template Expert, as shown in Figure 8-21.

Figure 8-21: Template Expert dialog box, before a template is selected.

2. **In the Available Templates pane, select Block (Blue).**

3. **Click OK.**

   The Template Expert disappears and, after a few seconds, the Block Sample formatting is applied to your report. The result looks like Figure 8-22.

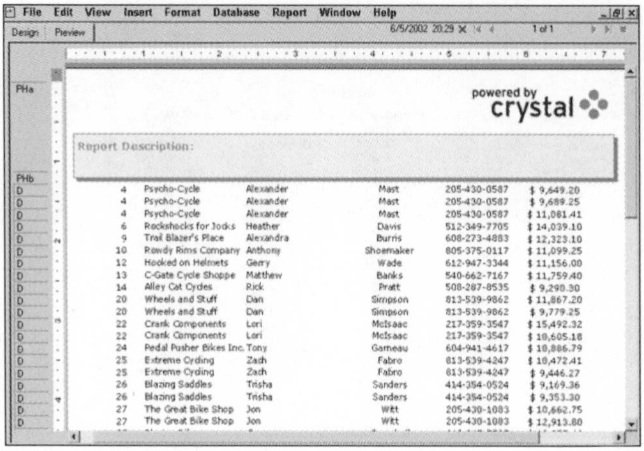

Figure 8-22: Big Orders report with Block Sample (Blue) formatting applied.

In this case, the template's headings have overridden the original headings. The detail rows are unchanged.

If the formatting that the template has given you is close to what you want but not exactly perfect, you can now switch to Design mode and make any needed changes. This should be much less work than would be needed to apply all the formatting from scratch.

Applying a template to a report you are creating

When you create a report using Standard Report Creation Wizard, the Wizard steps you through a series of views:

✔ First is the Data view, where you select the tables you will include in your report.

✔ Next is the Fields view, where you specify the fields from the selected tables that you will use.

✔ Third, you specify Grouping, which separates records into groups in the report, such as grouping customers by country.

✔ Fourth, you specify any summaries that you want to include in the report, such as totals or averages of numerical data.

✔ Fifth, in Group Sorting view, you can choose to sort records within groups.

✔ Sixth, Chart view enables you to add a chart to the report to show the data in an alternate, and possibly more intuitive, way.

✔ Seventh, you specify Record Selection, which filters out records that you don't want, so that you can concentrate on the records that you do want.

✔ Eighth and finally, you specify the template you want to use from the Template view of Standard Report Creation Wizard.

Standard Report Creation Wizard, which is shown in Figure 8-23, looks similar to Template Expert, which was shown in Figure 8-21. This is not surprising, because they serve similar purposes.

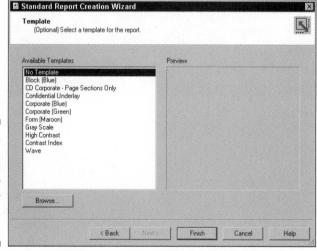

Figure 8-23:
The templates currently available for use in a report.

Chapter 9

Crystal Repository

. . . .

In This Chapter

▶ Adding folders and objects to Crystal Repository

▶ Adding repository objects to reports

▶ Modifying objects

▶ Updating connected repository objects in reports

▶ Deleting items from the repository

. . . .

Crystal Repository is a new feature of Crystal Reports 9. It delivers two benefits to the report developer. Its primary benefit is that it saves you from reinventing the wheel. After you create an object, whether it is a text object, a bitmapped image, a custom function, or an SQL command, you can store it in the repository. From there, you can add it to any other reports that you or your colleagues create.

An additional advantage of the repository is that it remains connected to all the reports that have drawn objects from it. This means you can take an object from the repository into a report, update it, and then return it to the repository. All other reports that contain that object are automatically updated. This saves you from having to keep track of which versions of a particular object are in which reports. You have to manually update the object only once, rather than in all the reports that use it.

The repository holds the master copy of any object it contains. Repository objects can't be modified while they're in the repository. To update an object, you must move it into a report, modify it there, and then move it back into the repository. This eliminates the possibility of object corruption in the repository due to concurrent access by two users.

The repository shipped with Crystal Reports is stored in an Access database. You can create a repository using a different DBMS if you want, as long as it's ODBC-compliant.

Storing Your Valuables in Crystal Repository

After you create an object in one report, you can put it into the repository, where it will be available for reuse in other reports and by other developers. Adding a report object to the repository is easy, but the methods differ depending on the type of object. The following sections describe these methods.

Adding folders to your repository

If you keep the objects in the repository organized, it will be easier to find them when you want to add them to your reports. To impose order, you can add folders and subfolders in a tree structure to hold objects in the repository. You have complete freedom in organizing those folders any way you want. The first step is to launch Repository Explorer:

1. **Open a report, any report.**

2. **On the Standard toolbar, click the Repository Explorer icon.**

3. **Expand the Crystal Repository node.**

   The Images and Text Objects folders appear.

4. **Expand the Images node.**

   You see whatever images and text objects are currently in the repository. You can now add a folder or subfolder to one of the existing folders.

5. **To add a top-level folder, right-click the Crystal Repository node and choose New Folder.**

   To add a subfolder, right-click the folder that will hold the subfolder instead of right-clicking the Crystal Repository node.

6. **Give the folder a name and then press Enter.**

Adding text and bitmapped objects to the repository

To illustrate how to add a text object or a bitmapped object to the repository, use the Customer Orders by State or District, Mexico report from Chapter 6. Figure 9-1 shows what it looks like.

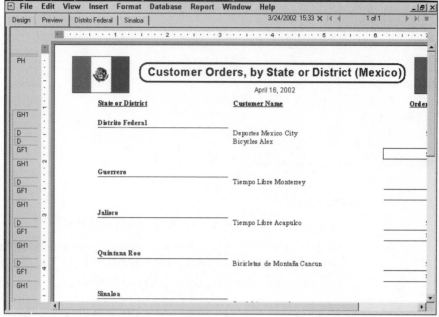

Figure 9-1:
The
Customer
Orders by
State or
District,
Mexico
report.

Suppose you'll be creating other reports about sales in Mexico, and you want to retain the Mexican flag in the repository. The flag is an image, but you're likely to be putting other flags as well as other kinds of images in the repository. To keep things straight, create a Flags subfolder of the Images folder, and then place the Mexican flag image into it:

1. **In Repository Explorer, right-click the Images folder and choose New Folder.**

   A new folder appears.

2. **Name the folder, and then press the Enter key.**

   To follow along with the example, name the folder Flags.

3. **To add an image to your newly created repository subfolder, select the image and then drag it to the subfolder in Repository Explorer.**

   For the example, select the image of the Mexican flag and drag it to the Flags folder.

4. **Enter a name for the object. You may also want to add the author and a description, although that information is optional.**

   I entered the information shown in Figure 9-2.

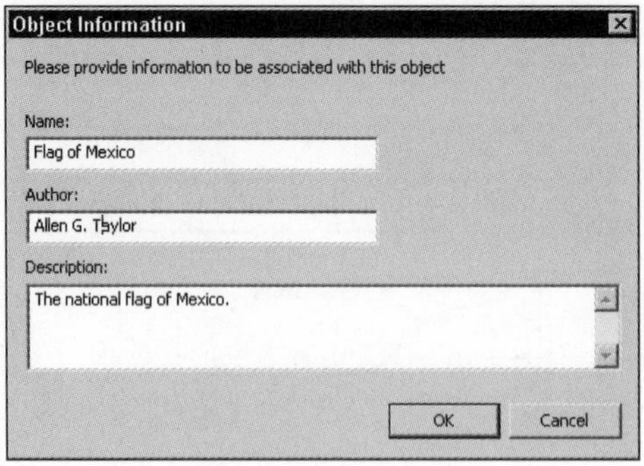

Figure 9-2:
Give the
object a
name.

5. **Click OK.**

   The object is added to the folder in the repository.

6. **Verify that the object is in the repository by right-clicking the folder you just dropped it into and choosing Refresh.**

   Your new object should now appear in the Repository Explorer tree.

You can add a text object in a similar manner. Just drag it to the appropriate folder in Repository Explorer and name it. From that point on, the object is resident in the repository and is connected to the report that you took it from.

Adding custom functions to the repository

You can create custom functions for use in formulas that you create with Formula Workshop. Formula Workshop and the creation of custom functions are covered in Chapter 12.

Putting custom functions in the repository and thus allowing them to be reused is a great laborsaver. Adding a custom function from Formula Workshop to the repository is easy, but I will not go into it here. Chapter 12 gives a step-by-step procedure.

Adding SQL commands to the repository

Relational databases are created and manipulated by commands in SQL. You can add such commands to the repository in much the same way that you add text objects, image objects, or custom functions to the repository. In Chapter 20, I give an overview of SQL commands and how to add an SQL command to the repository. For a more complete exposition of SQL, refer to my *SQL For Dummies* (published by Wiley Publishing, Inc.).

Using Repository Objects in a Report

Moving an object from the repository to a report is essentially the reverse of moving an object from a report to the repository. There is one method for text and image objects, a second method for custom functions, and a third method for SQL commands.

To add a text object or an image object to a report, follow these steps:

1. **On the Standard toolbar, click the Repository Explorer icon.**

2. **Expand the Text Objects or Images folder, whichever is appropriate.**

3. **Drag the desired object into your report, at the location where you want it.**

   That's all there is to it.

Adding a custom function to a report is only a little more complicated:

1. **On the Expert Tools toolbar, click the Formula Workshop icon.**

2. **In Formula Workshop, expand the Repository Custom Functions node.**

3. **Right-click the desired custom function and choose Add to Report.**

   The function is now added to the report. If the function you added requires other functions for its operation, those functions are automatically added too.

Adding an SQL command is similar to adding a custom function:

1. **On the Expert Tools toolbar, click the Database Expert icon.**

2. **In Database Expert, expand the Repository folder.**

3. **Right-click the command you want to add and choose Add to Report.**

   The SQL command is now part of your report.

Modifying a Repository Object

After an object is in the repository, it's available for inclusion in multiple reports. When these reports are opened, the repository is checked to see whether the object has been updated since the last time the report was open. If the object has been updated, the new version is downloaded to the report.

Because you don't have any control over when other users might be opening reports that contain an object that you want to modify, Crystal Reports doesn't allow the modification of repository objects. To update or in some other way modify a repository object, you must first change the object in a report. After the change is complete, you can add the object back to the repository. The next time anyone opens a report that contains that object, your updated object will be the one that's supplied.

To see how to modify a text object in the repository, follow these steps:

1. **Open a report in Design view.**

   You might want to open the Mexico Orders, with Running Totals report from Chapter 6. However, for this example, any report will do.

2. **From the Text Objects folder of Crystal Repository, drag the Copyright — tag line object into the Report Footer.**

3. **Right-click Copyright — tag line in the repository and choose Properties. Note the current version number.**

4. **In Design view in the report, right-click the Copyright object you just dragged into the report and choose Disconnect from Repository.**

5. **Double-click the Copyright object, and then modify the text.**

6. **Drag the modified text object from the report back to the Copyright — tag line object in Repository Explorer.**

   The Add or Update Object dialog box appears.

7. **Make sure that the Update the Report Object in the Repository option is selected, and then click OK.**

   The Modify Item dialog box appears.

8. **Click OK.**

9. **Right-click the Copyright — tag line again and choose Properties.**

   Notice that the version number is incremented by 1.

Updating Reports Automatically Using Connected Repository Objects

You may want to set an organization-wide policy that whenever a repository object is updated, all the reports that use that object will receive the update the next time they're opened. This guarantees that all reports that use a repository object are using the same version. On the other hand, people creating reports might not want to surrender control of their report to who-ever makes a repository update. In this case, they would not want their reports to be automatically updated when they're opened after a repository update. Crystal Reports can be configured to work in either of these two ways. In addition, you can decide on an individual basis whether or not you want a specific report to receive updated repository objects.

To have all reports that use repository object receive updated objects when they're opened, configure Crystal Reports in the following manner:

1. **Choose File⇨Options.**

   The Options dialog box appears.

2. **Click the Reporting tab.**

3. **Select the Update Connected Repository Objects When Loading Reports option.**

4. Click OK.

From now on, whenever any report is opened, the version numbers of the repository objects it contains will be compared against the current version numbers of those objects in the repository. If the repository contains a newer version, it will replace the older version in the report.

If you don't want the automatic update feature, make sure that the Update Connected Repository Objects When Loading Reports option is *not* checked.

To update the repository objects in a single report rather than globally for all reports, note the dialog box that you use to open a report. Figure 9-3 shows an example. At the bottom of the dialog box is an option that reads Update Repository Objects. If you select this option, repository objects in the report will be updated when the report is opened. If you don't select the option, the report's repository objects will not be updated.

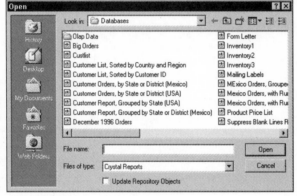

Figure 9-3: Note the Update Repository Objects option.

Deleting Objects from the Repository

Sooner or later, repository objects become obsolete and should be deleted. However, you don't want just anyone deleting repository objects that other people might want to continue to include in their reports. Removal of a repository object is simple. You can do it in three easy steps:

1. On the Standard toolbar, click the Repository Explorer icon.

2. Move to the appropriate folder in the Repository Explorer and select the object you want to remove.

3. Press the Delete key, and then click the Yes button to respond to the confirm Delete dialog box.

The object is removed.

Any reports that already include a deleted object will still contain it, but the object can't be included in any reports from this point on.

Wow. That seems drastic and potentially dangerous. How do you control who has permission to delete repository objects?

Remember, the repository is stored in a relational database. Relational databases have built-in protections against unauthorized tampering. One of those protections is that the database administrator assigns permissions to all users. One of those permissions is the right to delete records from database tables. Only those users who have been granted delete permission may delete objects from the repository. The DBA should choose such people with care.

Part III
Advanced Report Types and Features

The 5th Wave   By Rich Tennant

"I did this report with the help of a satellite view atmospheric map from the National Weather Service, research text from the Jet Propulsion Laboratory, and a sound file from 'The Barfing Lungworms' new CD."

In this part . . .

_T_his part introduces you to the major leagues of report creation. With the knowledge you gain here, you'll be able to produce reports that are the ultimate in sophistication. You uncover ways to select the data that your report will include and sort it for maximum under-standability. You make reports that use formulas and almost think for themselves. Cross-tab reports expose correlations in your data. OLE enables you to include data from nontraditional data sources. OLAP introduces you to multidimensional reporting. Charts and graphs tell your story in a way that words can't express.

Chapter 10

Displaying Your Favorite Hit Parade with Group Sort

In This Chapter

▶ Sorting groups by performance rather than by name

▶ Selecting by percentage

▶ Sorting groups in reverse

▶ Troubleshooting problems with group sorts

An old saying in the sales business is that you get 80 percent of your sales from 20 percent of your customers. It's called the 80/20 rule, and it's not restricted to sales. Some people or things are more productive than others doing the same work. If you identify the most productive salespeople, machinery, or whatever, you can analyze the factors that make them so effective and perhaps apply what you learn to increase productivity overall.

In Chapter 6, you find out how to sort records and group them. A valuable extension of these capabilities is producing a report that shows only the top producers. In this chapter, you find out how to do just that.

Sorting Groups Based on Performance

In Chapter 6, you create a report for Xtreme Mountain Bikes Inc. that shows the dollar totals of individual sales orders, sorts the orders by customer name, groups records by state, and sorts the groups by state. That report (refer to Figure 6-13) is not very helpful to the Vice President of Sales, who is trying to get a feel for which customers are buying the most.

Adding drill-down capability (refer to Figure 6-14) shows which states are responsible for the most sales, on a percentage basis, but doesn't tell us which customers are the best. To get the information you want, in the easiest-to-understand form, a Top N report is probably your best choice. To build one, follow these steps:

1. **Choose File⇨New. In Crystal Reports Gallery, choose Standard, and then click OK.**

   Standard Report Creation Wizard appears.

2. **Find the xtreme database, and then select the Customer and Orders tables, as shown in Figure 10-1.**

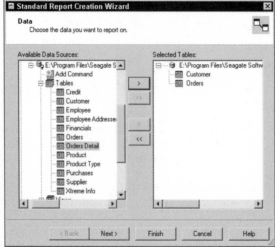

Figure 10-1: Customer and Orders tables selected from Standard Report Creation Wizard.

3. **Click Next to display the Links view.**

   You see the Customer table connected to the Orders table by the Customer ID field.

4. **Click Next to display the Fields view.**

5. **Move Customer Name, Region, and Order Amount to the Fields to Display pane.**

6. **Click Next to display the Grouping view.**

   The Vice President of Sales wants to list the five top U.S. customers, along with their state and the total amount of their orders. The easy way to do this is to group the records by Customer ID, hide order detail, sort by the sum of the order amount for each customer, and include the top five customers in the report.

7. **Move Customer.Customer Name to the Group By pane and specify descending order.**

    This puts the customer with the highest total first.

8. **Click Next to display the Summaries view.**

9. **In the Summarized Fields pane, specify Sum of Orders.Order Amount. In the pull-down list below that pane, specify Sum.**

10. **Click Next to display the Group Sorting view, which is shown in Figure 10-2.**

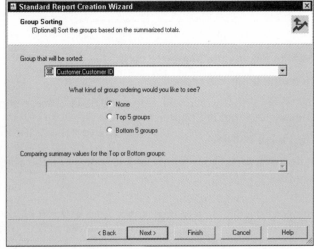

Figure 10-2:
Group
Sorting
view,
showing the
Top 5
Groups
option.

11. **Select Top 5 Groups. In the Comparing Summary Values for the Top or Bottom Groups pull-down list, select Sum of Orders.Order Amount.**

12. **Click Next to display the Chart view, and then click Next again to display the Record Selection view.**

13. **You're interested in only U.S. sales at present, so fill out the Record Selection view as shown in Figure 10-3.**

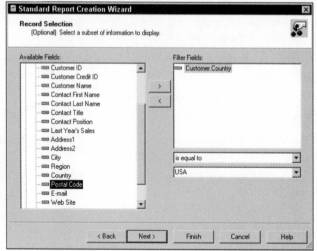

Figure 10-3:
Record
Selection
view with
USA
selected.

14. **Click Next to display the Template view.**

15. **Select a template for the report.**

    To follow along with the example, select the Block (Blue) template. Templates are covered in Chapter 8.

16. **Click the Finish button.**

    Crystal Reports builds your report, and it appears on the screen, as shown in Figure 10-4.

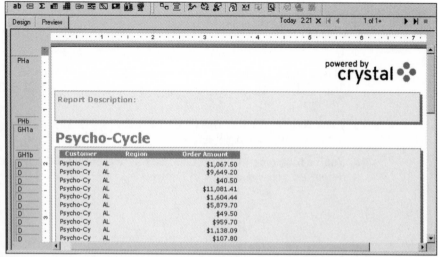

Figure 10-4:
Top Five
USA
Customers
report, as
created by
Standard
Report
Creation
Wizard.

It's not exactly what the Vice President of Sales had in mind. You need to make the following adjustments:

- ✔ Give the report a title.
- ✔ Delete the *Powered by Crystal* line, which appears at the top of every page.
- ✔ Change the Region column heading to State, and center the state data under it.
- ✔ Expand the space allocated for the customer's name in the group header.
- ✔ Hide the individual entries for each order.
- ✔ Display the sum of the orders for each displayed customer.

To make the needed adjustments, follow these steps:

1. **Switch to Design mode.**

2. **Right-click the Powered by Crystal graphic in the page header and choose Cut.**

   (The graphic is actually a hyperlink to the Crystal Decisions Web site.).

3. **On the Insert Tools toolbar, click the Insert Text Object icon, and drag the rectangular placement frame to the page header area above the shaded rectangle that says *Report Description*.**

4. **In the newly placed text field, type** Top Five USA Customers.

5. **Expand the text field and center it. Increase the font size of the text to 22 to make the heading easier to read.**

6. **In the Report Description area, drag a text object from the Insert Tools toolbar to the line below the words *Report Description*.**

7. **In the text object, type** The Top Five USA Customers.

   Things are going well.

8. **Change the Region column heading to State and center the two-character state abbreviations below it.**

   Make the change to the column heading in group header. To center the state abbreviation, click one of the state fields in the Details section, and then click the Align Center icon on the Formatting toolbar.

9. **Center the group headers and details columns on the page, expanding the space allotted to the Customer Name field at the same time.**

At this point, the report looks like Figure 10-5.

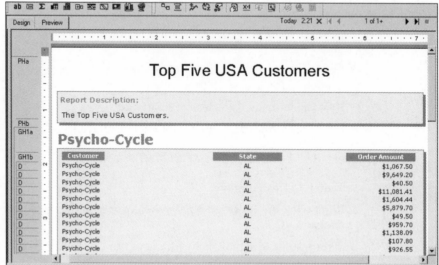

The next thing you should do is hide the lines for individual orders and display a group total in the Group Footer section:

1. **Pull down the lower boundary of the shaded rectangle drawing object from Group Footer 1a to Group Footer 1b.**

This enables you to put a group sum in the Group Footer 1a space.

2. **Click the Insert Summary icon.**

The Insert Summary dialog box appears.

3. **Make the selections as shown in Figure 10-6.**

These selections are as follows: summarize the Orders.Order Amount field; use the Sum summary operator; and choose Group #1 for the summary location. Crystal Reports automatically places the sum field in the appropriate place in the Group Footer 1a section, below the Order Amount heading.

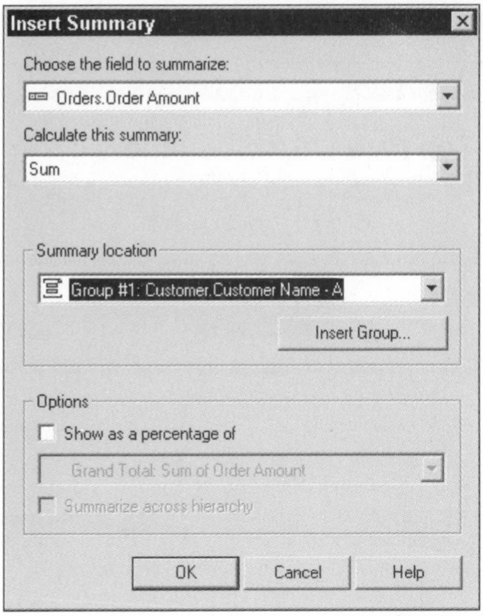

Figure 10-6:
The summarization of Order Amount for each group.

The next thing to do is to hide all the detail lines:

1. **Right-click in the area to the right of the Details section and choose Hide (Drill-Down OK).**

   The report now looks like Figure 10-7. This is still not quite what you want. The customer name is bigger and bolder than it needs to be for a one-line entry. The state information has been hidden, and you still have only one customer per page. These defects are easy to correct.

2. **Click the Insert Summary icon.**

   The Insert Summary dialog box appears.

3. **Make the selections as shown in Figure 10-8.**

   These selections are: summarize the Customer.Customer Name field; use the Maximize summary operator; and choose Group #1 for the summary location. Crystal Reports automatically places the Customer Name field in the appropriate place in the Group Footer 1a section, below the Customer Name heading.

4. **Repeat Step 3 for the Customer.Region field to insert it below the State heading.**

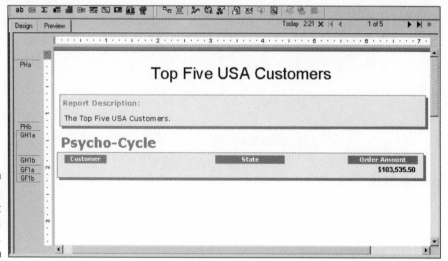

Figure 10-7:
The report
with Details
hidden.

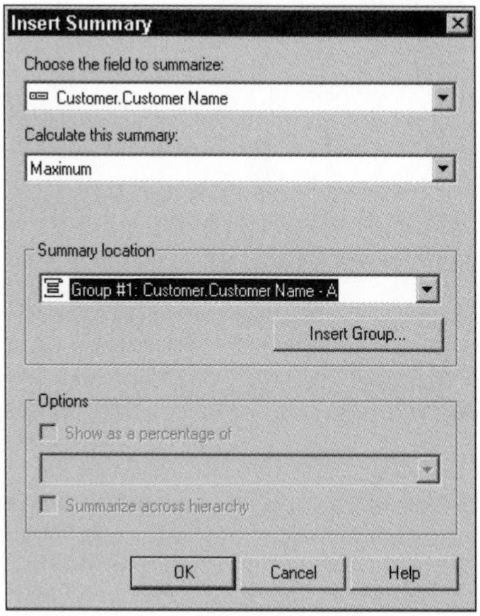

Figure 10-8:
Putting the
Customer
Name in the
Group
Footer.

5. **With the Region still selected, click the Align Center icon to center the state abbreviation below the State heading.**

6. **Delete the Customer.Customer Name field from Group Header 1a.**

    This leaves each group with all the information you want and none of the extra stuff you don't want to display.

Summary fields do more than just compute sums

The Insert Summary dialog box in Figure 10-6 specifies the Sum summary. Many other summary functions appear in the pull-down list, some of which you might want to use, depending on your application.

For numeric fields, the summary options are Sum; Average; Sample variance; Sample standard deviation; Maximum; Minimum; Count; Distinct count; Correlation with; Covariance with; Median; Mode; Nth largest; Nth smallest; Nth most frequent; Pth percentile; Population variance; Population standard deviation; Weighted average with.

For text fields, a smaller array of choices are available, namely, Maximum; Minimum; Count; Distinct count; Mode; Nth largest; Nth smallest; Nth most frequent.

These choices give you just about any type of summarization you'd ever want.

Now all you have to do is remove the page breaks between groups. The page breaks were set by a formula in the Group Footer #1 specification. To delete the formula, follow these steps:

1. **Right-click in the area to the left of the Group Footer #1a section and choose Section Expert.**

   The Section Expert dialog box appears, as shown in Figure 10-9. Group Footer #1a is selected.

2. **Move the Group Footer #1a selection up one row to Group Footer #1.**

   Note that for the Group Footer #1 section, the New Page After box is checked, and a color change in the formula icon for that selection indicates that this action is controlled by a formula.

3. **Click the Formula icon.**

   Formula Format Editor appears, as shown in Figure 10-10.

4. **Delete the** `not onlastrecord` **formula (in the lower part of the screen).**

5. **Click the Save and close icon.**

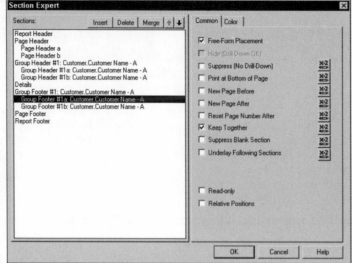

Figure 10-9:
You want to remove page breaks between groups.

Figure 10-10:
You want to delete this formula.

6. **Uncheck the New Page After box, and then click OK.**

   This gives you the five top customers, their states, and the amounts each has purchased, as shown in Figure 10-11.

7. **Save this report as Top5USAfinal.rpt.**

Figure 10-11:
The
completed
report.

Going with the Percentages

Sometimes, it's more helpful to know who is responsible for the largest percentage of an organization's total sales rather than the specific dollar amount. The Group Sort Wizard handles summaries expressed as percentages as well as straight numbers. You can build a report from scratch, similar to the one you built in the preceding section, by following most of the same steps, with just a slight difference at the summarization step.

Rather than going through all that again here, though, you modify the completed report (shown in Figure 10-11) to display percentages rather than group totals. Follow these steps:

1. **In Design mode, right-click the Orders.Order Amount field in the Group Footer #1a section.**

   The menu shown in Figure 10-12 appears.

 2. **Choose Edit Summary.**

 The Edit Summary dialog box appears.

 3. **Select the Orders.Order Amount field to summarize; calculate the Sum summary, and select the box to the left of Show as a Percentage of.**

 4. **Click OK.**

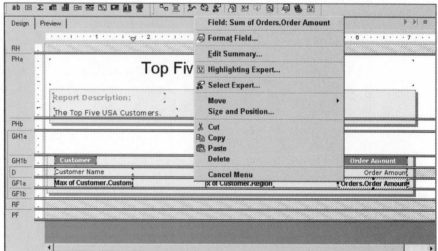

Figure 10-12: Menu for Orders. Order Amount field.

Now when you switch to Preview mode, you see the report shown in Figure 10-13. The five top customers are listed along with their percentage of Xtreme's total sales. This report tells you something that you did not get from the previous report, namely, that the accounts of the top five customers combined account for less than 15 percent of Xtreme's orders. This indicates that Xtreme is in the healthy situation of not being overly dependent on a small number of customers. Sales volume is distributed over a large customer base.

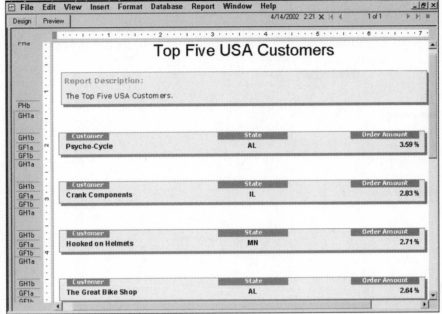

Figure 10-13: This report shows the top customers' percentage of Xtreme's total orders.

What If You Want the Top Seventeen?

The group sort that you used to produce the latest reports happened to ask for the top five customers. This was suspiciously convenient, because the Standard Report Creation Wizard gives you the option of selecting the top five or the bottom five, but not the top ten, or top seventeen, or any other number. If you want to create a report that returns some number of groups other than five, use Group Sort Expert.

 When you click the Group Sort Expert icon on the Expert Tools toolbar, the Group Sort Expert dialog box appears, as shown in Figure 10-14.

The default values for the current report are shown. The type of sort is Top N, based on Sum of Orders.Order Amount, where N is 5. If you want to see the percentage sales of the top 17 customers instead of the top 5, just replace the 5 with a 17 in the Where N Is box, and then click OK. The only task that remains to make this a complete report is to change the references to *Five* in the page header to *Seventeen*. Figure 10-15 shows the result.

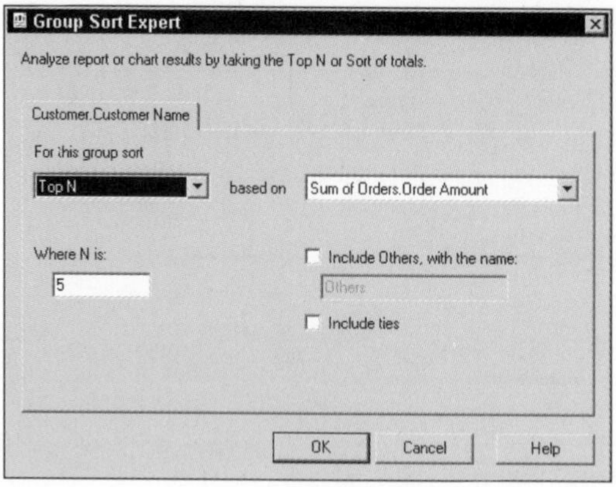

Figure 10-14:
You can sort
in several
ways.

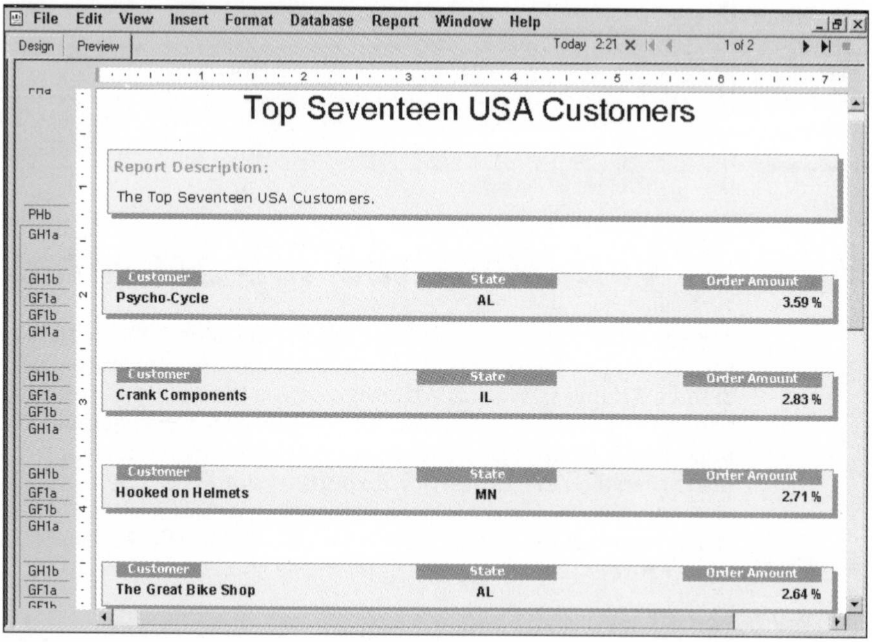

Figure 10-15:
Top
Seventeen
report.

Hmmm. Maybe you're not finished after all. Now the report extends over two pages, and it seems redundant to repeat column headings above each customer line. Also, the space between records is excessive. You can tighten up the report as follows:

1. **In Design mode, right-click the area to the left of Page Header b and choose Insert Section Below.**

   One way to tighten up your report is to move the column headings from the Group Heading section to the Page Heading section. This means you have to expand the Page Heading section by adding a new subsection, in this case, Page Header c.

2. **Drag the column headings up from Group Header 1b to Page Header c, placing them at the top of the Page Header c space.**

3. **Drag the bottom of the section up to the bottom of the column headings.**

4. **Drag the bottom of the shaded box Drawing Object that provides the background color down into the Page Footer section.**

5. **Drag the top of the box down to the bottom of the Group Header b section.**

6. **Right-click in the area to the left of Group Header a to display the shortcut menu, and then use it to suppress Group Header a.**

   This eliminates Group Header a, which is doing nothing but taking up space. At this point, the report looks like Figure 10-16.

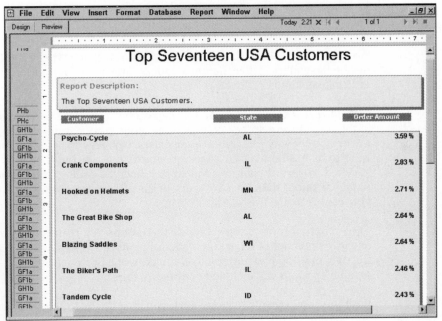

Figure 10-16:
The revised
Top
Seventeen
report.

A Choice of Group Sorts

From what you have seen so far, you've probably guessed that everything you can do for the top performers, you can do also for the bottom. In this section, you take a closer look at the Group Sort Expert dialog box. Figure 10-16 shows it with the group sort list pulled down. The options on this menu are No Sort, All, Top N, Bottom N, Top Percentage, and Bottom Percentage.

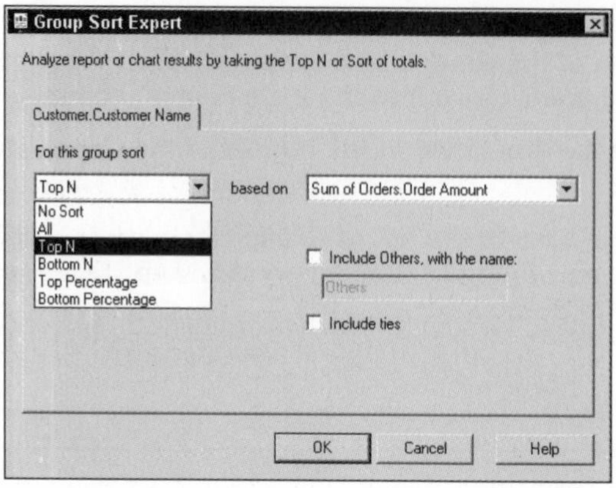

Figure 10-17: Group Sort Expert dialog box, showing group sort list.

We have already seen what Top N does. Bottom N does the same thing, but for the tail-enders rather than the leaders. The other four options require a little explanation.

The No Sort option does what it says: nothing. It leaves the lines of the report in the order in which the corresponding groups appear in the database. You might wonder why this option even exists. One reason might be that you want to build a new report based on an existing one, but the existing report is sorted. If you want your new report to reflect the order of the records in the database rather than the sort order of the old report, one way to get what you want is to use the No Sort option.

The All option sorts and displays all the groups, not restricting the display to any given number. A report built according to this option would contain all the data of a Top N report, plus all the data of a Bottom N report, plus data on all the groups not included in either of those.

With the Top Percentage group sort, you specify the top percentage that you want to see in the report. For example, if you wanted to see whether the 80/20 rule applies to your organization, specify a Top Percentage group sort, and enter 80 in the Where Percentage Is box. If you have, for example, 90 customers, the 80/20 rule holds if the report lists about 18 customers (representing 20 percent of the total).

To report on the customers who order the least amount of product, use the Bottom Percentage group sort. For Xtreme Mountain Bikes Inc., the companies in this report need help or should be replaced by companies that can do a better job.

Troubleshooting Group Sort Problems

Because Group Sort Expert walks you through the process of sorting and summarizing group data, there aren't many ways for you to get into trouble. However, you should keep a few things in mind when adding group sort capability to a report:

- You can't perform a Top N, Bottom N, or other type of group sort unless your report contains a summary value. So, if you have trouble creating a Top N or Bottom N report, make sure that you're basing the sort on a summary value.

- Creating a subtotal for a group may not work if the report data is being drawn from tables linked in a one-to-many relationship. For such a case, you may have to use a running total rather than a subtotal. If you're not getting the summary values you want, and your report is drawing data from multiple tables, check to see whether the tables have a one-to-many relationship. If such a relationship exists, try using a running total rather than a subtotal for each group. (Chapter 6 explains the use of running totals.)

- Sometimes, you'll want to shrink the size of a section by dragging up its lower boundary. If you find that the section will shrink only so much and no more, an invisible object might be in the section. You can't shrink a section past the border of an object that the section contains, even if you can't see the object. Check carefully to see whether the border of a drawing object or an empty text object is hidden under the boundary line that you're trying to drag up.

Chapter 11

Making Correlations with Cross-Tab Reports

F or some people, a summarization of one sort or another is far more valuable than reams of detailed data. However, reports with summaries in group footers or the report footer don't always display summaries in a form that is good for comprehension and decision-making. In some of these cases, a cross-tab object can present the data in a form that's both easy to understand and capable of conveying the *significance* of the data.

The main advantage of a cross-tab is that it can put multiple summaries together in a compact form. You can draw inferences from a single cross-tab on a single page, that displays separate summaries that are nonetheless related.

Creating a Cross-Tab Object to Summarize All Report Data

Suppose that the Sales Manager at Xtreme Mountain Bikes Inc. would like to see how the various product categories are contributing to total sales volume in Canada. A cross-tab report is ideal for presenting that information in a way that can be easily viewed and comprehended. Follow these steps:

1. **In Crystal Reports Gallery, select Cross-Tab, and then click OK.**

   Cross Tab Report Creation Wizard appears.

2. **Select the Customer, Orders, Orders Detail, Product, and Product Type tables from the xtreme database.**

3. **Move the tables to the Selected Tables pane.**

4. **Click Next to display the Link view.**

   The display should show the five tables connected to each other by the fields that they have in common.

5. **Click Next to display the Cross-Tab view, which is shown in Figure 11-1.**

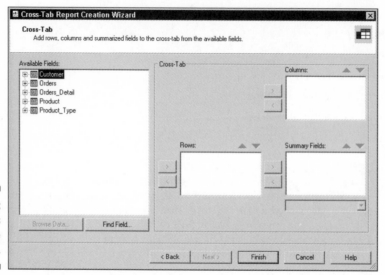

Figure 11-1:
The tables
you have
selected.

6. **In the Available Fields pane, expand the Customer node and select Region. Then click the right-facing arrow to the left of the Rows pane.**

   Each row of the cross-tab now corresponds to a region, which in this case is a province of Canada.

7. **In the Available Fields pane, expand the Product_Type node, and drag Product Type Name to the Columns pane.**

   Each column of the cross-tab now corresponds to a product type.

To get the report to make the summaries you want, follow these steps:

1. **In the Available Fields pane, expand the Orders node. Drag Order Amount to the Summary Fields pane.**

   The default value in the pull-down list below the Summary Fields pane displays Sum, which is the type of summary you want for this report.

2. Click Next to display the Chart view.

You can add a bar, line, or pie chart to the report, if you want.

3. Select Bar Chart, just to see what it will give you.

When you select a chart type, the wizard suggests a chart title that you can override if you want. It also asks that you verify several other assumptions that it has made about what you want the chart to show.

4. Change the Chart Title to Sales by Province and Product Type, **as shown in Figure 11-2.**

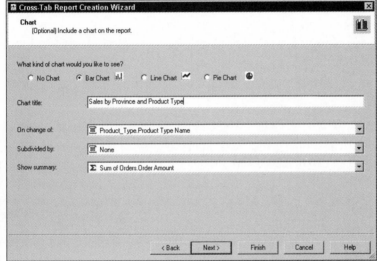

Figure 11-2:
Chart view, with a descriptive chart title.

5. Click Next to display the Record Selection view.

For this report, you want to deal with records only from Canadian customers.

6. In the Available Fields pane, expand the Customer node and move Country to the Filter Fields pane. In the pull-down lists that appear below the Filter Fields pane, select is equal to **and** Canada.

7. Click Next to display the Grid Style view, which is shown in Figure 11-3.

A good assortment of styles is available, some more appropriate than others for various kinds of reports.

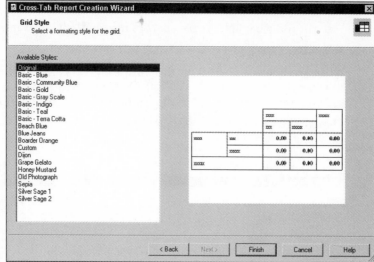

Figure 11-3:
A mock-up
of the
Original
style.

8. **Retain the Original style, and then click the Finish button.**

   The report is displayed in Preview mode. The upper part of the report is
   shown in Figure 11-4.

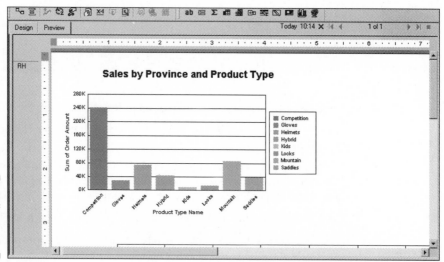

Figure 11-4:
The top of
the cross-
tab report.

This chart should be of interest to the Sales Manager. It shows that
Competition bikes are outselling Mountain bikes by a factor of almost three
to one. It also shows that Xtreme is deriving almost as much revenue from

the sale of helmets as it is from the sale of mountain bikes. This kind of information can be a great help to decision makers.

Moving down the page to the actual cross-tab shown in Figure 11-5, you can see that most sales are coming from British Columbia. This may also be important information for the Sales Manager.

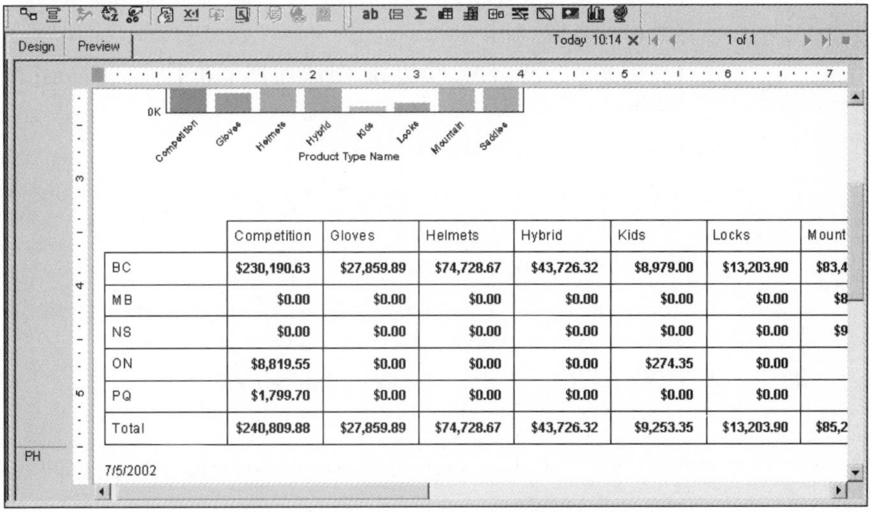

Figure 11-5: Main part of the cross-tab report.

	Competition	Gloves	Helmets	Hybrid	Kids	Locks	Mount
BC	$230,190.63	$27,859.89	$74,728.67	$43,726.32	$8,979.00	$13,203.90	$83,4
MB	$0.00	$0.00	$0.00	$0.00	$0.00	$0.00	$8
NS	$0.00	$0.00	$0.00	$0.00	$0.00	$0.00	$9
ON	$8,819.55	$0.00	$0.00	$0.00	$274.35	$0.00	
PQ	$1,799.70	$0.00	$0.00	$0.00	$0.00	$0.00	
Total	$240,809.88	$27,859.89	$74,728.67	$43,726.32	$9,253.35	$13,203.90	$85,2

The overall totals for each province are off the screen on the right edge of the report, with a grand total in the bottom-right corner. With this cross-tab object and its accompanying chart, the manager can quickly see the relevant facts and make decisions based on those facts.

Summarizing the Contents of a Group with a Cross-Tab

Where a cross-tab object is located in a report is related to the data it contains. For example, if the cross-tab should include all the data in the database for customers in Canada, as in the preceding section, the cross-tab must be located in either the report header or the report footer. This makes sense — the displayed data is a summary of data from all the Canadian provinces, so it must appear in a report section that encompasses data from all those provinces.

It's also possible to create individual cross-tab objects for each group in a report. For example, you can create a report similar to the preceding one, but with summaries for each province rather than one overall summary for all of Canada. Follow these steps:

1. **In Crystal Reports Gallery, select Standard and then click OK.**

   Because there's more to this report than just a cross-tab, you need to create the report using Standard Report Creation Wizard rather than Cross-Tab Wizard.

2. **Place the Customer, Orders, Orders Detail, Product, and Product Type tables in the Selected Tables pane.**

3. **Click Next to display the Link view.**

   The links between these tables are straightforward, so the wizard has assumed them correctly.

4. **Click Next to display the Fields view.**

   Your report won't include any fields other than those in the cross-tabs, so there's no need to select any fields here.

5. **Click Next to display the Template view.**

   You won't use a template either.

6. **With No Template as the default choice, click Finish.**

   This creates a report with nothing in it but a date and a page number.

To continue building the report:

1. **Switch to Design mode.**

2. **Expand the Print Date field in the Page Header to make it big enough to display a date.**

3. **Add a text field in the Report Header to hold the report title. To do so:**

   a. **Right-click the area to the left of the Report Header section and choose Don't Suppress.**

   b. **On the Insert Tools toolbar, click the Insert Text Object icon and drag the text rectangle down into the Report Header.**

   c. **Type the report title, and then expand the rectangle across the entire width of the page.**

      To follow along with the example, type **Sales of Product Types by Province**.

   d. **On the Formatting toolbar, click the Align Center icon to center the text. Enlarge the font and give the text the Bold attribute to make it more readable.**

4. **On the Expert Tools toolbar, click the Group Expert icon.**

   The Group Expert dialog box appears.

5. **Expand the Customer node and then move Region over to the Group By pane. Click OK.**

   This creates Group Header 1 and Group Footer 1.

6. **Drag the bottom boundary of the Group Header section down to make room for the cross-tab that you'll be placing there.**

7. **On the Insert Tools toolbar, click the Insert Cross-Tab icon.**

   Cross-Tab Expert appears.

8. **In the Available Fields pane, drag Customer Name from the Customer table to the Rows pane, Product Type Name from the Product Type table to the Columns pane, and Order Amount from the Orders table to the Summarized Fields pane, as shown in Figure 11-6.**

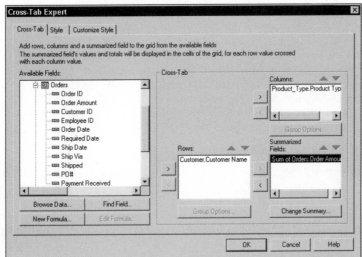

Figure 11-6:
Cross-Tab
Expert, with
fields
selected.

9. **Click OK.**

   The dialog box disappears and the cursor becomes a rectangle.

10. **Drag the rectangle from the left edge of the Group Header section to just below the Group Name field.**

11. **Switch to Preview mode.**

    The report now looks like the one shown in Figure 11-7.

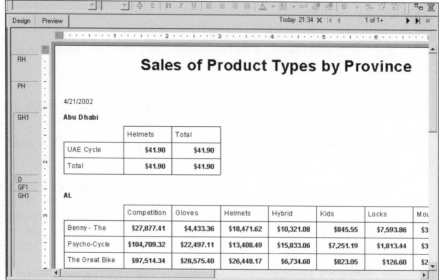

Figure 11-7:
Cross-tab
report, first
version.

You have cross-tabs all right, but they're not the ones you want. The first is for the customer in Abu Dhabi, and the second is for customers in Alabama. There are 3684 records in all. You want the report to show only customers in Canada. To do that, you have to work on the report just a little bit more:

1. **On the Expert Tools toolbar, click the Select Expert icon.**

   The Choose Field dialog box appears.

2. **Expand the Customer node, and then select Country. Click OK.**

   The Select Expert dialog box appears, with the Customer.Country tab on top.

3. **In the pull-down lists, select** is equal to **and** Canada. **Click OK.**

   You want to select only Canadian customers.

4. **When the dialog box asks whether you want to use saved data or refresh the data, click one of the options.**

   In this case, it doesn't matter which you choose because the database has not changed since the last time you ran the report.

   The report, which is shown in Figure 11-8, now contains only Canadian customers, but there's a formatting problem. Below the cross-tab for British Columbia, there are a large number of detail lines, all of which are empty. You should get rid of these so that the cross-tabs for all the provinces are displayed one below another.

5. **Right-click in the area to the left of the Details section and choose Suppress (No Drill Down).**

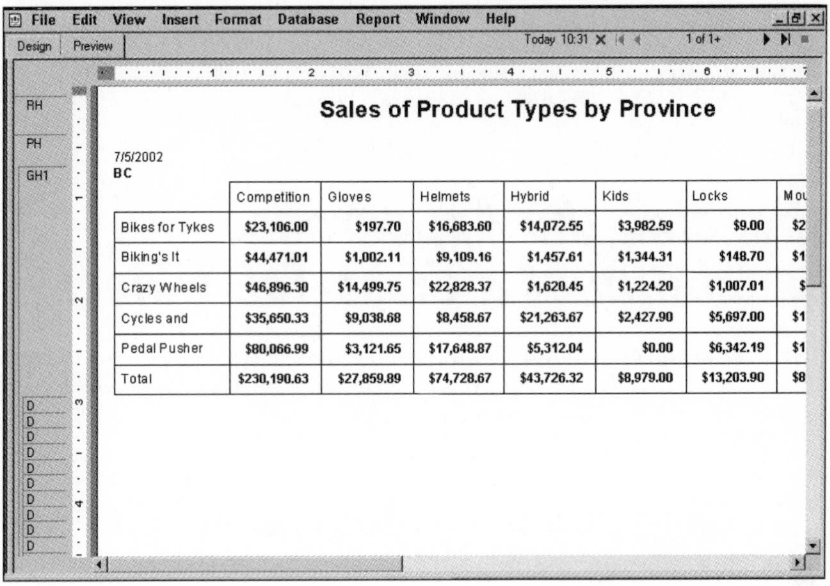

Figure 11-8:
Cross-tab
report,
second
version.

The report shown in Figure 11-9 appears. The data for Manitoba is right
below that for British Columbia, and the data for Nova Scotia is right
below Manitoba's. This is what we want.

6. **Save this report as Sales of Product Types by Province.**

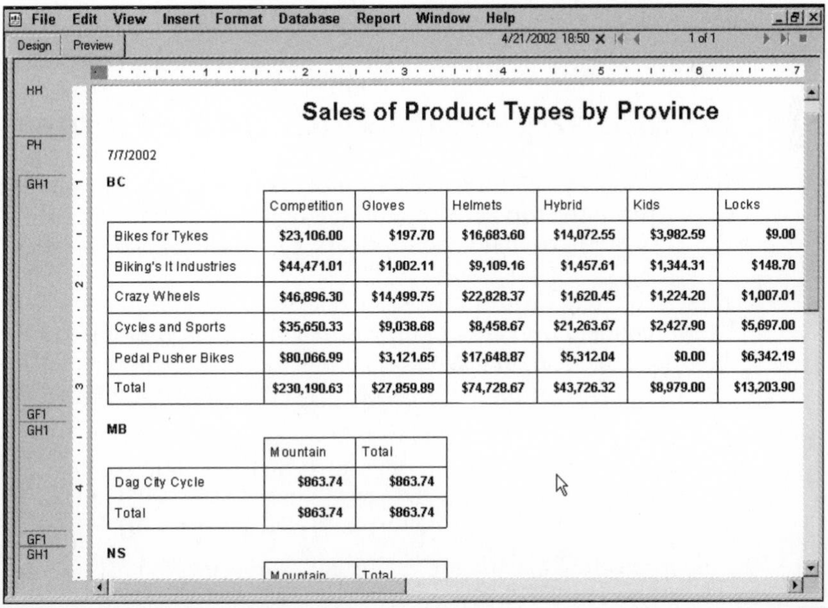

Figure 11-9:
Cross-tab
report, final
version.

As you saw in the preceding section, you can add cross-tabs to a report header or report footer. This section showed you how to add cross-tabs to group headers or group footers. You can't put a cross-tab in page headers, page footers, or details sections.

Enhancing the Appearance and Readability of a Cross-Tab Object

You can do a number of things to enhance the appearance of a cross-tab report. In this section, you experiment with achieving different effects in the reports you just created.

Changing the width and height of cross-tab cells

The width and height of cross-tab cells are easy to change in Design mode. Merely select the cell you want to change and drag its width or height handle in the direction you want. If you drag a width handle, all the cells in that column are changed along with the cell you're dragging. If you drag a height handle, all the cells in the same row are changed in the same way. This retains size consistency across columns and rows. It's not uncommon to need to enlarge cells to display all that they contain because the default size assigned by Cross-Tab Wizard is often not adequate.

Formatting entire rows and columns

You can apply formatting to an entire cross-tab object by right-clicking the blank area at the top-left corner of the object and choosing Format Cross-Tab. The Format Editor dialog box appears, as shown in Figure 11-10.

You can specify various things, such as Read-only and Lock Position and Size. By switching to the Border tab, you can specify border lines, drop shadows, and foreground and background colors. Click the Hyperlink tab and you can associate your cross-tab with a Web site, an e-mail address, or a disk file.

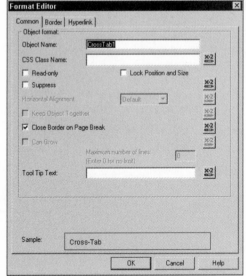

Figure 11-10:
Format
entire
cross-tab
objects
here.

Formatting individual fields

To format an individual field, right-click it and choose Format Field. This displays a version of the Format Editor tailored to the data type of the field you're formatting. For example, a currency field displays font options and currency format options in addition to the Common, Border, and Hyperlink options that appear when you're formatting an entire cross-tab.

You can give multiple cross-tab cells the same formatting by selecting them simultaneously using shift-click, and then applying formatting in the same way you would for a single cell.

Suppressing selected cross-tab data

Sometimes the cross-tab objects you create may contain empty rows or columns because of a lack of data. For readability, you may want to suppress these empty rows and columns. To do so, right-click the blank area in the upper-left corner of the cross-tab object and choose Cross-Tab Expert. One of the tabs for this Expert is Customize Style. Click that to display the dialog box shown in Figure 11-11.

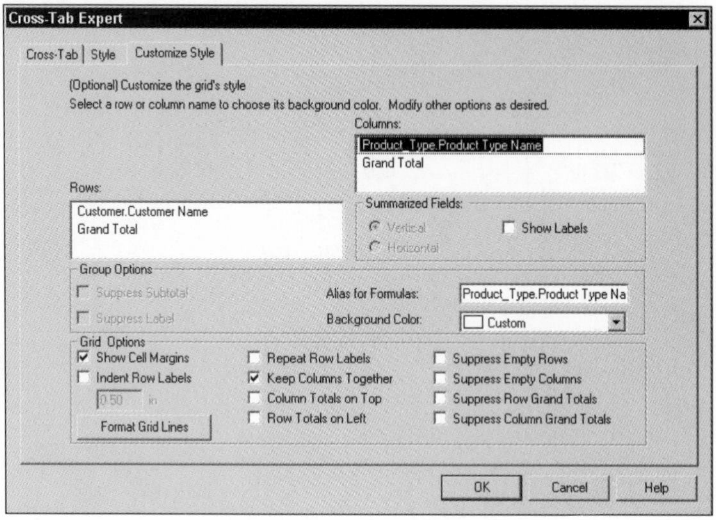

Figure 11-11:
Suppress
the display
of empty
rows and
columns.

As you can see from the figure, you can suppress not only empty rows and columns, but also row and column grand totals. If your report has subtotals, you can suppress those too. A variety of other customizations are also available.

Printing cross-tabs that span multiple pages

It's not uncommon for a cross-tab object to be wider or longer than the specified page size. Crystal Reports automatically formats the report on as many extra (extension) pages as needed. Column headings are repeated on all such extra pages. By default, row labels are not repeated. If you want row labels to be repeated on extension pages, select the Repeat Row Labels option on the Customize Style tab of Cross-Tab Expert (shown in Figure 11-11).

Chapter 12

Adding Formulas to Reports

● ●

In This Chapter

▶ Understanding formula syntax

▶ Writing formulas with Formula Workshop

▶ Deleting formulas you no longer want

▶ Using data types in formulas

▶ Manipulating data with variables in formulas

▶ Altering reports at runtime with control structures

● ●

*Y*ou can create a report by dragging database fields onto a blank report, adding text and images, and performing a variety of summaries. Such reports are fine for many applications, but sometimes you want to do more than merely summarize data. You might want to process it in some way before displaying it. Crystal Reports' formula capability gives you much more latitude in creating the report you want. If you're already a programmer, using formulas will be easy. If you're not a programmer, you may be surprised to see how soon you can do useful things with formulas.

Formula Overview and Syntax

You can use formulas in a number of ways. One common use is to perform a calculation that modifies the contents of a database field. Suppose you have a database table named Product that holds data, including the price, on all the products you sell. To calculate a 10 percent discount from your normal price, you can use a formula such as

```
{Product.Price} * .9
```

This formula follows Crystal Reports syntax. Crystal Reports is unusual in that you can write formulas that obey either of two syntaxes. Because the two syntaxes are equivalent, you can use whichever syntax you find easier. The preceding formula, written with Basic syntax, looks like this:

```
formula = {Product.Price} * .9
```

Crystal Reports Basic syntax is similar to Visual Basic syntax. If you're a Visual Basic programmer, you may be more comfortable using Basic syntax. If you're not particularly biased toward Visual Basic, you may want to use Crystal Reports syntax instead.

Crystal Reports syntax is, logically enough, the original formula syntax used by early versions of Crystal Reports. You can do a few things with Crystal Reports syntax that you can't do with Basic syntax, but for the most part, neither has an advantage over the other. In the example formulas in this book, I use Crystal Reports syntax.

Lessening the Workload with Functions

Crystal Reports has a number of predefined functions that you may find useful. You can include these functions in formulas to reduce the size and complexity of the formula code that you have to write yourself. For example, suppose that you have a database application with a data entry form in which users enter a customer's name and address information. In the Region field, users should enter a two-letter state or province code, in uppercase. If the user accidentally fails to use uppercase, you can correct the problem with Crystal Reports' UpperCase function:

```
UpperCase ({Customer.Region})
```

This formula converts whatever is in the Region field of the Customer table. If the contents are already in uppercase, no change occurs. If any of the letters are lowercase, they're changed to uppercase. By using this function, you don't have to bother with checking the case of an entry, and then correcting it if necessary. I discuss functions in greater detail when I talk about the Formula Editor component of Formula Workshop later in this chapter.

Creating a Custom Function Using Formula Workshop

You can access Formula Workshop from the Expert Tools toolbar. When you click the Formula Workshop icon, the screen shown in Figure 12-1 is displayed.

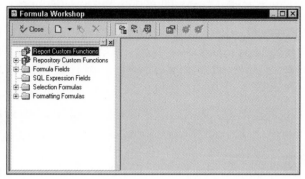

Figure 12-1:
The main categories of functions and formulas for inclusion in your report.

The Workshop tree in the left pane of Formula Workshop displays several folders: Report Custom Functions, Repository Custom Functions, Formula Fields, SQL Expression Fields, Selection Formulas, and Formatting Formulas.

Custom functions are a new feature of Crystal Reports 9. After you create a formula, you can give it a name and save it as a custom function. You can then use the custom function again in the same report or in other reports. To create a custom function, follow these steps:

1. **Open the report where you want to use the function.**

   To follow along with the example, open the Top5USAfinal report from Chapter 10.

2. **On the Expert Tools toolbar, click the Formula Workshop icon to open Formula Workshop.**

3. **Right-click the Report Custom Functions branch on the Workshop tree and choose New.**

   The Custom Function Name dialog box appears, asking you to enter a name for the custom function you are about to create.

4. **Enter a meaningful function name.**

Name the function ConcatWith1Space. You'll use this function to concatenate a customer contact's first and last name, with one blank space in between.

5. **Click the Use Editor button.**

The Custom Function Editor appears, as shown in Figure 12-2. On the right is a Function tree pane, with various predefined functions that you can include in your custom function, and an Operators tree pane. You can use the operators to combine function elements or operate on function elements.

The Functions pane on the left holds a collection of predefined functions. The Operators pane on the right displays an array of operators.

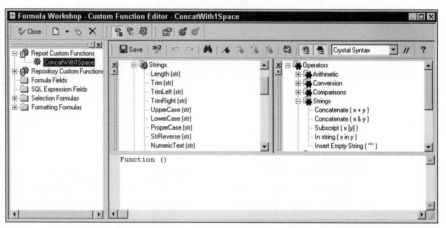

Figure 12-2: Custom Function Editor is waiting for you to specify what the function will do.

6. **If the functions and operators are not already displayed, expand the Functions and Operators nodes.**

You can drag the functions or operators you need down to the formula entry area to build up a custom function, or you can type the function into the formula entry area directly.

7. **Drag the elements you need down from the Functions and Operators panes or type your function directly.**

To follow along with the example, expand the Strings branch in the Operators pane (because concatenation is a string function). You can specify concatenation in two ways: (x + y) and (x & y). You can drag either one down into the formula entry area. However in many cases, such as in this example, it's easier to just type the formula rather than drag pieces of it from the trees in the panes above the formula entry area.

8. **In the pane below the Tree panes, type the parameter declarations and the body of the function as given below. Note that the word *Function ( )* is already there.**

   The parentheses are to enclose any parameters that the function might use. If the function has no parameters, the parentheses remain, enclosing nothing.

   For the example, you want to concatenate the contact first name and the contact last name from the Customers table, with one blank space between them. The two parameters, x and y, represent the two names you want to concatenate. They are both declared as string variables. Type the following:

   ```
   Function (StringVar x, StringVar y)
   (x + " " + y);
   ```

   This function concatenates a string with a blank space, and then concatenates the result with a second string.

9. **Click the Close button, and then click Yes because you should save your changes.**

This is just what you need to create a full name for customer contacts. It may also be useful in a number of other contexts. After you create a custom function, you can use it in many places with any two string arguments.

Formula Editor

You can't use a custom function directly in a report. Instead, you must wrap the function in a formula. Therefore, the next order of business is to create a formula that takes your general concatenation function and applies it specifically to concatenating the first and last names of customer contacts:

1. **Click the Formula Workshop icon.**

2. **In the Workshop tree on the left edge of Formula Workshop, right-click Formula Fields and choose New.**

   The Formula Name dialog box appears.

3. **Enter a name, such as ContactFullName.**

4. **Click the Use Editor button.**

   Formula Editor appears, as shown in Figure 12-3. It looks a lot like Custom Function Editor, but they do have some differences.

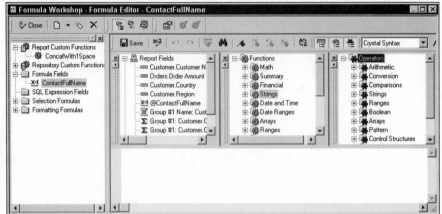

Figure 12-3:
Use Formula
Editor to
create a
formula.

In the Workshop tree on the left, notice that ConcatWith1Space is listed under Report Custom Functions. Note also that ContactFullName is listed under Formula Fields, even though you haven't added functionality to it yet. The formula exists; it just doesn't do anything yet.

As with Custom Function Editor, there's a Functions tree, which contains standard functions that you can include in your formula, and an Operators tree, which contains operators that you can use in your formula. You can drag these functions and operators down to the appropriate spot in the formula you're building, or you can type them by hand. In many cases, it's easier to type them than it is to drag them. Formula Workshop also has a Report Fields tree, which Custom Function Editor doesn't have. You can drag fields from the Field tree for inclusion in the formula you're building.

You don't need any of these handy tools in the example, because you already did most of the work of building this formula by creating the ConcatWith1Space custom function. All you need to do now is the following:

1. **Drag your custom function from the Workshop tree down to the formula pane.**

   To follow along with the example, drag ConcatWith1Space.

2. **Click the Close icon.**

The next step is to add the contact's full name to the report. You do that with the help of Formula Expert.

Formula Expert

Currently, the Top Five USA Customers report lists the customer names, states, and order totals for the five U.S. customers who have purchased the most merchandise from Xtreme Mountain Bikes Inc. At each of these customer sites, you want to insert the full name of the contact person between the Customer Name and the State columns:

1. **Switch to Design view.**

2. **Move the State column to the right to make room for the new column that will contain the contact's full name.**

3. **On the Expert Tools toolbar, click the Formula Workshop icon.**

4. **Expand the Formula Fields node in the Workshop tree, and then click the ContactFullName formula.**

   Formula Expert appears in Formula Workshop. The Custom Function Supplying Logic pane has two entries, Report Custom Functions and Repository Custom Functions.

5. **Expand the Report Custom Functions node, and then click ConcatWith1Space, which appears as shown in Figure 12-4.**

   In the Function Arguments pane, the x and y arguments from the ConcatWith1Space custom function await values. For this report, you want x to be Customer.ContactFirstName and y to be Customer.ContactLastName.

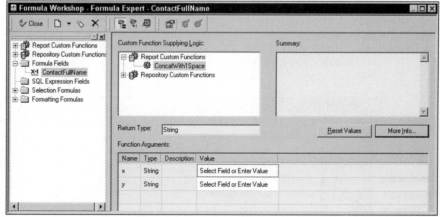

Figure 12-4: Details of the ContactFull Name formula.

6. **Click the Value field of the x row and then select Choose Other Field from the drop-down menu that appears.**

   The Choose Field dialog box appears.

7. **In the Customer table, select Contact First Name, and then click OK.**

   The selected field appears in the Value column for the x row.

8. **Click the Value field of the y row and then select Choose Other Field from the drop-down menu.**

9. **In the Customer table, select Contact Last Name, and then click OK.**

   The selected field appears in the Value column for the y row.

10. **Click the Close icon.**

    The formula is saved and Formula Workshop closes.

Next, you add the full name of the contact to your report.

1. **On the Insert Tools toolbar, click the Insert Text Object icon, and drag the resulting placement frame to a spot in Group Footer 1a, between the Customer column and the State column.**

2. **Drag ContactFullName from Field Explorer to the placement frame.**

3. **On the Formatting toolbar, click the Bold icon.**

   Now the font in this column matches the font in the other columns.

4. **Switch to Preview mode to confirm that the names of the customer contacts appear where you want them.**

   You can always switch back to Design mode and adjust the position of the new column.

5. **In Group Header 1b, add the header titled *Contact*.**

   An easy way to do this is to copy the State header, paste it above the ContactFullName column, and then edit it to read *Contact* instead of *State*. Figure 12-5 shows the result.

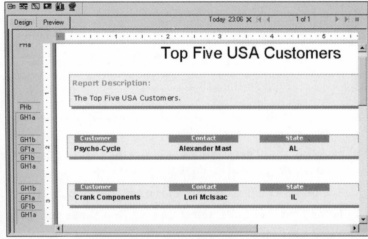

Figure 12-5:
The report
with a
column
created by
formula
rather than
by database
field.

SQL Expression Editor

SQL Expression Editor is another incarnation of Formula Workshop. It's similar to Formula Editor but is used to build SQL expressions from tables, functions, and operators. With an SQL expression, you can issue commands to the database that underlies your report — but you can retrieve no more than one database record at a time. With an SQL command, you can retrieve multiple records in a single operation.

Chapter 20 covers the use of SQL commands, but to handle SQL properly, you have to know much more about it than is mentioned in this book. For a thorough treatment, read my *SQL For Dummies* (published by Wiley Publishing, Inc.).

The SQL Expression Editor view of Formula Workshop looks exactly like the Formula Editor view of Formula Workshop, except for the name in the title bar. You work with it in the same way too. The only difference is that the expression that you build must adhere to legal SQL syntax. This is an advanced feature that you'll probably not use until you have gained considerable experience with both Crystal Reports and SQL.

Selection formulas

The two kinds of selection formulas are group selection and record selection. By applying a group selection formula to a report, you can restrict retrieval to a single group or specific desired groups. With a record selection formula, you can restrict retrieval to specific records. For example, in a report that groups sales figures by state, you can use group selection formula to pull out the sales for a specific state. Similarly, you can use a record selection formula to retrieve selected records.

Group selection

In this section, you look at an example of a group selection formula. First, open the Customer Report, Grouped by State or District (USA) report from Chapter 6 (and shown in Figure 6-13). Note that the first page shows sales for Psycho-Cycle in Alabama, because Alabama is the first state or district in an alphabetical sort on Region. Note also that right side of the tab bar indicates that the report has multiple pages.

This is the full report, with results for all Xtreme customers in the United States. Suppose that you wanted to print a report for only a single state, North Carolina. Follow these steps:

1. **On the Expert Tools toolbar, click the Formula Workshop icon.**

2. **Expand the Selection Formulas node in the Workshop tree to display the Group Selection and Record Selection options. Select Group Selection.**

   Group Selection Formula Editor appears in the Workshop. You want to retrieve the records where the value of the Region field is NC.

3. **Drag Customer.Region from the Report Fields pane down to the blank pane at the lower right of Group Selection Formula Editor.**

   You want to set that field equal to NC.

4. **After the Customer.Region field, type an equals sign.**

   Alternatively, you can expand the Comparisons node in the Operators pane and drag down an equals sign.

5. **Finish the formula by typing after the equals sign the two-letter state abbreviation, surrounded by single quotes.**

   Type **'NC'** to follow along with the example. The resulting formula is shown in Figure 12-6.

Figure 12-6: The Group Selection formula for North Carolina customers.

6. **Click the Check icon to check your formula for syntax errors.**

7. **Click the Save icon to save the formula.**

8. **Click the Close icon to close Formula Workshop.**

Now when you look at the report, it consists of only a single page, showing information for only North Carolina.

Record selection

For record selection, you can follow substantially the same procedure that you did for group selection. Suppose that you want to see all transactions in Customer Report, Grouped by State or District in which the order amount was greater than $10,000. First, delete the Group Selection formula from the preceding section. (Because North Carolina had no orders exceeding $10,000, a blank report will result if Group Selection is still in effect.) Then, follow this procedure:

1. **On the Expert Tools toolbar, click the Formula Workshop icon.**

2. **Expand the Selection Formulas node in the Workshop tree to display the Group Selection and Record Selection options. Select Record Selection.**

   Record Selection Formula Editor appears in Workshop. You want to retrieve records where the value of the Orders.Order Amount field is greater than 10,000.

3. **Drag Orders.Order Amount from the Report Fields pane down into the blank pane at the lower right of Group Selection Formula Editor.**

4. **Type > (greater than sign) after the Orders.Order Amount field.**

5. **Finish the formula by typing an amount after the equals sign.**

   Type **10000** to follow along with the example. The resulting formula is shown in Figure 12-7.

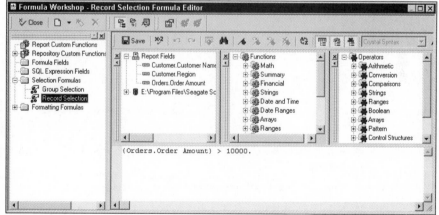

Figure 12-7: Record selection formula for orders greater than $10,000.

6. **Click the Check icon to check the formula for syntax errors.**

7. **Click the Save icon to save the formula, and then click the Close icon.**

Now when you look at the report, only orders greater than $10,000 are shown. They're spread over ten pages, indicating that only ten states have customers with orders in excess of $10,000.

Formatting formulas

You can use formatting formulas to change various aspects of the format of a report. In this section, you take another look at the Customer Report, Grouped by State or District report (used in the previous section):

1. **Open Formula Workshop.**

2. **Expand the Formatting Formulas node in the Workshop tree.**

   A number of subnodes appear, including the Page Header node.

3. **Expand the Page Header node.**

   The screen now looks like Figure 12-8.

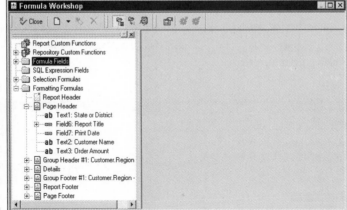

Figure 12-8:
Record
selection
formula for
orders
greater than
$10,000.

4. **Right-click the Report Title entry and choose New Formatting Formula.**

   The New Formatting Formula dialog box appears.

5. **Select Font Style, and then click the Use Editor button.**

6. **In the Functions pane of Format Formula Editor, expand the Font Style Constants node and double-click BoldItalic.**

   This puts the BoldItalic function (crBoldItalic) in the Formula pane at the bottom of Format Formula Editor.

7. **Click the Check icon to check the syntax.**

8. **Click the Save icon to save the new formula, and then click the Close icon.**

   When Formula Workshop disappears, you see that the report now has a bold and italicized heading

You can add or change the formatting of any aspect of a report in the same way. Do a little looking around in the Report Fields, Functions, and Operators panes of Format Formula Editor to get an idea of what's available.

Changing and Deleting Formulas

In earlier sections of this chapter, you use Formula Workshop to create a formula. It's just as easy to modify an existing formula. Display it in the Formula Workshop formula pane and make whatever modifications you want, then check it and save it. Deleting a formula is even easier. Select it in the Workshop tree, and then click the Delete icon on the Workshop's toolbar.

Data Types

Formulas deal with data, and databases may hold several different types of data. You can manipulate this data with formulas, but you must be careful to do it properly. For example, you can use the common addition, subtraction, multiplication, and division mathematical operators on number type data, but you can't multiply a number by a string. Specific operations apply to specific data types.

Simple data types

Some data types are more complex than others. The simplest data types are number, currency, string, date, time, datetime, and Boolean. Range types and array types are more complex. Look at the simple types first.

Number

The number type includes positive and negative integers and real numbers. When you enter number data, don't separate each group of three digits with commas. The only non-numeric characters allowed in a number are the decimal point and the negation sign. Following are examples of number type data:

```
42
-273
3.1415927
93000000.
```

You can perform addition, subtraction, multiplication, and division operations on number data. Just make sure that you don't divide by 0. Doing so will cause an error.

Currency

Currency data is similar to number data, except it starts with a dollar sign ($) and numbers to the right of the decimal point are rounded differently. Following are a few examples of currency type data:

```
$19.95
-$4000000000.
$64000
```

String

Character strings use different operators than those you use with numbers and currency. You can't add two strings, but you can concatenate them. You can convert a string to all uppercase or all lowercase, which is something you can't do with a number.

Strings must be enclosed in either single or double quotes. Here are a few strings:

```
"I Left My Heart in San Francisco"
"$19.95"
'You can put "quoted text" within a string.'
'You can even include an apostrophe in a string''s text'
```

As you can see, sometimes you must use quotes in an unusual way to keep from confusing the string parser. (The *string parser* is the part of Crystal Reports that analyzes and interprets strings, one character at a time.) Also note that anything within quotes is a string, even if it looks like a number or a currency value.

Date, time, and datetime

As you might surmise, the date data type holds dates, the time data type holds times, and datetime data type holds a combination of the date and time. Date and time data types are somewhat redundant because the date-time data type can hold dates without times and times without dates. You might want to use the date or the time data type anyway, though, because data in those two types takes up less storage space in memory and on the hard disk than the same quantity stored as a datetime data type.

Datetime values are not strings or numbers. They are literals, which are handled differently from the way either strings or numbers are handled. Datetime literals are enclosed in pound (#) signs. This differentiates them from strings, which are quoted, and numbers, which are not enclosed in anything. Following are some examples of values that can be stored in the datetime data type:

```
#July 20, 1969#
#20 Jul 1969 4:18 pm#
#7/20/1969 16:18:00#
#7/20/1969#
#4:18 pm#
```

Boolean

Boolean data is named after the British mathematician George Boole, who invented Boolean algebra, which gave logic a mathematical foundation. Boolean data has only two values, True and False. Crystal Reports accepts Yes and No as synonyms for True and False. Boolean logic has been critical to the development of the digital computer, which uses ones and zeros to represent True and False.

Range data types

Crystal Reports enables you to restrict the values of data elements to a specified range for all data types except Boolean. For example:

> A range of `70 To 100` includes values between 70 and 100. Both 70 and 100 are included in the range.

> `70_To_100` includes values between 70 and 100. Both 70 and 100 are excluded.

> `70_To 100` includes values between 70 and 100. 70 is excluded but 100 is included.

UpTo 100 includes all numbers up to and including 100, but none beyond.

"A" To_"Z" includes all character strings starting with an uppercase letter, except for strings starting with "Z".

UpFrom #1/1/2000# includes all dates after the once-dreaded Y2K day.

Array data types

Arrays are ordered lists of values that are all the same type. In Crystal Reports, an array can be a simple type or a range type. Array elements are enclosed in square brackets. For example:

```
[2, 3, 5, 7, 11, 13]
```

is an array containing the first six prime numbers.

```
["Mercury", "Venus", "Earth", "Mars"]
```

is an array containing the string values of the names of the terrestrial planets in our solar system.

You can subscript an array by specifying the index in square brackets after the array. (A *subscript* specifies a particular element of an array.) For example:

```
[2, 3, 5, 7, 11, 13] [3]
```

specifies 5, the third element in the array.

You can also specify a range of elements, as follows:

```
["Mercury", "Venus", "Earth", "Mars"] [3 To 4]
```

This creates a new array, ["Earth", "Mars"].

Variables in Formulas

In the discussion of Formula Workshop, I used the x and y variables to act as placeholders for specific values in the ConcatWith1Space custom function. Whenever the formula parser encounters a variable in a formula, it looks for the value represented by that variable, and then plugs the value into the formula. Because the value of a variable can be changed by the user or assigned in the formula, variables give Crystal Reports considerable flexibility.

Declaring a variable

Before you can use a variable, you must declare it, to make Crystal Reports aware of it. When you declare a variable, you must specify three things: its name, its scope, and its data type. The name can be something simple, such as *x* or *y*. It can also be something more descriptive, such as *topic*.

When you declare a variable's data type, stick Var on the end of the type, such as StringVar or NumberVar. Scope may be local, global, or shared. If a variable is declared locally, it is valid only in the formula in which it is declared. If a variable is declared globally it is available to all the formulas in a report that declare it (except for subreports). A *shared variable* is available to all formulas in a report that declare it, including subreports. Subreports are covered in Chapter 13.

Assigning a value to a variable

After you declare a variable, you can assign it a value. Here's an example:

```
//Declare topic1 to be a global variable of String type that
//specifies a book topic.
Global StringVar topic1;
topic1 := "Crystal Reports";
```

You can also declare a variable and assign it a value in a single statement, as follows:

```
Global StringVar topic2 := "SQL";
```

You can now use the variable in a formula.

Control Structures

Control structures enable you to alter the flow of execution from a strict sequential order to something else. For example, you can branch one way or another with an If-Then-Else control structure. You can branch multiple ways with a Select Case structure. You can loop through an expression or a set of expressions multiple times with a For or While Do structure. You can implement business logic (or illogic) with these structures.

If-Then-Else

The If-Then-Else control structure is useful when you want to do one thing if a condition is true and another thing if the condition is false. Suppose that you want to give a 5 percent discount to customers who order more than $10,000 worth of products in a single order. Before printing their invoice, you can have Crystal Reports make the calculation for you as follows:

```
//Give 5% discount for orders > $10,000
If {Orders.Order Amount} > 10000.
Then
     {Orders.Order Amount} = {Orders.Order Amount} * 0.95
Else
     {Orders.Order Amount} = {Orders.Order Amount};
```

If the condition is satisfied, Order Amount is multiplied by 0.95, giving a 5 percent discount. Otherwise, Order Amount is unchanged. The change to Order Amount applies only to this report. The data in the database is not affected.

The Else clause is required, even though it doesn't change anything. The data type of the result returned from the Else clause must match the data type of the result returned by the Then clause. If you leave out the Else clause and the condition is not satisfied, the formula returns the default value for the data type.

Select Case

Use the Select Case control structure when there are more than two alternatives to choose from and you want to do a different thing in each case. Suppose that the 5 percent discount you offered your customers last month resulted in a huge increase in sales, so you decide to expand the offer this month. A Select Case statement will do the job:

```
//Give volume-based discounts
Select {Orders.Order Amount}
    Case 15000. To 1000000.:
         {Orders.Order Amount} = {Orders.Order Amount} * 0.93
```

```
Case 12000. To 14999.99:
    {Orders.Order Amount} = {Orders.Order Amount} * 0.94
Case 10000. To 11999.99:
    {Orders.Order Amount} = {Orders.Order Amount} * 0.95
Default:
    {Orders.Order Amount} = {Orders.Order Amount};
```

If an order is between $15,000 and $1,000,000, a 7 percent discount is applied. Lesser discounts are applied for smaller orders. Below $10,000, no discount is applied. If an order comes through for more than $1,000,000, there must be a mistake, so no discount is applied. The Default clause is optional. If you omit it, the value of the selection condition is not changed. It isn't changed in the preceding example either, but by making it explicit, you avoid confusion.

For loop

Like the If-Then-Else structure and the Select Case structure, the For loop alters the flow of execution, but it alters it in a different way. Whereas the If-Then-Else and the Select Case constructs cause execution to take one path of execution rather than another, the For loop causes execution to pass through a single piece of code multiple times.

The For loop is the best tool to use when you want to execute a section of code a predetermined number of times. Suppose that you have a character field named Size in a table named Product, and you want to know how many instances of the letter x it contains. You can find out with a formula containing a For loop:

```
Local NumberVar Index;
Local NumberVar Xcount := 0;
Local NumberVar StringLength := Length ({Product.Size});

//loop through the characters in Size and count x's
For Index := 1 to StringLength Step 1 Do
(If ({Product.Size} [Index] = "x") THEN
    (Xcount := Xcount + 1;)
 Else (Xcount := Xcount;)
);
Xcount
```

In the preceding example, Product.Size is treated as a string array, and Index is the subscript that points to each character in the array in turn. Execution steps through the Size field, one character at a time, counting the occurrences of *x* as it goes. If *x* occurs three times in the Size field, Xcount holds a 3. The last line in the formula returns the value of Xcount.

While Do loop

Whereas the For loop is designed for situations in which you know or can compute the number of iterations of the loop you want to execute, the While Do loop is ideal when you don't know the number of iterations. The While Do loop depends on the truth value of a condition. As long as the condition remains true, execution continues to loop. When the condition turns false, the current iteration of the loop is completed and looping terminates. If the condition is initially false, the loop is not executed at all.

Suppose that in the preceding example, you wanted to know the character position of the first *x* rather than the total number of instances of *x* in the string. Because you don't know how far into the string the first *x* occurs, if at all, a While Do loop is appropriate:

```
Local NumberVar Index := 1;
Local NumberVar Xpos := 0;
Local NumberVar StringLength := Length ({Product.Size});

//Find location of first x in Product.Size
While Index <= StringLength And Xpos = 0 Do
(If ({Product.Size} [Index] = "x") THEN
    (Xpos := Index;)
 Else (Xpos := Xpos;)
);
Xpos
```

Note that if Index were initially greater than StringLength, the loop would be skipped.

Do While loop

The Do While loop is similar to the While Do loop, but whereas the While Do loop doesn't execute if the condition is not initially satisfied, the Do While loop is always guaranteed to execute at least once, regardless of whether or not the condition is satisfied. Sometimes you want the behavior of While Do, and other times you want the behavior of Do While. Crystal Reports gives you both.

With a Do While loop, you can accomplish the same character location task that was illustrated in the While Do loop. The code is just a little bit different:

```
Local NumberVar Index := 1;
Local NumberVar Xpos := 0;
Local NumberVar StringLength := Length ({Product.Size});

//Find location of first x in Product.Size
Do
(If ({Product.Size} [Index] = "x") THEN
     (Xpos := Index;)
 Else (Xpos := Xpos;)
While Index <= StringLength And Xpos = 0
):
Xpos
```

In this case, the loop is executed once, and the first character of Product.Size is checked to see whether it's an "x". This occurs even if the condition is not satisfied because execution doesn't reach the condition until after the loop has been executed once. Thus, if by some mischance the value of Index was greater than StringLength, an "x" located beyond the end of the Product.Size string would cause Xpos to take on a non-zero value. This could be misleading and cascade into a significant error. It's important to choose loop type based on whether or not you want the loop to execute at least once, regardless of whether the condition is satisfied or not.

Chapter 13

Creating Reports within a Report

*I*n other chapters, you see how to build reports based on the data contained in several related tables in a database. This is wonderful, but sometimes you want to build a report that displays data from two or more sources that are unrelated or related only indirectly. Crystal Reports meets that need by enabling you to embed one report in another. The embedded report is called a subreport. Subreports allow you to take data from diverse sources and present it on one or a small number of pages, for ease of comprehension.

Combining Unrelated Reports

A standard report created by Crystal Reports can't display data from two tables that are not linked, but a subreport can. You use subreports when you have data tables that are unrelated or have an indirect relationship.

The easiest kind of primary report/subreport combination to produce is one in which the two reports are unrelated but nonetheless of interest to the reader. Because the primary report and the subreport are not directly related to each other, you don't need to worry about linking them. Aside from the details of building the primary report and the subreport, your main concern is the placement of the subreport within the primary report.

You can embed a subreport within another report in two ways. One way is to open the primary report and create a subreport within it from scratch. The other way is to embed an existing report into another report as a subreport. In this section, you look at an example of embedding an existing report into a primary report.

In Chapter 10, you create the Top Five USA Customers report. In Chapter 5, you create the Big Orders report, which lists the highest value orders from customers all over the world. The management at Xtreme Mountain Bikes Inc.wants to see the results of both these reports in a single report. Crystal Reports makes this easy to do; just add the Big Orders report to the Top Five USA Customers report as a subreport. From this report, it will be easy to tell not only which customers have a large cumulative total of purchases but also which of them tend to buy in large lots.

To start, follow these steps:

1. **Open the report that you want to use as the main report.**

   To follow along with the example, open the Top Five USA Customers report. My report file is named TopFiveUSAfinal.rpt and is shown in Figure 13-1. This summary report fits on a single page. The Big Orders report also fits on a single page, so putting it into the report footer of the Top Five USA Customers report will produce a handy two-page report.

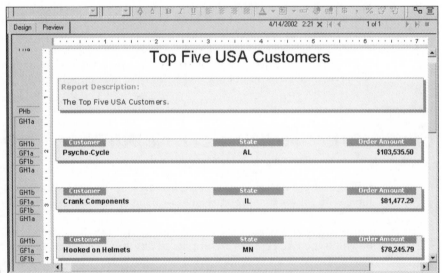

Figure 13-1: The Top Five USA Customers report.

2. **Switch to the Design tab.**

   The report sections are displayed, as shown in Figure 13-2. The report footer appears gray, indicating that it's suppressed. To display anything in this section, you must first reverse the suppression.

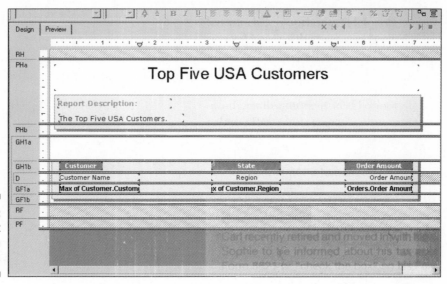

Figure 13-2:
The report
in Design
mode.

3. **Right-click the area to the left of the report footer section and choose Don't Suppress.**

   Now when you put something in the report footer, it will be displayed.

4. **On the Insert Tools toolbar, click the Insert Subreport icon.**

   The Insert Subreport dialog box appears.

5. **Select the Choose a Report option.**

6. **Click Browse.**

   A standard Open dialog box appears.

7. **Use the controls in the Open dialog box to find and select the report that you want to use as the subreport. Then click the Open button to enter the subreport in the Report File Name box.**

   To follow along with the example, find and open the Big Orders report.

8. **Click OK.**

9. **Drag the placement frame that appears at the cursor location into the Report Footer.**

   This gives you the layout shown in Figure 13-3.

10. **Switch to Preview mode.**

   The Big Orders report, you may recall, uses a parameter field into which users can enter a value that they want to set as a lower limit for what would be considered a big order. Thus, when you switch to Preview mode, you must enter a lower limit value into the dialog box that appears before you can view the report.

Figure 13-3:
Design view
of the report
and
subreport.

11. If your report has a parameter field, a dialog box appears. Enter a value and then click OK.

To follow along with the example, enter 10000 for the lower limit value. Page 1 of the report is unchanged, but now page 2 shows the Big Orders report, which includes all orders of $10,000 or more, as shown in Figure 13-4.

Top Five USA Customers

4/26/2002

Customer ID	Customer Name	Contact First Name	Contact Last Name	Phone	Order Amount
4	Psycho-Cycle	Alexander	Mast	205-430-0587	$9,689.25
4	Psycho-Cycle	Alexander	Mast	205-430-0587	$9,649.20
4	Psycho-Cycle	Alexander	Mast	205-430-0587	$11,081.41
6	Rockshocks for Jocks	Heather	Davis	512-349-7705	$14,039.10
9	Trail Blazer's Place	Alexandra	Burris	608-273-4883	$12,323.10
10	Rowdy Rims Company	Anthony	Shoemaker	805-375-0117	$11,099.25
12	Hooked on Helmets	Gerry	Wade	612-947-3344	$11,156.00
13	C-Gate Cycle Shoppe	Matthew	Banks	540-662-7167	$11,759.40
14	Alley Cat Cycles	Rick	Pratt	508-287-8535	$9,290.30
20	Wheels and Stuff	Dan	Simpson	813-539-9862	$11,867.20

Figure 13-4:
Page 2 of
the report
and
subreport.

With a subreport, information that doesn't need to be directly related to information in the primary report can be presented in a compact and convenient form.

Underlay formatting for side-by-side location of subreport

In the preceding example, you inserted a subreport at the bottom of the primary report. For some applications, you'll want the subreport alongside the primary report for comparison. For this type of formatting, you use the underlay feature.

Underlaying is a useful feature in several contexts aside from positioning a subreport next to corresponding information in a primary report. When you underlay the material in a section, the material in the following section is overlaid on top of it. This may seem like a strange thing to do. Wouldn't underlaying just make the material in both sections unreadable? Normally, that would be true, but you can use a trick to make underlaying worthwhile.

Offset the overlaid material to the right of the underlaid material. One such use would be to place a chart immediately to the right of the data that it is taken from. Another use is to place a subreport immediately to the right of related material in the primary report.

Both the Big Orders report and the Top Five USA Customers report are too wide to fit comfortably side-by-side on a standard 8½ x 11-inch sheet of paper in portrait mode. However, if you know ahead of time that you want to combine two reports as a primary report/subreport combination, you can format them in such a way that they will work together to effectively convey the information that you want to deliver to your readers:

1. **Place your subreport in the Report Header or a Group Header section.**

2. **Click the Section Expert icon.**

   The Section Expert dialog box appears.

3. **Select the section into which you have placed the subreport.**

4. **Select the Underlay Following Sections option, and then click OK.**

   The subreport will now underlay the following sections.

Make sure that you've formatted the subreport such that it's offset far enough to the right that it doesn't interfere with any of the content of the primary report.

Drilling down in a subreport

As explained in Chapter 6, drilldown is an important capability that enables you to take detailed information contained in a summary report and hide it but still make it available to users. If hidden detailed information is available in a summary report, the user's cursor changes to a magnifying glass when it passes over the summary field. If you then double-click while the cursor is a magnifying glass, the detailed information is displayed. When you have a subreport in a report, drilldown works a little differently.

Subreport drill down versus report drill down

When you pass the cursor over a subreport, the cursor changes to a magnifying glass, whether or not the subreport supports drilldown. If you double-click, a preview tab for the subreport appears to the right of the preview tab of the primary report. No additional detail appears in the report (yet), and the cursor changes back to the normal pointer.

Now that you have entered the subreport, drilling down works like it does in a primary report. When you move the cursor over a summary field that supports drilldown, the cursor once again changes into a magnifying glass. Double-click, and the detailed information that supports the summary appears. A drill-down tab for that information also appears to the right of the subreport preview tab.

Handling tab overflow

With the tabs for the primary report, including possible drill-down tabs, and the tabs for the subreport, including multiple possible subreports, it's quite possible the tab bar will not have enough space to display all the tabs. To deal with this situation, click the left and right arrows on the tab bar to move left and right, respectively, through the tabs. In addition, click the red *x* when you want to close the current tab and open the tab immediately to the left. This is a helpful tool for getting rid of tabs that you no longer need.

Figure 13-5 shows the tab bar, including drill-down tabs, left and right movement arrows, and the x icon that closes the current tab.

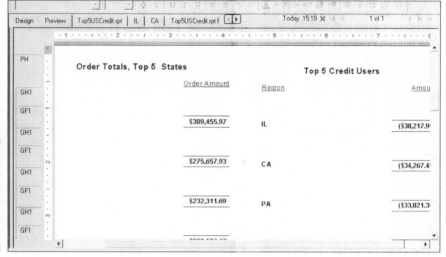

Figure 13-5:
Click the
arrows to
move
through the
tab bar.

Linking a Subreport to a Primary Report

One of the most valuable uses of a subreport is to have it supplement the information displayed in the primary report. To have the data in the subreport correspond to the related data in the primary report, you must link the subreport to the primary report.

You can establish the link by using a field that's shared by the tables that form the basis of the primary report and the subreport. Alternatively, you can form the link using formula fields.

Suppose that you have a primary report that holds the name and address information for Xtreme's customers in Michigan. Another report, which will be the subreport, holds the order data for Michigan customers.

The primary report, called MIcust, is a simple report. The fields from the Customer table have been dropped into text fields to allow formatting of lines that contain more than one database field, such as City, Region, and Postal Code. A filter has been applied such that only customers with a Region of MI appear in the report.

The subreport, called MIorders, contains Order Date, Order Amount, and Ship Date for all orders made by Michigan customers.

Subreports need not be linkable

The example in the "Linking a Subreport to a Primary Report" section shows how to link a subreport to a primary report when the linking field is shared by both reports. However, sometime you'll want to combine two reports that don't have a column in common. Such reports can't be linked in the usual way, but may nevertheless be linkable using a formula field.

Suppose that one of your reports is based on a table that has a First Name field and a Last Name field. The other report you want to use is based on a table that has a Full Name field. No other fields in the two tables are even close to being the same.

A solution to the problem would be to create a formula in the first report that concatenates the First Name and the Last Name fields with a single blank space in between. The resulting full name could then be used as a linking field with the Full Name field in the second table. In Chapter 12, I cover formulas in detail.

To create the full report, follow these steps:

1. **Open the primary report, MIcust.**

   Figure 13-6 shows what the report looks like in Design view.

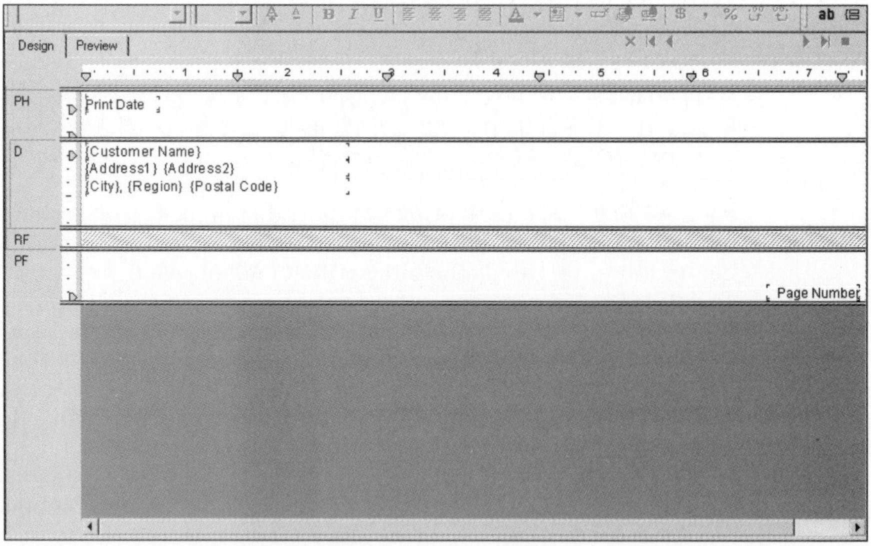

Figure 13-6:
Design view of the MIcust report.

2. **Choose Insert⇨Subreport.**

   The Insert Subreport dialog box appears.

3. **Find MIorders and specify it in the Report File Name box of the Insert Subreport dialog box.**

   You can specify an existing report to use as a subreport or call upon Report Wizard to create a new report to be used as a subreport. For the example, assume that MIorders has already been created. Figure 13-7 shows the Design view of MIorders.

   By now, you know enough about report creation that you do not need a step-by-step description of how to do it. To follow along, create a report that looks like Figure 13-7 and that filters out all orders except those where the value of Region is 'MI'.

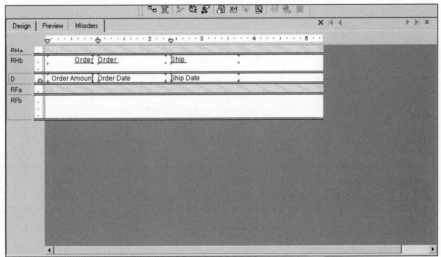

Figure 13-7:
Design view
of the
MIorders
report.

4. **Click OK to dismiss the Insert Subreport dialog box and return to the Design view of MIcust.**

   A placement frame appears at the pointer.

5. **Drag the frame into the Details section, to the right of the Customer Name field.**

   MIcust now looks like Figure 13-8 in Design mode and like Figure 13-9 in Preview mode.

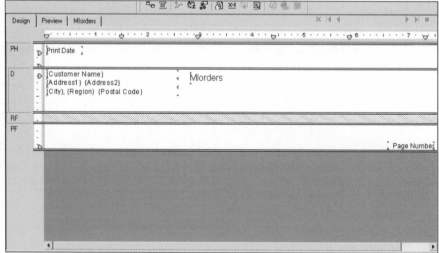

Figure 13-8:
Design view
of the
report,
with the
subreport.

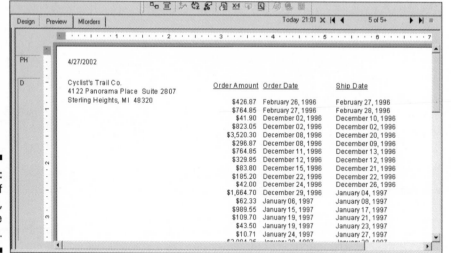

Figure 13-9:
Preview of
the report,
with the
subreport.

I used Record Sort Expert to sort the subreport by order date and used
Format Editor to remove the default border line around the subreport. (To
invoke Format Editor, right-click the MIorders rectangle in the MIcust Design
view of the report and choose Format Subreport.)

Boosting Efficiency with On-Demand Subreports

On-demand subreports can be valuable when you have a report that contains multiple subreports. The primary report doesn't actually contain the subreports. Rather, it contains hyperlinks to the subreports. The subreports are not read from the database until the user clicks the hyperlink. This way, only viewed subreports travel from the database server to the user's client, reducing the load on the network from what it would be if the user downloaded the full report, including all subreports.

To make MIcust an on-demand subreport, follow these steps:

1. **Place MIorders into your primary report, select it, and then click Format ⇨Format Subreport on the main menu.**

   The Format Editor dialog box appears.

2. **Click the Subreport tab, which is shown in Figure 13-10.**

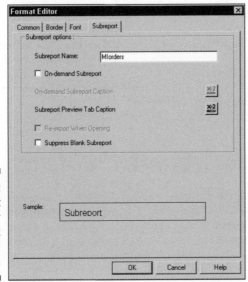

Figure 13-10:
The Format
Editor
dialog box
Sub-
report tab.

3. **Select the On-demand Subreport option.**

4. **Click OK.**

   Instead of including each customer's orders in the report, there's now a hyperlink to each order. The report size has shrunk to a single page.

Clearly, on-demand subreports will not work with printed reports. On-demand subreports require a database connection.

Passing Data between Reports

Crystal Reports allows you to pass data from a primary report to a subreport or from a subreport to its primary report. This is accomplished with shared variables used in formulas. A shared variable is common to a report and all its subreports.

You must declare a shared variable in a formula in the main report, and then declare it in any subreports that need to exchange data with the main report by way of the shared variable. You may want to pass a shared variable from a primary report to a subreport for display in the subreport or as a selection criterion in the subreport.

A shared variable must be declared and assigned a value in a formula in the main report and declared in a formula in a subreport before the value can be passed from the main report to the subreport. To pass a value from the subreport to the main report, you must also make both declarations, but you make the value assignment in the subreport.

Troubleshooting Subreport Problems

Sometimes reports containing subreports can give odd results because of the order in which reports are processed. Formulas in the main report are processed before subreports. Thus, if you set the value of a shared variable in a subreport and then pass the variable to a group footer in the main report, you may find that the main report is using the value of the shared variable from the previous group rather than the current group.

To avoid this problem, create an additional group footer in the main report, such as Group Footer 1b. Place the subreport in Group Footer 1a and retrieve the value of the shared variable in Group Footer 1b. This associates the shared variable with the proper subreport.

Reports that contain subreports process more slowly than reports that do not. However, you can do a few things to lessen the problem:

✔ If your report contains multiple subreports, consider changing the subreports to on-demand subreports. This way, only the subreports that the user is interested in are downloaded from the server. This could have a major effect on system response time.

✔ For linked subreports, make sure that the linking field is indexed. Doing so can give a tremendous boost to performance.

✔ If you're linking a report to a subreport using a formula field, make sure that the formula field is on the main report and that it corresponds to a database field in the subreport. Requiring a formula calculation in the subreport will cause processing to migrate from the server to the client, using network bandwidth and performing calculations on a slower machine.

Chapter 14

Combining Report Elements with OLE

*T*he primary purpose for a report is to present database data to users in a form that's easy to understand. Crystal Reports gives you all the tools you need to do that. Sometimes, however, you want a report that does more than just present database data. You might want to include text from a word processing file, or data that resides in a spreadsheet, or a graphical image stored as a bitmapped image file. To allow the sharing of various kinds of information in different kinds of files, Microsoft developed the OLE (Object Linking and Embedding) architecture.

Overview of OLE

Reports that you create with Crystal Reports can serve as OLE container applications. That is, they can contain OLE objects that were created by other applications called OLE server applications. Microsoft Word and Microsoft Excel are examples of OLE server applications. You can take text from a Microsoft Word file as an OLE object and place it into a Crystal report. Similarly, you can take an Excel spreadsheet as an OLE object and place it into a Crystal report.

Crystal Reports can also function as an OLE server application. You can place a Crystal report as an OLE object into a Word text file, an Excel spreadsheet, or any other OLE-compatible container application.

OLE is unusual in that an OLE object that has been placed in a document such as a Crystal report maintains a relationship with the application that created it. The nature of that relationship depends on whether the OLE object is static, embedded, or linked.

Static OLE objects

A *static OLE object* is a snapshot of an object that has been copied from the original application to the container application. You can place a static OLE object in a Crystal report, but after you do, you can't edit it or change it in any way. A static OLE object doesn't maintain any connection to the application that created it.

Embedded objects and linked objects

An *embedded OLE object* is similar to a static OLE object in that the entire object is downloaded to the container application, along with an awareness of which server application it comes from. It differs from a static OLE object in that it can be edited in the container application. When you double-click an embedded OLE object, it becomes editable. The server application takes over the menus and toolbars to allow editing. So, if you embed an Excel spreadsheet into a Crystal report, you can edit the spreadsheet from Crystal Reports using Excel menus and toolbars.

Any modifications you make to an embedded OLE object are not reflected back in the original file in the OLE server application. If you want to change the original, you can't do it by way of an embedded OLE object.

Linked objects don't move to the container application. Instead, the container contains a pointer to the linked object, which remains in the server application. This link means that whenever the original object in the server application is updated, the linked object in the container application is updated too. Suppose, for example, that your server application is Excel, and you update the data in the linked spreadsheet. The next time you run your Crystal report, it will pull the latest data from the Excel file to display in the report.

Linking is best if you want your report to always reflect the latest data and if you want the data in multiple applications to remain synchronized. The pointer also takes up less space than embedding a large spreadsheet or Word document. Reports containing linked objects are less portable than reports containing embedded objects, however, because the original server application must be present on the machine running Crystal Reports. An embedded object is completely self-contained, not needing any link to its original source file.

Embedding or Linking a File as an OLE Object

Just as there are several types of OLE objects, there are several ways to insert an OLE object into a Crystal report. You can embed or link an entire file or part of a file into a report as an OLE object.

In this section, I cover embedding and linking entire files. In the next section, I deal with embedding and linking part of a file.

The file to be embedded can be an existing one or you can create one on the spot. In this section, you see how to embed a file in both ways. First, in the following steps, you create an OLE object based on a new file.

1. **Display your target report in Design mode.**

2. **Choose Insert⇨OLE Object.**

   The Insert Object dialog box appears, as shown in Figure 14-1. It lists the various types of files that you can insert as an OLE object.

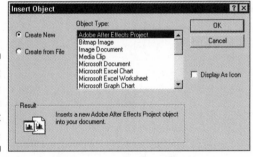

Figure 14-1: Some of the available object types.

3. **Select the Create New option.**

   You can create an OLE object file or an OLE object based on an existing file. In the next set of steps, you find out how to do the latter.

4. **In the list box, select an object type.**

5. **Click OK.**

   An object placement frame appears at the cursor position.

6. **Drag the placement frame to the appropriate section of the report.**

   The tool for creating the type of object you have chosen appears. For example, if you chose Bitmap Image, the Paint drawing tools appear.

7. Create the object.

This procedure creates an embedded OLE object. It is editable, and you can add it to the repository if you want. Just right-click the object to display a menu that lists all the things you can do with it.

If you want to create an OLE object based not on a new file but rather on an existing file, the procedure is a little different:

1. Display your target report in Design mode.

2. Choose Insert⇨OLE Object.

The Insert Object dialog box appears.

3. Select the Create from File option.

This specifies that you want to create an OLE object based on an existing file.

4. Specify the file that you want to link or embed.

Either type the file's full name, including its path, or browse for it and then select it. See Figure 14-2.

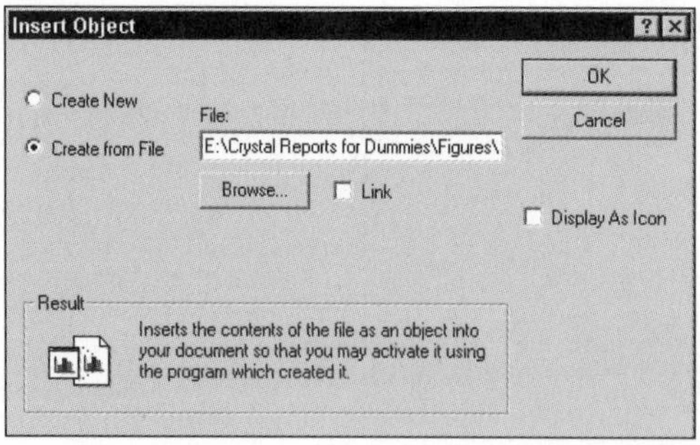

Figure 14-2:
Insert
Object
dialog box,
when
inserting
an object
based on an
existing file.

5. If you want to link to the existing file rather than embed it, select the Link option.

6. Click OK.

An object placement frame appears at the cursor's position.

7. Drag the placement frame to the appropriate spot in the appropriate section of the report.

Embedding or Linking an Object Taken from a File

To embed or link an object from an OLE server application — rather than an entire file — into a report, follow these steps:

1. **Copy the object to the Windows clipboard.**

2. **On the Crystal Reports menu, choose Edit➪Paste Special.**

   The Paste Special dialog box appears.

3. **Select Paste or Paste Link.**

   If you select Paste, the clipboard object is embedded in your report. If you select Paste Link, the object is linked.

When a linked object is updated in the OLE server application, it's updated in your report. Such an update to the object in the server application does not affect an embedded object.

Editing OLE Objects

Static OLE objects can't be edited, but you can edit both embedded and linked OLE objects easily.

To edit an OLE object from Crystal Reports, just double-click it. The appropriate editing tools for that kind of object appear and you can proceed to edit the object. If the object is embedded, the changes you make will not be made to the original object, back in its OLE server application. If the object is linked, the original object *will* be changed.

Chapter 15

Creating and Updating OLAP Reports

In This Chapter

▶ Defining and applying OLAP

▶ Retrieving OLAP data with Crystal Reports

Computer geeks have a maddening tendency to refer to things by inscrutable acronyms, sometimes even pseudo-acronyms, such as SQL, which does not stand for Structured Query Language. The letters in BASIC, FORTRAN, and COBOL once stood for something, as did the letters in the late, lamented SNOBOL. OLAP is a new entry in the list of obscure computer acronyms. OLAP is an acronym for On-Line Analytical Processing. In this case, the name does bear some resemblance to what the technology is actually about.

What's OLAP, and Why Might I Need It?

OLAP is On-Line because it happens in real time, while the user is sitting in front of the screen, and there is a direct connection to a database. Results to user actions are immediate (more or less). It is analytical processing, which means that the main function of OLAP is to quickly analyze huge quantities of data and deliver meaningful information to the user. The information is in a form that the user can readily comprehend and then take action on.

Who uses OLAP?

Huge amounts of data are stored in relational databases belonging to organizations of all sizes and types. You can retrieve information from these databases using queries written in SQL or using a graphical approach such as Query By Example (QBE), which gets translated into SQL and then executed. This is great as long as you are an SQL guru or someone equally skilled in

QBE usage. OLAP is for people who don't even know what a nested SELECT is, let alone a LEFT OUTER JOIN. OLAP is a tool designed for managers who must make decisions, based on a needle of information buried in a haystack of data. OLAP gives people who are not database specialists the capability to find that needle quickly.

Creating multidimensional views

A spreadsheet gives you a two-dimensional view of the data you're displaying. So do most of the reports you create with Crystal Reports. An example is a company's income and expense line items in rows, and months or quarters in columns. Another example is an instructor's course records, with student names in rows and assignment grades and examination scores in columns. Many common situations can be represented very well with two dimensions. Others, however, require three or even more dimensions to convey what the data means.

OLAP is designed to work with these more challenging data sets. A multidimensional OLAP representation of complex data is called an *OLAP cube*. Even though the word *cube* implies three dimensions, an OLAP cube can have more than three dimensions.

What does *SQL* stand for?

SQL is an industry standard data sublanguage descended from a precursor language developed in the 1970s by IBM for internal use only. That rough prototype language went by the acronym SEQUEL, pronounced "sequel." The acronym stood for Structured English QUEry Language. It was called that because statements in SEQUEL looked a lot like English language statements, but they were more structured than English.

When IBM released their first relational database product (SQL/DS) in 1981, they wanted to deliver a commercial quality data sublanguage to go with it. They performed a major overhaul on SEQUEL, creating what was essentially a new language. On the one hand, they didn't want the new commercial language to be confused with the prototype SEQUEL. But on the other hand, they wanted to give some indication as to where the new language came from, so they dropped the vowels and called it SQL, pronounced "ess-que-ell." Many people persist in pronouncing SQL as "sequel," and it's probably fruitless to try to correct them at this late date.

The name Structured Query Language implies that SQL is a structured language, which it is not. It breaks the cardinal rule of structured languages by allowing branches to remote locations. Its statements do look like a structured form of English, but it is not a structured language, query or otherwise. So the answer to the question in the title of this sidebar is that SQL doesn't stand for anything, just like C, C++, and C# don't stand for anything. They are the names of languages, and they stand for nothing more than themselves.

What kinds of reporting tasks might require more than two dimensions? Suppose the company displaying income and expense data by month wants to expand the report to show the data for the last ten years. Income and expense could be one dimension; January through December could be a second dimension, and the years could be the third dimension.

Suppose the instructor's course is a distance-learning course with clusters of students meeting in 15 different cities. An OLAP cube can have student names in one dimension, assignment grades and examination scores in a second dimension, and student location in a third dimension. Any application in which more than two aspects of the data are important is a candidate for storage in an OLAP cube and presentation in an OLAP report.

OLAP Reporting with Crystal Reports

Crystal Reports does not create OLAP cubes. That is a job for the DBMS that Crystal Reports is working with. Crystal Reports currently creates reports based on six data sources:

- ✔ Hyperion Essbase Cube
- ✔ IBM DB2 OLAP Server Services
- ✔ Microsoft OLE DB Provider for OLAP Services
- ✔ Microsoft OLE DB Provider for OLAP Services 8.0
- ✔ Informix MetaCube
- ✔ Crystal Analysis Server

The most common type of Crystal Reports OLAP report is an OLAP grid. An *OLAP grid* looks like a two-dimensional slice through a three-dimensional cube. Multiple slices give the report a third dimension.

Depending on how you want to look at the data, you may slice a cube in different directions. This process, called slicing-and-dicing, allows you to play with the data until you display it in the most informative way. Reports based in an Informix MetaCube are not grid-based but have their own format.

Creating a three-dimensional report

To demonstrate how to create an OLAP report, you'll slice and dice some data from a cube based on the Xtreme database. Among the files that come with Crystal Reports 9 is a Crystal Analysis Server cube named Xtreme.hdc. It's on your hard disk, probably at a location similar to

```
C:\Program Files\Seagate Software\Crystal Reports\Samples\En\Databases\Olap Data
```

Here's a step-by-step procedure for creating an OLAP report based on the Xtreme.hdc cube:

1. **Choose File⇨New. In Crystal Reports Gallery, select the OLAP option, and then click OK.**

   The OLAP Report Creation Wizard appears.

2. **Click the Select Cube button.**

   The Crystal OLAP Connection Browser appears, as shown in Figure 15-1.

Figure 15-1:
OLAP
servers
that are
currently
connected.

3. **If the source of your cube is listed on the OLAP Cube tree, do the following:**

   a. **Select the source.**

   b. **Click Open.**

   c. **Proceed to Step 5.**

4. **If the source of your cube is not listed, do the following:**

   a. **Click the Add Server button.**

   The New Server dialog box appears, as shown in Figure 15-2.

   b. **Specify the location of your cube, either on a remote server, as a local .CUB file, or as a HTTP cube on the World Wide Web.**

   c. **Click OK.**

5. **Verify that the wizard has correctly identified the cube's name and location, as shown in Figure 15-3. Click Next.**

   The Wizard's Rows/Column page appears.

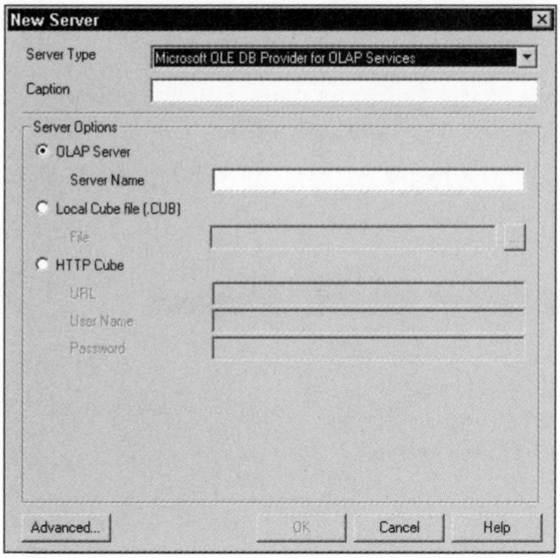

Figure 15-2:
Specify the server that holds your OLAP cube in the New Server dialog box.

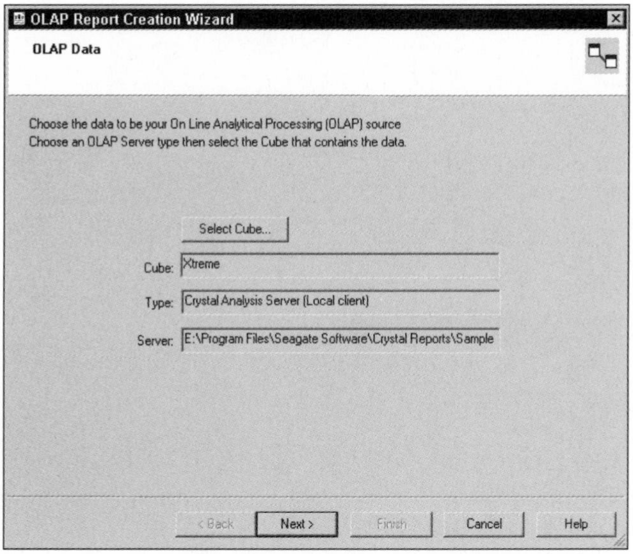

Figure 15-3:
OLAP Wizard with a cube selected.

6. Structure the OLAP grid the way you want it.

This cube has three dimensions: Monthly, Customer, and Product. The wizard suggests that Customers be shown in rows and Products in columns. The third dimension, Monthly, can be the basis for slices through the cube. You don't have to accept the wizard's suggestions. You can, for instance, drag Customers to the Columns pane and Products to the Rows pane, or either to the Dimensions pane.

For this example, I chose to leave the dimensions where they are, as shown in Figure 15-4.

7. **Select the member in the Columns pane. Click the Select Column Members button below the Columns pane.**

To follow along with the example, select Product. The Member Selector appears, as shown in Figure 15-5.

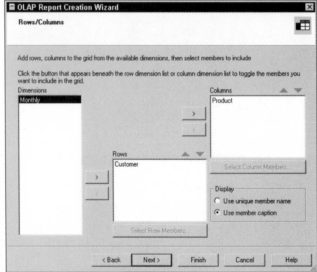

Figure 15-4:
OLAP
Wizard,
Rows/Colum
ns page.

Figure 15-5:
Member
Selector,
showing the
Product
dimension
of the cube.

8. **Expand the displayed tree node. Select the specific members you want to display on the report, and then click OK.**

   I expanded All Products. This lists all Xtreme Mountain Bike Inc. products. Next, you'll display the bicycles of interest. I then selected Descent, Endorphin, Mozzie, Nicros, and Rapel.

9. **Select the member in the Rows pane. Click the Select Row Members button below the Columns pane.**

   In this example, I selected Customer. The Member Selector for rows appears.

10. **Expand the displayed tree node. Select the specific members you want to display on the report, then click OK.**

    I expanded USA, and selected CA for California.

11. **Click Next.**

    The Wizard's Slice/Page page appears, as shown in Figure 15-6. The Wizard suggests that you deal with the Monthly dimension by making a slice based on the year totals for the customers and products in the cube.

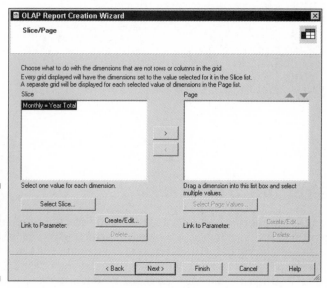

Figure 15-6:
OLAP
Wizard,
Slice/Page
page.

12. **Accept the wizard's suggestion, and then click Next.**

    For this example, keep it simple.

13. **Select a style from the Wizard's Style page, and then click Next.**

    I chose the simple and classic Original style.

14. **If you want to include a chart in your report, select a chart type from the Wizard's Chart page. Fill in appropriate entries for Chart Type, On Change of, and Subdivided by.**

I chose not to include a chart for this example.

15. **Click the Finish button.**

A completed report with no associated chart appears, as shown in Figure 15-7. Some tweaking is needed because for the USA slice, some of the order numbers are too large to fit in the boxes provided. These are easy to expand, however, by switching to Design mode and dragging the right handles of the Value fields horizontally to the right.

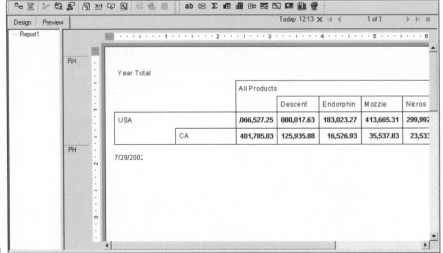

Figure 15-7: The OLAP report based on Xtreme cube.

Updating an OLAP report

Because an OLAP report is based on an OLAP cube created by a database management system, any change in the underlying cube can cause errors in the production of the report. The report may even come out blank if, for example, the location of the OLAP cube has changed and Crystal Reports can no longer find it. Other problems occur if, for example, a dimension has been removed from the cube or a field used by the report is removed.

To reconnect a report to a cube whose location has changed, perform the following steps:

1. **In the report, select the grid by clicking the border.**

2. **Choose Database⇨Set OLAP Cube Location.**

   A dialog box appears, saying, "Warning: It is not possible to undo this command. Would you like to perform the command anyway?"

3. **If you're sure that your OLAP cube location has changed and that your report is no longer valid, click the Yes button.**

   The Set OLAP Cube Location dialog box appears, displaying what Crystal Reports currently thinks the cube location is.

4. **Specify the new OLAP Server location by clicking Select. Use the Crystal OLAP Connection Browser that appears to locate the cube, and then click Open. When the connection is established, click OK.**

5. **When Crystal Reports asks whether you want to have the other grids in the report refer to the new location, click the Yes button.**

   Another dialog box appears, stating, "You have changed the data source for the OLAP cube objects. We suggest that you also change the relational database location to use this new data source. Would you like to do this now?"

6. **Click the Yes button.**

   The Set Datasource Location dialog box appears.

7. **In the Replace with pane, make a new connection to the relocated cube.**

8. **Click the Close icon.**

Your OLAP cube is now reconnected to its source database at its new location.

Chapter 16

Enhancing Reports with Charts

· ·

In This Chapter

▶ Adding visual impact to a report with charts

▶ Finding out about the different chart layouts

▶ Placing charts in the right spot

▶ Creating charts

▶ Troubleshooting problems with chart format and placement

· ·

The essential purpose of a report is to communicate meaning to its readers. Lines of text and columns of numbers undeniably communicate meaning, but sometimes they don't do so as forcefully as a visual image. A picture can sometimes be worth much more than a thousand words.

Choosing the Best Chart Type for Your Data

Crystal Reports gives numbers and statistics an added dimension of communication with its charting capabilities. Numerical data represented visually in a chart can much more readily reveal trends or show relative sizes. Different types of data are best displayed with different types of charts, and Crystal Reports offers a wide variety to accommodate just about any data set you may have. This section provides a brief summary of each chart type.

Side-by-side bar chart

The *side-by-side bar chart* represents data as a series of bars, lined up side-by-side and extending vertically from the bottom or horizontally from the left edge of the chart. This type of chart is an excellent choice for displaying comparative values, such as the annual sales volume for a company's major divisions for a period of several years. Not only sales totals but also any trends in sales would be evident.

Figure 16-1 is an example of a two dimensional, side-by-side bar chart of the percentages of a person's carbohydrate, fat, and protein intake for a one-week period.

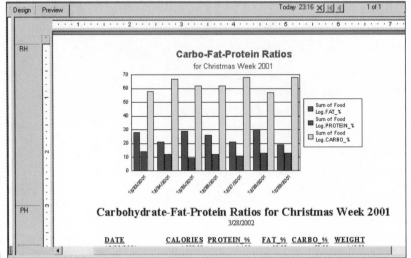

Figure 16-1:
2-D side-by-side bar chart.

Another option is the 3-D side-by-side chart, which is shown in Figure 16-2.

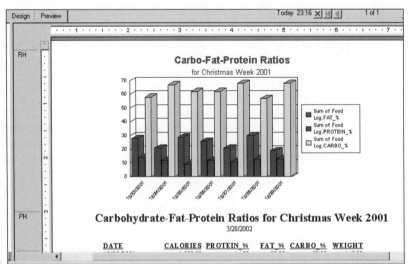

Figure 16-2:
3-D side-by-side bar chart.

Stacked bar chart

The *stacked bar chart* also represents multiple series of data as vertical or horizontal bars, but each value for all series is represented by a single bar, with the value of the second series stacked on top of the value of the first series, the value of the third series stacked on top of the second series, and so on. This type of chart, like the side-by-side bar chart, is a good choice for showing the total value of multiple series of data, while also showing how the relative contribution of each series changes with time. Figure 16-3 shows a 2-D stacked bar chart. 3-D stacked bar charts are also available.

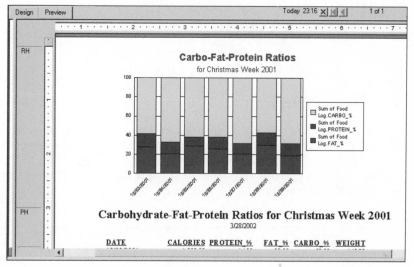

Figure 16-3: 2-D stacked bar chart.

Line chart

A *line chart* displays one or more lines that each connect a series of points. This type of chart is excellent for showing the value of a single variable as it changes over time or the values of several variables with comparable scales. Figure 16-4 shows a line chart of calories consumed daily for the week starting December 23, 2001. Note the large increase in consumption on December 25.

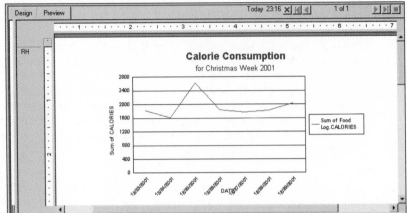

Figure 16-4:
Line chart.

Area chart

In an *area chart,* areas that are filled in with colors or patterns represent the values of variables. This type of chart is good for showing the percentage contribution of a small number of variables to a total. Figure 16-5 shows an area chart displaying the same information that the previously displayed bar charts presented.

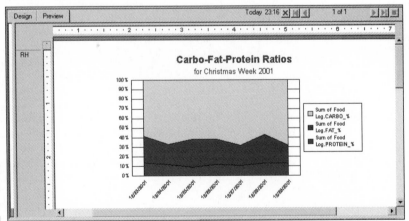

Figure 16-5:
Area chart.

This chart makes it abundantly clear that the bulk of this person's diet was carbohydrates in the time period plotted, with a relatively small amount of protein consumption.

Pie chart

Pie charts are two-dimensional circular charts that display one series of data values, where each value determines how large a sector of the pie that element of the series receives. You might use a pie chart to show the relative contribution each operating division makes to a corporation's sales. Or you might use it to look at food consumption. Figure 16-6 is a pie chart that looks at only the fat data for Christmas week 2001. It shows that fat consumption did not vary much from one day to the next.

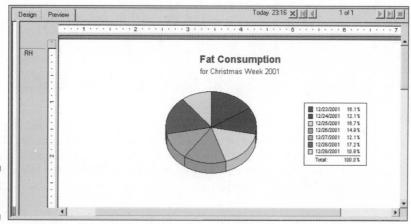

Figure 16-6:
Pie chart.

Doughnut chart

A *doughnut chart* is similar to a pie chart, but the center of the pie is cut out, leaving a 3-D ring that encircles a number that gives the total value of all the sectors of the doughnut. Figure 16-7 is the doughnut chart for the same data illustrated by the pie chart in Figure 16-6. The doughnut's bites are equivalent to the pieces of the pie.

3-D riser chart

The *3-D riser chart* is a cool way to represent several series of data points. If the number of series and the number of data points are both under about ten, a 3-D riser chart can convey a lot of meaning — and look great too. Values are represented by three-dimensional objects rising out of a three-dimensional plane. Various shapes of objects are available.

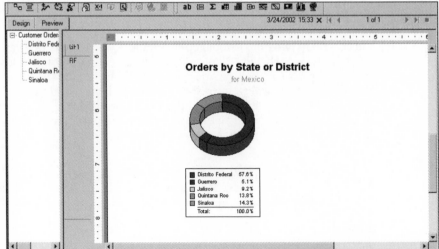

Figure 16-7:
Doughnut
chart.

Figure 16-8 shows a 3-D riser chart for the Christmas week carbohydrate, fat, and protein data. It uses octagon-shaped risers, which I think are the best looking of the several available riser shapes. For some data sets, however, one of the other shapes may be better. Try them all out and see which one communicates your data best.

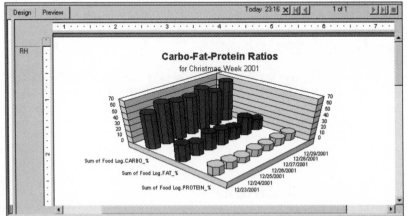

Figure 16-8:
3-D riser
chart.

3-D surface chart

The *3-D surface chart* represents several series of data points with a multi-color surface that sits over a three-dimensional plane. As with the 3-D riser chart, the 3-D surface chart is most meaningful if there are fewer than about ten series and ten data points within each series.

Figure 16-9 is an example of a 3-D surface chart. It gives the data a different look from that obtained with the 3-D riser chart.

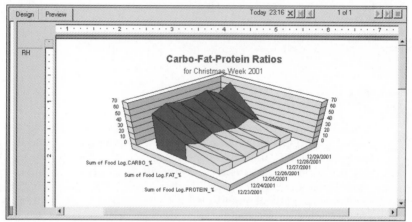

Figure 16-9:
3-D surface chart.

XY scatter chart

XY scatter charts are effective when you have a large number of data points and you want to see, for example, whether any clusters show up in the data and, if so, how compact the clusters are. These graphs are also good at showing whether two variables are correlated. If they are, you'll be able to draw a line with a characteristic slope through the average location of the points. The slope indicates the nature of the relationship. The closeness of the points to the line indicates the strength of the relationship.

This chart in Figure 16-10 plots carbohydrate consumption on the vertical axis against fat consumption on the horizontal axis. The two are definitely correlated, because they fall closely on a straight line. The variation from a perfect linear relationship is caused by varying protein consumption (not shown) from day to day.

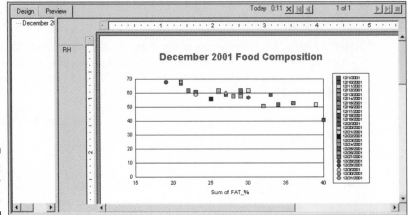

Figure 16-10:
XY scatter
chart.

Radar chart

A *radar chart* is a polar graph that looks somewhat like a radar screen or a plot of an antenna's radiation characteristics. Arrayed around the perimeter are the changing values that generate the chart. The magnitudes of the one or more series of data depicted by the chart are shown by how far they extend from the center toward the perimeter. This type of chart is good for showing how several quantities vary with respect to each other as time or some other variable changes.

The chart in Figure 16-11 shows the same data as the XY scatter chart, but in a very different form. In this chart, it is clear that on 12/10/2001 the person consumed much more fat than usual and much less carbohydrate.

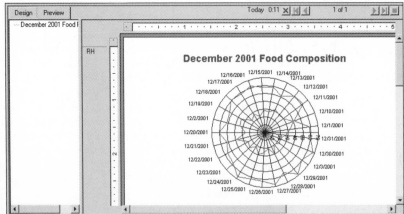

Figure 16-11:
Radar chart.

Bubble chart

A *bubble chart* is similar to an XY scatter chart, except the markers that indicate data points are circles that vary in size. The larger the value of that data point, the bigger the circle. The value of one variable is plotted against the X-axis; the value of a second variable is plotted against the Y-axis, and the value of a third variable is indicated by the size of the bubble. Use this type of chart when you have three series of data that vary with time or with some other fourth variable.

The bubble chart in Figure 16-12, like the XY scatter chart, shows a definite linear relationship between carbohydrate and fat. In addition, the bubble chart explicitly shows the magnitude of the protein variable. It shows that 12/10/2001 had a relatively high value for protein and that 12/21/2002 had a relatively low value.

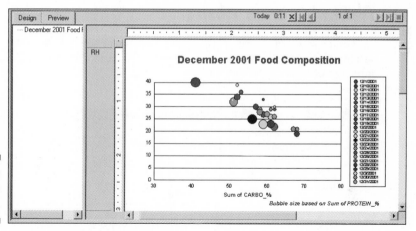

Figure 16-12:
Bubble
chart.

Stock chart

A *stock chart* is familiar to anyone who reads the financial section of a newspaper. It's used to show the daily price ranges of stocks and of indexes such as the Dow Jones Industrial Average. For a given date, a line extending from the lowest value the variable had that day to the highest indicates the range of a variable. Crystal Reports gives you a similar chart, but without the little tic marks for the opening and closing prices.

This type of chart is good for showing the differences between two variables. In Figure 16-13, it is immediately obvious that there is a relatively large difference between carbohydrate consumption and fat consumption on 12/24/2001, 12/27/2001, and 12/29/2001, and a relatively small difference on other days that week.

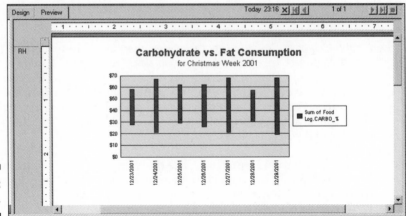

Figure 16-13:
Stock chart.

Numeric axis chart

Numeric axis charts come in six types, as you can see in Figure 16-14. They are the numeric axis bar, line, and area charts, and the date axis bar, line, and area charts.

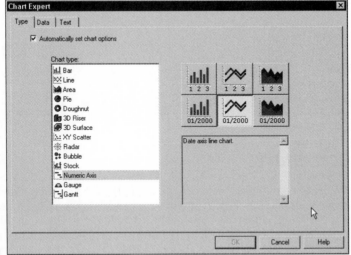

Figure 16-14:
Chart
expert,
showing the
six numeric
axis chart
types.

These charts are similar to the ordinary bar, line, and area charts, except their x-axis must be a numeric or date type. The ordinary, bar, line, and area charts are more flexible, but the numeric axis charts may be somewhat simpler to create, assuming that you want the horizontal axis to represent either numbers or dates.

Figure 16-15 is a numerical axis chart showing two months worth of data on the composition of a person's food intake. As you can see, the person consistently consumes more carbohydrates than anything else, followed by fats, and then proteins.

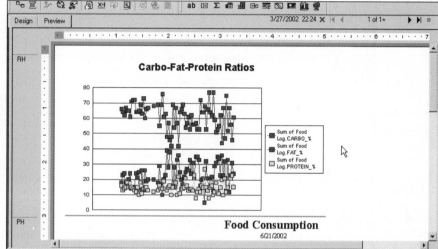

Figure 16-15: Numerical axis chart showing diet composition for a two-month period.

Gauge chart

A *gauge chart* displays a graphic that looks like an automobile speedometer gauge, with a rotating hand indicating the value of the reported quantity. This type of chart is appropriate only when you have a small number of values to display If you have too many, the gauges get stacked one atop the other in a jumbled mess.

Figure 16-16 shows a gauge chart of a person's food intake for March 15, 2002. It's clear that protein consumption for that day was about 15 percent, fat consumption about 24 percent, and carbohydrate consumption at approximately 61 percent. This person is apparently eating a high proportion of fruits and vegetables, and very few hamburgers and potato chips.

Gantt chart

Project managers often use *gantt charts* to track progress. Figure 16-17, for example, shows five weeks of data on how quickly Xtreme Mountain Bikes Inc. ships their products. Each bar represents the interval of time between the entry of an order and when that order was shipped. As you can see, some orders are shipped promptly, but others are not. Management can examine which orders were shipped after an excessive delay, and possibly make changes that will enable the faster shipment of such orders. The number of orders illustrated in this chart is probably more than is reasonable for a Gantt chart. Choosing a smaller sample would make it easier to see which specific orders have problems.

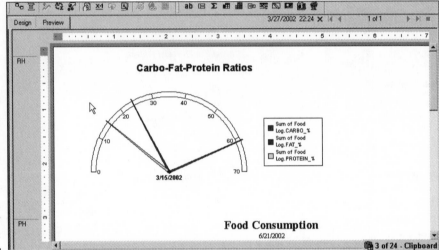

Figure 16-16: Gauge chart showing intake of protein, carbo-hydrate, and fat for 03/15/2002.

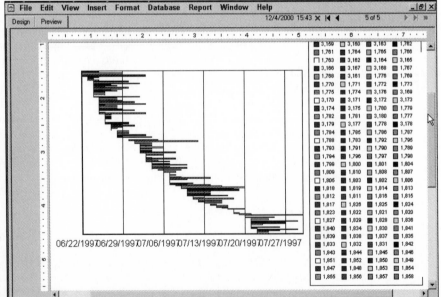

Figure 16-17: Gantt chart showing order turnaround for a five-week period.

Different Chart Layouts for Different Data Types

Crystal Reports deals with four different types of data sets. The most basic is data retrieved from the database and sent more or less directly to the Details section of the report. No grouping or summarization is involved. The Advanced chart layout deals with this kind of data. With the Advanced layout, you can filter the data with one or two conditions. You can also group values in several different orders, plot a value for each data record, plot a grand total for all records, and base charts on formulas or running total fields.

The Group layout gives a higher-level overview than an Advanced layout. It displays summary information when the value of a specified field changes. Logically enough, you can use the Group layout only with reports that have at least one group and at least one summary field for that group.

The Cross-Tab layout is specifically for charting a cross-tab object. Chapter 11 is devoted to cross-tab reports, so I will not say any more about Cross-Tab layouts here.

The OLAP layout is the structure of a chart based on an OLAP grid. I cover OLAP in Chapter 15, so I will not say any more about OLAP layouts at this time. The OLAP layout makes a lot more sense after you know what an OLAP grid is.

A Chart's Placement Affects the Data It Can Represent

A report has multiple sections: a Report Header section, a Page Header section, zero or more Group Header sections, Details sections, as well as Report, Page, and Group Footer sections. Charts can appear in the Report Header and Footer or in Group Headers and Footers.

A chart in the Report Header or Report Footer section draws its data from the entire report. A Chart in a Group Header section draws its data from only that group.

With a chart in the Report Header or Report Footer, you can graphically convey the main point of the report. With charts in either a Group Header or Group Footer, you can show a chart that displays the important information specific to each group.

Figure 16-18 shows a Group Header chart located above data for one of Xtreme Mountain Bikes Inc.'s customers in California. It shows the values of the sales that Xtreme's various salespeople have made to this customer.

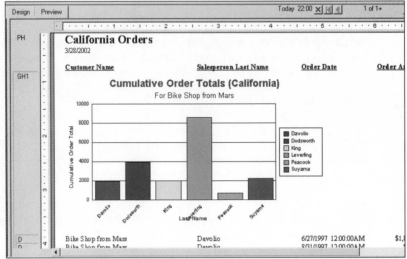

Figure 16-18:
A chart in the Group Header section.

Using Chart Expert

The tool you use to create all the charts shown in this chapter is Chart Expert. You can open Chart Expert by clicking the Chart Expert icon on the Standard toolbar or by choosing Insert⇨Chart on the main menu. The Chart Expert dialog box appears.

Whirlwind tour of the Chart Expert dialog box

The default tab that you see when you first open Chart Expert is the Type tab.

Type tab

The Type tab is shown in Figure 16-19. On this tab, you can select the type of chart you want to include in your report. As you can see, six different bar charts (three 2-D charts and three 3-D charts) are available. The other types of charts have multiple variants as well.

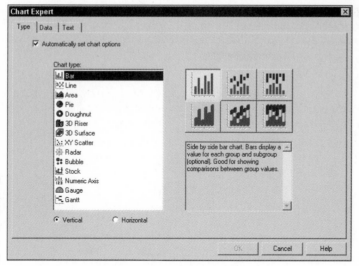

Figure 16-19:
Type tab of
Chart
Expert.

If you leave the Automatically Set Chart Options check box checked, you don't have to worry about the other tabs. The Chart Expert makes default assumptions and displays your chart immediately. In many cases, the result will not be exactly what you want, so you usually have to uncheck this box.

When you select the Vertical option, the bars rise vertically from the bottom of the chart. When Horizontal is selected, the bars move horizontally from left to right. These options don't appear when you have selected a chart that doesn't distinguish between vertical and horizontal (such as a pie chart).

Data tab

The Data tab, which is shown in Figure 16-20, has three areas: Placement, Layout, and Data. In the Placement area, you specify where the chart will go in the report. It can go in a group header or footer or in the report header or footer. The Layout options were described previously, in the "Different Chart Layouts for Different Data Types" section. In the Data area, you specify what data to show in the chart and what event will trigger the chart display. The triggering event is the change in the value of some field.

Options tab

The third tab in the Chart Expert dialog box is Options, which is shown in Figure 16-21. The areas on this tab are Chart color, Data points, Customize settings, and Legend. You can specify a chart color of either Color or Black and White. Black and White, for use with black-and-white printers, uses different patterns to show the different areas.

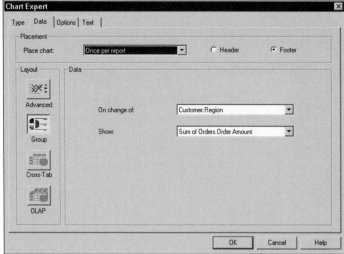

Figure 16-20:
Data tab of
Chart
Expert.

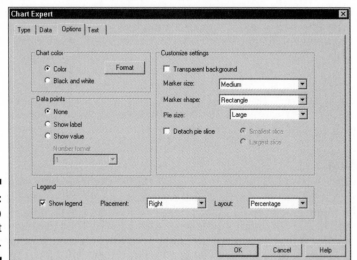

Figure 16-21:
Options tab
of Chart
Expert.

Even if you have a black and white printer, it may be better to specify color anyway. The different colors will show up as different shades of gray on a black-and-white printer and may be easier to interpret.

The Data points area allows you to put labels or values in the vicinity of points on the graph. Sometimes these are helpful, but often they just clutter up the chart, without adding much additional information. That's probably why None is the default selection.

The Customize settings area has a Transparent background check box. You would use this if you were going to underlay content beneath the chart, so that the underlaid content would be visible. You can select from several marker sizes, marker shapes, and pie sizes. The defaults are good choices to start with. Also in this area is the Detach Pie Slice option. Select it if you want to pull out the largest or the smallest slice out of the pie.

On charts, a *legend* is not a tale of heroic deeds handed down from long ago. It's an explanation of what the various elements of the chart represent.

Text tab

The final tab in the Chart Expert dialog box is the Text tab, which is shown in Figure 16-22. This is where you add some text to the chart. The two areas are Titles and Format. In the titles area, the Auto-text boxes are checked by default. This means that Chart Expert selects a title for you, based on the fields the chart uses. Usually the default choice is not the best, although it is somewhat descriptive. The Format area at the bottom of the dialog box displays the default fonts chosen for the different types of text objects on the chart. You can select a different font for each of the Title, Subtitle, Footnote, and Legend title categories by clicking the Font button. This displays a Font dialog box that you can use to specify the font you want.

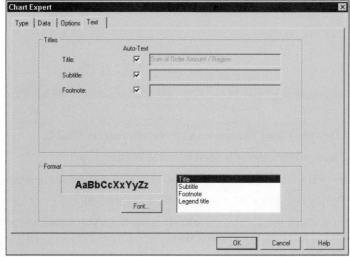

Figure 16-22:
Text tab
of Chart
Expert.

Creating a chart

In this section, you run through the steps of using Chart Expert to create a chart. It's not difficult after you do it a few times, but in the beginning there are behaviors that might have you scratching your head. Before you can create a chart, you must have a report and the report must have data upon which the chart will be based:

1. **Open a report and switch to Design mode.**

   For the example, use the Customer Orders, by State or District (Mexico) report from Chapter 8 as the basis for the chart. The chart will show the relative contributions of the various states or districts. Figure 16-23 shows what you should see.

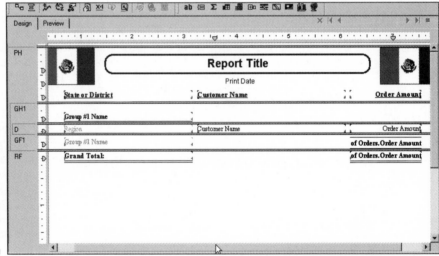

Figure 16-23: Customer Orders, by State or District (Mexico) report.

2. **Click the Chart Expert icon or choose Insert➪Chart.**

   The first decision you need to make is chart type.

3. **Switch to the Type tab, if necessary, and make your selections.**

   To follow along with the example, make the following choices:

   a. **Click to remove the check mark from the Automatically Set Chart Options check box.**

   This means you can have full control over how the chart will look.

      b. In the Chart type selection pane, select Pie, because the pie chart is probably the best choice for showing the fraction of sales orders coming from each of the states.

      The Vertical and Horizontal options at the bottom disappear because they don't apply to pie charts.

  4. Switch to the Data tab and make your selections.

    To follow along with the example, make the following choices:

      a. You want to place the chart in the report footer, so in the Placement area, select the Footer option.

      Once per report is the only option in the pull-down menu because for this example I specified summary data for each state or district, not for individual customers within each state or district.

      b. Keep the default layout of Group.

      The Group layout is okay because this will be a summary report, pulling one number from each group.

      c. In the Data area, keep the default choices of On change of: Customer.Region and Show: Sum of Orders.Order Amount.

      Again, Crystal Reports has guessed correctly. You want the pie chart to start a new segment when Customer.Region changes. Customer.Region is the field that contains the state or district names. Also, the quantity you want to depict with the chart is the Sum of Orders.Order Amount field. The Chart Expert didn't have to be too smart to select this field because it's the only numeric field in the report.

  5. Click the Options tab and make your selections.

    To follow along with the example, make the following choices:

      a. In the Chart color area, select the Color option.

      b. In the Data points area, select the Show Label option.

      c. In the Customize settings area, select Detach Pie Slice and then Largest Slice.

      d. In the Legend area, select the Show Legend option, keep Right Placement, and leave Layout as Percentage.

  6. Click the Text tab and make your selections.

    To follow along with the example, make the following choices:

      a. Uncheck the Title Auto-Text box and replace the default title with Orders by State or District.

      b. Uncheck the Subtitle Auto-Text box and type for Mexico.

   c. **In the Format area, accept the defaults or change them to fonts
   you like better.**

7. **When you're finished, click OK to add the chart to your report.**

   The bottom of the report page now looks like Figure 16-24. The pie chart
   is displayed, the largest slice is pulled out, and the legend appears on
   the right.

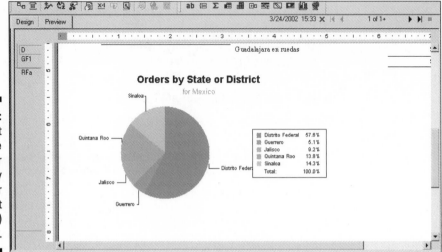

Figure 16-24:
Pie chart
for the
Customer
Orders by
State or
District
(Mexico)
report.

Drilling down from a chart

You've just created a chart based on a report in which the details were
hidden. Because the details were hidden and not suppressed, you can drill
down to see them by hovering the cursor over the subtotal fields in each
group footer. When the cursor changes from the arrow shape to the magnifying glass shape, double-clicking causes the drilldown and you can then see
the detail of the group.

You can do the same thing with the chart. When you hover over one of the
pie slices in the chart, the cursor changes to the magnifying glass drill-down
cursor and you can double-click. You see the same detail that you would see
if you had drilled down from the associated group footer. At the same time, a
new tab appears to the right of the Preview tab, corresponding to the group
you drilled into. From now on, when you want to view the detail information
for that group, you need only click its tab.

Figure 16-25 shows the chart with the drill-down cursor hovering over the Sinaloa pie segment. Double-clicking shows the detail for that state.

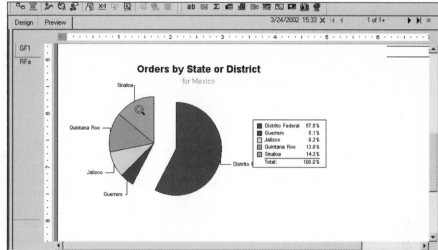

Figure 16-25:
Report
chart, with
drill-down
cursor.

Changing a chart

After you've created a chart on a report and viewed it, you may want to change it. Perhaps the audience for the report has changed and a new chart type would be more appropriate. Perhaps some changes would improve the chart. Here is how you do it:

1. **Right-click somewhere in the chart and choose Chart Expert.**

   Chart Expert appears, with all the options and other selections that you have made.

2. **If you want to change the type of chart, do so on the Type tab.**

3. **If you want to change the layout, do so on the Data tab.**

   You can change any of the parameters that you originally set when you created the chart.

4. **When you've made all your changes, click the Chart Expert's OK button.**

   The changes are instantly incorporated into the chart.

Troubleshooting Chart Problems

Sometimes the chart you're creating for a report just doesn't turn out the way you expect it to. This is less likely to happen as you gain experience with Crystal Reports, but in the beginning, it may occur frequently. Some problems are the result of not being fully aware of how to take advantage of Crystal Report's powerful features. Other times, you might envision a report that's simply not possible, regardless of the power of your report writer. Often, problems occur when you try to squeeze too much information into too small a space.

Selecting data so that a chart is both readable and meaningful

Earlier in this chapter, you created a chart that shows the cumulative sales orders for all the states and districts in Mexico in which Xtreme Mountain Bikes Inc. has customers. Suppose that you want to create a similar chart for the United States. The report would be essentially the same, but with a different selection condition (Customer.Country is equal to USA instead of Mexico). However, if you build the same report in the same way, but this time for the USA rather than Mexico, you might get something like Figure 16-26.

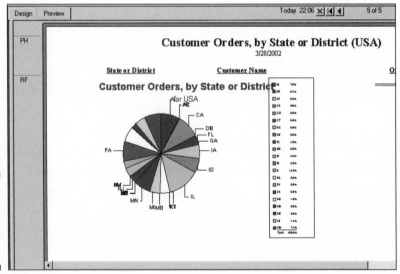

Figure 16-26: Too scrunched up to be readable.

You have too many states to make a good pie chart, so this graph doesn't communicate very well. Perhaps you should display only the states with the ten largest sales volumes. That would produce a reasonable chart.

The placement of chart elements matters

When you created the chart for Mexico, you kept the default legend placement on the right side of the page. If you select a bottom placement, however, your chart will look quite different, as shown in Figure 16-27.

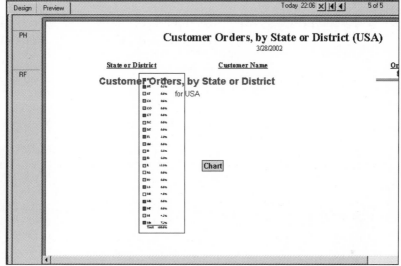

Figure 16-27: Customer Order chart for USA. What happened?

The legend at the bottom is so tall that it takes up all the space allocated for the chart. The chart itself is completely eliminated. If you ever encounter bizarre behavior such as this, check to see whether one element of the chart is hogging the area that rightfully belongs to another element. If you find that to be the case, you can usually find a way to rearrange things so that everything is displayed.

Chapter 17

Adding Geographic Detail with Maps

Many reports contain geographic information. Comprehending the significance of the information in such reports is enhanced when you add maps that show how the information relates to the relevant geographic locations. For example, the Xtreme database contains information on customers located in various cities, regions, and countries around the world. A sales manager may want to know which localities have a concentration of customers or a lack of customers, high sales volume or low sales volume.

All the reasons that make charts a valuable addition to a report apply to maps as well. For data that has a geographical connection, maps are even more valuable. If you can identify a fact, such as a sales total, with a particular city, state, or country, you lock that fact into the reader's mind much more securely than you would if you displayed only a table of numbers.

Crystal Reports has a built-in feature for adding maps to reports, with several different layouts and map types. The various choices enable you to create a map that does the best job of communicating important parts of your report.

Crystal Reports Maps

To create a map with Crystal Reports, you must first have a data source with one or more geographical fields, such as city, region, or country. Depending on the specific data you have and how you want to display it geographically, you can choose the kind of map that will have the most impact on readers. You can choose both the map layout and the type of map.

Map layouts

Four map layouts are available: advanced, group, cross-tab, and OLAP. Each layout is designed for a specific kind of report, as follows:

- ✔ The group layout is usually best when your report has groups and you want to associate a map with each group.
- ✔ The cross-tab layout is designed to be a part of a cross-tab report.
- ✔ The OLAP layout is designed for use with a report containing an OLAP grid.
- ✔ The Advanced layout is for any map that doesn't fall into the other three categories. It works well for reports that don't have groups or summaries, as well as reports that do.

Map types

In addition to the four map layouts, you can choose one of five map types. If the data you're reporting on has a geographic component, one of these map types will prove to be the best way to show the geographical relationships of the data. The major value of Crystal Reports maps is their capability to associate some numerical quantity, such as a sales total, with a geographic location. This gives a memorable visual impression that is likely to be retained better than a simple recitation of fact.

Ranged type

For numerical quantities that can take on an almost infinite number of values, such as sales totals, it's helpful to aggregate records with similar values into *bins,* each one of which holds the records for a range of values that's a subset of the total range of values. By assigning each bin a different color, shade of gray, or other indicator of magnitude, geographical regions on a range type map can be associated with a quantity, making comparisons easy. You can establish bin size in four ways:

- ✔ **Equal count:** With an equal count range type map, the same number of regions (or as close to the same number as possible) appears in each bin. For example, if the regions are the fifty states of the United States and ten different bins show ranges of sales volume, each of ten different shades of gray can be applied to five states. The five states with the highest level of sales would perhaps be shown as white, and the five states with the lowest level of sales would be shown as black, with progressively darker shades of gray in between, moving from high sales volume to low.

This map type is best when values are unevenly distributed among the regions. It prevents a situation in which most regions are the same color, with only one or a few that fall into different bins and thus have different colors.

✔ **Equal range:** This map type has bins of equal size (or as close to equal as possible) regardless of how many records fall into each bin. Equal range maps are most useful when the distribution of values being displayed is fairly uniform, with approximately equal numbers of records in each bin.

✔ **Natural break:** This map type applies only to reports that contain summary values. It assigns bin sizes to separate clusters in the data into separate bins.

✔ **Standard deviation:** This map type is used to show statistical analysis. It is best used with three bins. The middle bin shows regions associated with values within one standard deviation of the mean of the entire data set. The bins above and below hold the regions that are more than one standard deviation removed from the mean.

Dot density type

The *dot density type* map is good for giving the reader a general idea of where concentrations of records are located and the overall distribution of records. A dot is placed on the map for each record. A company might use this type of map to show the locations of their dealerships. The map would make it obvious which regions are adequately covered and which are not but wouldn't be good at conveying quantitative information.

Graduated type

The *graduated type map* is similar to the ranged type, except instead of giving an entire region a specific color or shade of gray based on the numerical value associated with that region, the graduated type puts a symbol in the middle of each region. The size of the symbol corresponds to the magnitude of the associated value. The default symbol is a circle, but you can use a different symbol if you want.

Pie chart type

The *pie chart type map* associates a pie chart with each geographic area being displayed. It's useful only when you're comparing the values of several related items in a geographic region. For example, if you want to know the relative sales levels of Xtreme's five major product categories in each region, a pie chart associated with each region on the map would give you a visual picture of that comparison. Pie charts make sense if the values of all the segments of the pie add up to 100 percent of the total.

Bar chart type

Bar charts associated with maps, like pie charts, are useful only when you're comparing the values of several related items in a geographical region. Unlike pie charts, the total of all the values represented by bars do not have to add up to 100 percent. You can use bar charts to show, for instance, the relative sales of bicycles and helmets for the regions of interest, ignoring the other products that Xtreme sells.

Map placement

Where you place a map on a report depends on the information you want it to display. If the map uses data taken from the entire report, you will want to place it in the Report Header or Report Footer section, so that the needed data is accessible to it. If you want a map to be associated with a specific group in the report, you should place the map in the Group Header or Group Footer for that group. You can also place a map in a subreport of your main report. (See Chapter 13 for information on subreports.)

Map Creation Walkthrough

To create a map, start with a report that has the kind of data that would benefit from a map. This means the report should have at least one geographical field, such as city, state, or country. It also should have at least one numerical field, the value of which varies from one geographical location to another. Certain kinds of maps, such as the pie chart and bar chart types, have additional constraints as noted previously.

Creating an advanced layout map

In this section, you use the Advanced layout to add a map to a report:

1. **Load the Customer Orders, by State or District (Mexico) report.**

   You create the report in Chapter 8 and enhance the report with a chart in Chapter 16.

2. **On the Insert Tools toolbar, click the Insert Map icon.**

   The Data tab of Map Expert appears.

3. **In the Placement area, select Once Per Report for the Place Map option, and then select the Footer option.**

   This places the map in the report footer.

4. **In the Layout area, click the Advanced icon.**

   The display of the Data area changes, as shown in Figure 17-1.

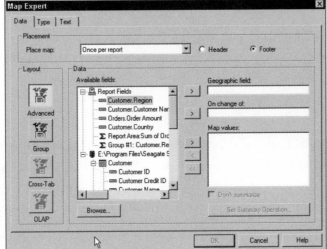

Figure 17-1:
Map Expert
with
Advanced
layout
selected.

5. **Drag Customer.Region from the Available fields pane to the Geographic field box.**

   The Customer.Region field automatically appears in the On Change of box also.

6. **Drag Report Area:Sum of Orders.Order Amount from the Available fields pane to the Map values pane.**

7. **Click the Type tab.**

   The default type is Ranged, which is what you want, so keep it. The other defaults are good too, so leave Number of Intervals at 5, Distribution Method at Equal count, Color of Highest Interval at White, and Color of Lowest Interval at Black.

8. **Verify that the Allow Empty Intervals option is checked.**

9. **Click the Text tab.**

10. **Type a Map title and legend titles, if appropriate, and then click OK.**

    Map Expert generates your map, as shown in Figure 17-2.

The five states or districts appear in five shades of gray as you specified. The top producing Distrito Federal is white — and a little difficult to see because it's only Mexico City. The state of Guerrero is black because it has the lowest order total. The three other states that have Xtreme customers have three different shades of gray.

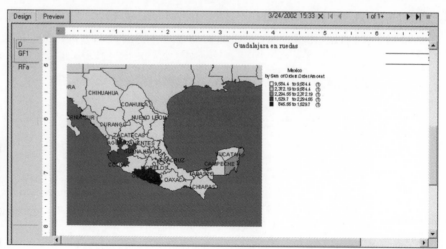

Figure 17-2:
The map
appears in
the report
footer.

Now you know how to add a map to a report. You can make various alternate choices — different types, different fields, different options — but the procedure for any of the Advanced layout reports is essentially the same. The procedure for the other layouts is a little different.

Creating a group layout map

To create a map with a group layout, your report must have at least one group and at least one summary field for that group. To illustrate this, you can use the Customer Orders, Grouped by State or District (USA) report that you create for the United States in Chapter 6 (refer to Figure 6-13). The Mexico report doesn't have enough states to show grouping.

To create a group layout map, do the following:

1. **Make sure that the Data tab of Map Expert is displayed.**

2. **In the Placement area, specify a placement of once per report in the footer.**

3. **Confirm that in the Layout area, Group is selected.**

4. **In the Data area, retain the On Change of: Customer.Region option and the Show: Percentage of Sum of Orders.Order Amount option.**

5. **Switch to the Type tab and verify that Ranged is selected, the Number of Intervals is 5, and the Distribution Method is Equal count.**

   Leave Color of Highest Interval as White, and Color of Lowest Interval as Black. Leave Allow Empty Intervals checked.

6. **Click OK.**

   The map shown in Figure 17-3 appears. It's clear that several states, including California, Alabama, and Pennsylvania, do substantial business. Similarly, states such as Maine, Georgia, and Utah do very little.

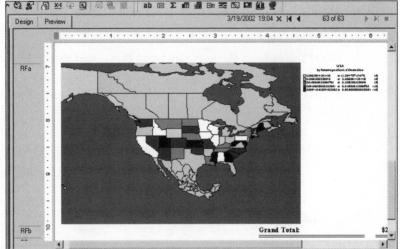

Figure 17-3:
Map
showing
distribution
of orders
from the
USA.

Creating a cross-tab layout map

To create a cross-tab layout, your report must have a cross-tab summary field and the rows or the columns must contain a geographical field. In Chapter 11, you build such a report that shows Xtreme's sales from several provinces of Canada (Sales of Product Types by Province). You can use that report as the base for a cross-tab layout map.

To create a map showing the relative sales figures for Canadian provinces that contain Xtreme customers, do the following:

1. **In the report footer, right-click on the cross-tab (assuming that there is a cross-tab in the report footer of your report) and choose Cross-Tab Expert.**

2. **Make sure that the Rows pane contains a geographic field, such as Customer.Region, the Columns pane contains another field, such as Product_Type.Product Type, and the Summarized Fields pane contains a summary field, such as Sum of Orders.Order Amount.**

3. **Click OK.**

4. **Click the Insert Map icon, or choose Insert⇨Map.**

   The Data tab of Map Expert appears.

5. Click the Cross-Tab icon to change the Data area to the Cross-Tab function.

6. In the Placement area, select Footer.

7. In the Data area, for Geographic field, select Customer.Region.

8. Leave Subdivided by with a value of None.

9. Verify that Map on contains Sum of Orders.Order Amount.

10. Click the Type tab, and then select the Ranged type.

11. Adjust the options the way you want them, and then click OK.

Crystal Reports draws your map, which should look something like Figure 17-4. It's easy to see that British Columbia has the largest order volume and Manitoba has the smallest.

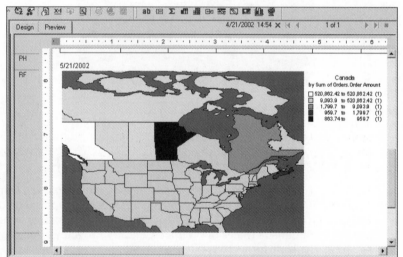

Figure 17-4:
Map is associated with a cross-tab.

Creating an OLAP layout map

The procedure for creating a map with an OLAP layout is similar to the procedure with a cross-tab layout. The main difference is that the report must contain an OLAP grid rather than a cross-tab object. One of the dimensions of the grid must be a geographical field. You create a report with an OLAP grid in Chapter 15, but it doesn't have a geographical dimension, so a map with an OLAP layout in that report would make no sense.

To add a map to a report that *does* have a geographical dimension, follow these steps:

1. **With any report that has a geographical dimension open in the workspace, click the Insert Map icon (on the Insert Tools toolbar).**

   The by-now-familiar Map Expert appears.

2. **In the Placement area, select either Header or Footer.**

3. **In the Layout area, click the OLAP icon if it's not already selected.**

4. **In the Data area, select a geographical field in the On Change of pull-down list.**

5. **If you will be adding a Pie chart or Bar chart to the map, select a field in the Subdivided by pull-down list. For a Ranged map, leave this option at None.**

6. **For a simple map, such as you are building here, leave the Other Dimensions option alone.**

7. **Click OK.**

   Crystal Reports draws the map you have specified, based on the information in the OLAP grid.

Including maps in subreports

You can include maps in subreports. The procedure for including a map in a subreport is the same as that for a report, except the subreport Design tab must be active. That makes so much sense, I almost hate to mention it. Oops. Too late. There it is, in indelible print.

Changing maps

Speaking of indelible print, after you add a map to a report, it's not cast in concrete. You can change it easily. Just right-click the map and choose Map Expert. Now you have the same control over the map that you had when you first created it.

Troubleshooting Map Problems

If you create a map and it doesn't look the way you expect it to, check to make sure that the Preview tab is active. If the Design tab is active, Crystal Reports displays a generic placeholder map in the location where the actual map is located.

If you create a map and all you see is a blank rectangle, make sure that you based the map on a geographical field. If you based it on a non-geographical field, Crystal Reports displays a non-geographical map — namely, nothing.

If you create a map of the Ranged type and you don't get the spectrum of colors or shades of gray that you expected, check to make sure that the distribution method you chose is appropriate for the data you're illustrating.

Part IV
Publishing Your Reports

The 5th Wave — By Rich Tennant

Ever the innovator, Larry beta-tests the Personal Belt Buckle Assistant/Wireless Fax

Hold on a second, Stu, I'm getting a fax.

In this part . . .

You will have a fine sense of accomplishment after you complete an excellent report that clearly conveys the information that you intended to deliver. However, your efforts will all be for naught if no one reads the report. Publishing your report to its intended audience is an important final step in the report-creation process. You can publish a report using various methods. You might make the report available on your organization's local area network, or you might print copies on a printer and distribute them. You might fax the report to people at remote sites, or you might put it up on a Web site. Crystal Reports supports all these methods of report distribution. Your handiwork will be visible to all who should see it. And in the case of posting on a Web site, your handiwork will be visible to the world.

Chapter 18

Getting Your Reports to Your Audience

*W*hen creating a Crystal Reports report, the ultimate goal is to get the report into the hands of people who can use the information that the report contains. These people may not have access to a computer running Crystal Reports, so several methods of distributing reports are available that don't depend on Crystal Reports being present. You can print the report on paper, send it directly from your computer via fax, or export it to a variety of destinations.

Printing Your Report

After you have completed report development, your report is ready to print. This is the easiest way to produce a finished report. Choose File⇨Print on the main menu or click the printer icon on the Standard toolbar. The dialog box shown in Figure 18-1 appears, telling you the name of the default printer and asking you which pages to print, how many copies, and whether to collate copies.

Figure 18-1:
Print
dialog box,
showing
default
assump-
tions.

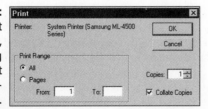

Make the appropriate responses, and then click OK. That's all there is to it. Your report is printed as you specified. Distribute the printed copies to the people who should get them. Now your job is truly finished.

Faxing a Report

Maybe the intended recipients of your report aren't close enough for you to hand them a printed report, and Federal Express is not fast enough to get it to them when they need it. For this case, you can fax the report directly from your computer, provided your computer is equipped with fax software and either has a modem connection to the telephone network or is set up to send faxes over the Internet.

To fax a report, you must change your default printer to a fax driver. Do this as follows:

1. **Choose File⇨Printer Setup.**

2. **Select your fax driver in the list of printer drivers installed on your computer.**

   If you don't find a fax driver among the list of installed printer drivers, it probably means that your computer is not set up to send faxes. You have to install fax software before you can fax any reports to recipients at remote sites.

3. **Click OK.**

4. **Click the Printer icon.**

   The Print dialog box appears. This time, your fax driver appears instead of your printer driver.

5. **Make the appropriate selections, and then click OK.**

   Your fax software appears.

6. **Follow the software's instructions to send your report to its intended recipients.**

Exporting a Report

Crystal Reports can send reports to a variety of destinations, in a format that is appropriate for those destinations. You can export a Crystal report to Microsoft Excel as a spreadsheet in the Excel .xls format or to Microsoft

Word as a word processing document in the Word .doc format. That's just scratching the surface, however.

Here's a list of file formats that you can export a report to:

Adobe Acrobat (.pdf)

Crystal Reports (.rpt)

HTML 3.2

HTML 4.0

Microsoft Excel 97-2000

Microsoft Excel 97-2000 (data only)

Microsoft Word (.doc)

ODBC

Record style (columns no spaces)

Record style (columns with spaces)

Report Definition

Rich Text Format (.rtf)

Separated Values (.csv)

Tab-separated text

Text (.txt)

XML

When you export a report to any format other than Crystal Reports format, you may lose some or all of the report's formatting. Crystal Reports will try to retain as much formatting as possible, but in some cases not much can be saved.

You may export a report to several destinations:

✔ An application

✔ A disk file

✔ A Microsoft Exchange folder

✔ Lotus Domino

✔ Lotus Domino Mail

✔ MAPI (Microsoft Mail)

If you choose to export to an application such as Microsoft Word or Microsoft Excel, Crystal Reports will launch the target application and open the report file in it. If you choose to export to a disk file, Crystal Reports will open a dialog box that allows you to specify a drive, directory, and file name for the report file. Using Lotus Domino Mail or MAPI, you can send a report directly to a person's electronic mailbox. Using Lotus Domino, you can send a report directly to a person's desktop.

Whether you are distributing your report as a printed document, fax, or computer file, Crystal Reports makes it easy for you to get the report out in a timely fashion and in the form you want.

Troubleshooting Output Problems

Little can go wrong when you're attempting to print a Crystal report to your system's printer. If you can print a document from your word processor or another application, you should be able to print from Crystal Reports. If you can't print from any of your applications, check to confirm that the printer is on and properly connected to your computer. Make sure that your printer is identified as your computer's default printer.

If you can't fax a Crystal report, make sure that your fax software is properly installed. Confirm that it works when sending a document from your word processor. If your system won't send a word processor document, the fault is not with Crystal Reports. Make sure that your fax driver is identified as your computer's default printer.

If you have trouble exporting a report, make sure that you have correctly specified the format and the destination. Like printing and faxing reports, exporting is pretty foolproof, after your set up your connections properly.

Chapter 19

Displaying Reports Online

As organizations become more interconnected electronically, an emerging trend is to communicate more over the network than by passing paper around. Organizational intranets have become the communications medium of choice in many cases. Beyond the organization's borders, extranets and the Internet have assumed ever more important roles. Crystal Reports takes advantage of this trend. Report features such as drill down and subreports require the reader to be online. It's not hard to drill down into a sheet of paper, but when you do, you don't see very much and it tends to ruin the surface of your desk.

Exporting to a Static HTML Page

Web pages, whether they're designed to be viewed by a small group of people on a company intranet or by a worldwide audience on the Web, are implemented using Hypertext Markup Language (HTML). A Crystal report can go online in several ways. Exporting to a static HTML page is the easiest but also the most limited. The only thing that gets exported is what is visible on the screen.

When you export a Crystal report to a static HTML page, take note of the word *static*. The data in the report is a snapshot of the data at the time of the export. The exported report will not be updated when the data in the original report changes. To display the changed data, you have to export the report again.

For many applications, there's no need to go beyond static HTML. In those cases, exporting is as easy as 1-2-3. Well, actually, it's as easy as 1-2-3-4:

1. **Open the report that you want to export, and display the screen — main report or subreport — that you want to present to your online audience.**

2. **Choose File⇨Export.**

   The Export dialog box appears.

3. **In the Format drop-down list, select HTML 4.0. In the Destination drop-down list, select Disk file. Then click OK.**

   The Select Export File dialog box appears, as shown in Figure 19-1.

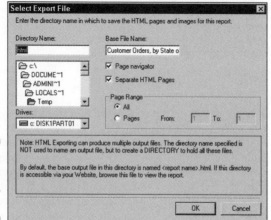

Figure 19-1:
Exporting
static HTML
is simple.

4. **Choose the drive and directory where you want to place the HTML file, make your formatting choices, and then click OK.**

   An HTML version of your report is created and stored in the directory you selected.

When you export a Crystal report to another format, such as HTML 4.0, you will likely lose some of the formatting of the original report. Crystal Reports does its best to preserve the original formatting, but the appearance of the exported report will probably not match the original exactly. If you're not happy with the way the exported report looks, you may have to make changes to the original to come up with a design that is less affected by the change of file type.

Figure 19-2 shows the top of the Customer Orders, by State or District (Mexico) report, as it exists in Crystal Reports. Note that the title is enclosed in a box with rounded corners.

After exporting the report to HTML 4.0, it appears as in Figure 19-3.

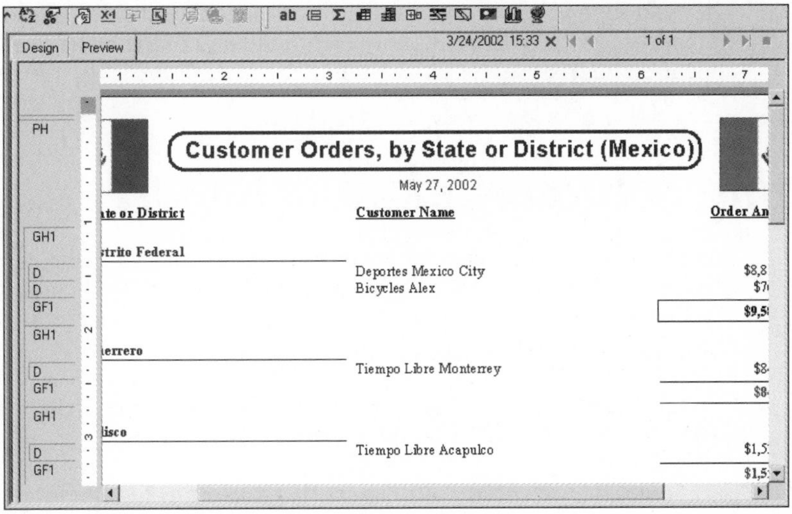

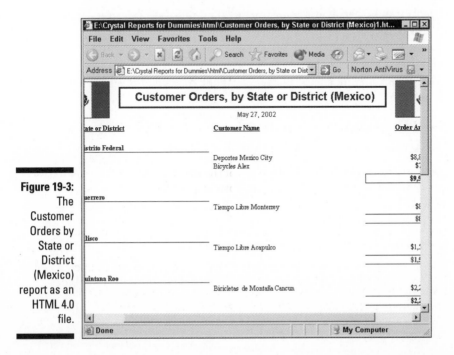

Figure 19-2:
The
Customer
Orders by
State or
District
(Mexico)
report in
Crystal
Reports.

The two reports look virtually the same, except that the corners of the box enclosing the title are no longer rounded. More complex formatting features, however, may not translate well in the exported report. Judge each case individually.

Figure 19-3:
The
Customer
Orders by
State or
District
(Mexico)
report as an
HTML 4.0
file.

After you save your report to a disk file, you can upload the file to your Web server in the same way that you upload any of the other files that appear on your site.

Adding a Hyperlink to a Report

One of the most valuable features of Web-based content is the capability to quickly move between pages by means of hyperlinks. By clicking a hyperlink associated with a word, a phrase, or an image, you can instantly display a new page that provides more detail.

Crystal Reports enables you to add hyperlinks to your reports, without having to become a HTML scripter. Here's how to do it:

1. **Select the object in your report that you want to turn into a hyperlink, and then click the Insert Hyperlink icon on the Expert Tools toolbar. (Or right-click the selected object and choose Format Field.)**

   The Hyperlink tab of Format Editor appears, as shown in Figure 19-4. If the Hyperlink icon on the Expert Tools toolbar appears dimmed, you can't use the object you selected as a hyperlink.

2. **Select the type of hyperlink that you want.**

3. **To link to a Web site, type a Web site address in the Hyperlink information box.**

4. **Click OK.**

As you can see from Figure 19-4, you can link to several places in addition to Web sites. Here's a brief description:

- **No Hyperlink:** Removes a hyperlink from the selected object.
- **A Website on the Internet:** Links to a Web site.
- **Current Website Field Value:** Select this when you want to link to the URL contained as a value in the selected object.
- **An E-mail Address:** Enables users to send an e-mail message to a recipient that you specify.
- **A File:** Links to a file on the user's computer.
- **Current E-mail Field Value:** Select this when you want to send an e-mail message to the address contained as a value in the selected object.

✔ **Report Part Drilldown:** Specifies which detail object will be displayed when the user drills down on a report part. (Report parts are explained in the next section.) This type of hyperlink works only with DHTML viewers such as Internet Explorer 4.0 and above or Netscape Navigator 4.72 and above.

✔ **Another Report Object:** Links directly to the object that the user specifies. The destination object may be in this report or in another report. Details up next.

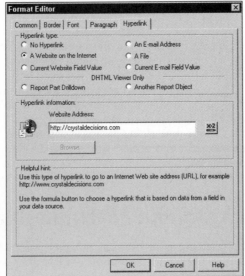

Figure 19-4:
The link is to
the Crystal
Decisions
Web site.

To link to another report object, follow these steps:

1. **Open the destination report, select the destination object in it, and copy the object to the clipboard.**

2. **Open the source report, and select the object that you want as the originator of the hyperlink.**

3. **Click the Insert Hyperlink icon.**

   The Hyperlink tab of Format Editor appears.

4. **Select Another Report Object.**

5. **In the Hyperlink information area's Select From box, paste the contents of the clipboard.**

   The Object Name and Datalink Context fields are filled in automatically.

6. **Click OK to establish the link.**

   Now users with DHTML viewers (such as Internet Explorer 4.0 and above or Netscape Navigator 4.72 and above) can link from the source object in the source report to the destination object in the destination report by clicking the hyperlink.

Crystal Enterprise

Crystal Enterprise is an enterprise-level companion product of Crystal Reports, designed for online viewing of reports by users across an entire enterprise. Hundreds or even thousands of users can view the same Crystal Reports report simultaneously. With Crystal Enterprise, you can expose reports to users who don't have Crystal Reports and who may not even have access to the database behind a given report. All such users need is a browser running on a workstation in your organizational intranet, an extranet, or on the World Wide Web. Unlike static HTML pages, reports viewed with Crystal Enterprise show the effects of updates to the underlying database without the need for re-exporting. Drill down also works in the same way it would if the report was viewed with Crystal Reports itself.

Crystal Launchpad and ePortfolio

The Crystal Launchpad, shown in Figure 19-5, has no functionality in itself but provides a hyperlink directory to the resources of Crystal Enterprise. As you can see from the figure, Crystal Launchpad is delivered to the user in a standard Web browser.

ePortfolio is an electronic portfolio of published reports. Figure 19-6 shows the ePortfolio main screen, with thumbnails of several reports. A user can view any report by clicking its thumbnail to move it to the preview area at the right edge of the screen. After confirming that the previewed report is the one you want, click the preview to launch Crystal Report Viewer, with the selected report displayed.

Crystal Report Viewer

Crystal Report Viewer, shown in Figure 19-7 with an inventory report on display, is similar to a Web browser. Users at a workstation running Crystal Report Viewer potentially have the same capability to interact with a report, including drill down, that they would have if they were viewing the report with Crystal Reports itself.

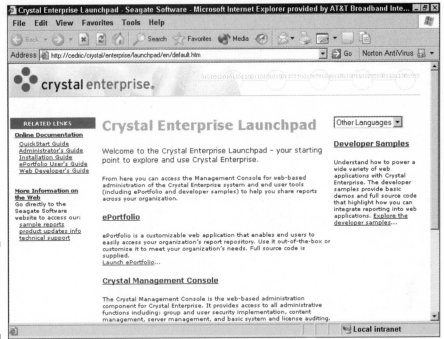

Figure 19-5:
Crystal
Launchpad
welcome
screen.

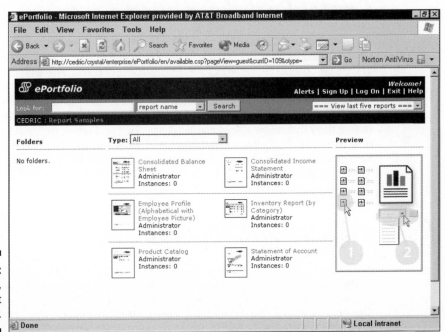

Figure 19-6:
e-Portfolio,
with report
thumbnails.

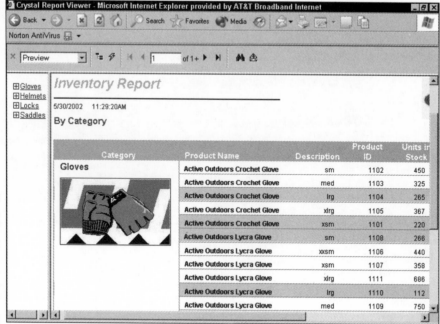

Figure 19-7:
Crystal
Report
Viewer, with
sample
inventory
report.

Crystal Publishing Wizard

To make a report accessible to users on a network who don't have Crystal Reports, you must *publish* the report. The easiest way to do this is with a part of Crystal Enterprise called Crystal Publishing Wizard. The wizard walks you step-by-step through a procedure that takes a Crystal report and adds it to the reports available through ePortfolio. This is an operation that would normally be accomplished by an organization's information systems department rather than by an individual report developer, so I won't go into detail on how to do it here. Crystal Publishing Wizard is just one of several components of Crystal Enterprise that can be used to manage an organization-wide report distribution system.

Report Parts and Navigation

Report Parts is a new feature in Crystal Reports 9. It enables the report designer to establish a hyperlink to a part of a report. When a user follows the link, only the specified report part is displayed, rather than the entire report. This facility gives the report designer total control over exactly what parts of a report are visible to users. It also serves as a method of navigating from one part of a report to another part of the same report or to a part of a different report.

You use the Report Parts Viewer to view Report Parts. This viewer, like Crystal Report Viewer, is essentially a customized browser. The difference is that with Crystal Report Viewer, the user sees an entire report; with the Report Parts Viewer, the user navigates from a report to an object in the same or another report. You can follow a series of links from one report to another, viewing only one part of each.

Setting up and enabling a series of Report Parts hyperlinks requires two distinct development efforts. In one, the report developer sets up the hyperlinks. In the second, the Web application developer adds code to the Web application to call Report Parts Viewer.

Regular hyperlinks can take a user from one section of a report to another, or from one report to another. Report Parts Viewer shows only the specific objects identified as the report parts rather than showing the entire report.

When you select the Report Part Drilldown option (in the DHTML Viewer Only area of Format Editor's Hyperlink tab), you're setting up an emulation of Crystal Reports drilldown for display in a DHTML viewer. When you drill down to a new object, however, you don't see anything but that object. The objects you can link *from* with the Report Part Drilldown option are summary field objects, group charts, maps, and fields in your report's group headers or group footers. Report Part Drilldown emulates in Report Parts Viewer the behavior of drilldown in Crystal Reports, with the difference that it displays only the specified destination object, not the page the destination object is on. Report Part Drilldown works only in a single report.

To link to an object in another report, select Another Report Object, rather than Report Part Drilldown, in the DHTML Viewer Only area. You can use the Another Report Object option for navigation within a report or between reports, rather than for drilldown.

Part V

Programming with Crystal Reports

The 5th Wave — By Rich Tennant

WELL, OBVIOUSLY ONE OF THE CELLS IN THE NAVIGATIONAL SPREADSHEET IS CORRUPT!

In this part . . .

As you know by now if you've read the previous parts of this book, it is possible to use Crystal Reports to produce informative, high-impact reports without writing a single line of program code. However, there's no denying that programming can add an element of flexibility, allowing you to present information in ways that would not otherwise be possible.

This part introduces — but does not delve too deeply into — the subject of programming with Crystal Reports. With the new SQL Commands facility, you can enter SQL statements directly into Crystal Reports, thus enabling you to specify, in the most discriminating terms possible, exactly what data to retrieve and display. In addition, Crystal Reports is tightly integrated into Microsoft's flagship programming environment, Visual Studio .NET. Anyone writing .NET applications will be able to seamlessly call upon the power of Crystal Reports to give their applications a report that conveys exactly the information they want to convey, with unrivalled clarity.

Chapter 20

SQL Commands

In This Chapter

▶ Creating SQL commands

▶ Adding an SQL command to a repository

▶ Modifying an SQL command

C rystal Reports 9 has a new feature called SQL Commands. SQL is an internationally accepted standard language for dealing with relational databases. Report writers such as Crystal Reports retrieve data from such databases. They do so by translating the data retrieval part of the report into an SQL statement that's sent to the database. The database executes the SQL statement, and then sends the result set back to the report writer, which formats and displays it.

As you may know, some concepts that you can express in one language are impossible to translate accurately into another language. I ran into this problem while trying to communicate with a taxi driver in Beijing, China using my community college Mandarin. I ended up on the wrong side of town, late at night. A similar problem can happen with database reports.

If you want to zero in on a particular data set, the specification of which is difficult or impossible to express using the admittedly handy wizards and dialog boxes that Crystal Reports provides, you may be able to get what you want by speaking the database's native language, SQL. SQL is not a particularly easy language to learn, although a book such as my *SQL For Dummies* (published by Wiley Publishing, Inc.) can make it about as easy as possible. If you make the effort to learn SQL, you will be able to extend the power of Crystal Reports. By using the new SQL Commands feature of Crystal Reports, you'll be able to add anything you want to your report. And if the information you want is buried somewhere in your database, you can retrieve it with SQL.

Creating an SQL Command

To create an SQL command, you must start with a report. Here's a step-by-step procedure for adding an SQL command to one of the sample reports that comes with Crystal Reports:

1. **With the Xtreme sample database connected, open the sample report called Formulas.rpt.**

   Mine is in `E:\Program Files\Crystal Reports\CRYSTAL En\Reports\Featured`. Yours is probably in a similar place.

2. **On the Expert Tools toolbar, click the Database Expert icon, or choose Database⇨Database Expert.**

   The Database Expert dialog box appears, as shown in Figure 20-1. The Xtreme sample database should be displayed in the Selected Tables pane, with the Customer and Orders tables listed under it.

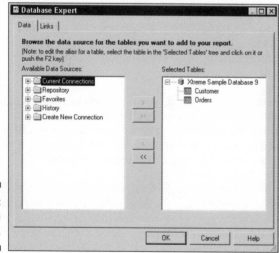

Figure 20-1:
Database
Expert.

3. **Connect to the xtreme database. In the Available Data Sources pane, double-click the Add Command node.**

   The Add Command to Report dialog box appears, as shown in Figure 20-2.

4. **Type the following SQL statement in the left pane:**

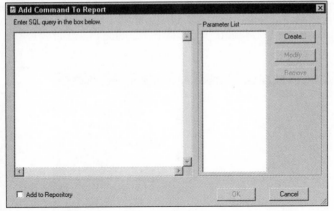

Add Command To Report

Enter SQL query in the box below.

Parameter List

Create...

Modify

Remove

Add to Repository

OK   Cancel

Figure 20-2:
This is
where you
add the SQL
statement.

```
SELECT
      Customer.[Customer ID],
      Customer.[Customer Name],
      Customer.[Last Year's Sales],
      Customer.Region,
      Customer.Country,
      Orders.[Order Amount],
      Orders.[Customer ID],
      Orders.[Order Date]
FROM
      Customer Customer INNER JOIN Orders Orders ON
            Customer.[Customer ID] = Orders.[Customer ID]
WHERE
      (Customer.Country = "USA" OR
      Customer.Country = "Canada") AND
      Customer.[Last Year's Sales] < 10000.
ORDER BY
      Customer.Country ASC,
      Customer.Region ASC
```

Figure 20-3 shows the Add Command to Report dialog box after the SQL command has been entered.

The specific database driver that your system uses may differ from the driver that my system uses. My system accepts square brackets around field names that contain blanks or other punctuation. Yours may accept single or double quotes instead. If your system has Access, look at the syntax of the SQL that it generates, and use the same thing. It's important that Crystal Reports be able to distinguish between field names and quoted strings such as `"USA"`. It also needs to be able to properly handle field names that include punctuation, such as `Last Year's Sales`.

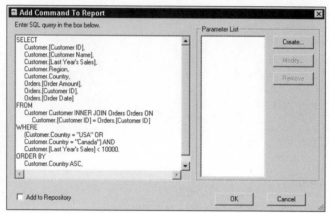

Figure 20-3:
The SQL command has been entered.

5. **Click OK.**

   You are returned to Database Expert.

6. **Click OK.**

   Database Expert displays the Link view.

7. **Click OK.**

   In my case, a Database Warning dialog box appears, stating "More than one database driver has been used in this report. If you want to change the database drivers, use Database/Set Location. Also, please make sure that no SQL Expression is added and no server-side group-by is performed." I'm not sure why this warning appears. Perhaps it's a bug in SQL Commands. At any rate, it doesn't seem to matter.

8. **Click OK.**

   A dialog box asks whether you want to refresh the data.

9. **Click OK.**

10. **If you see a few more dialog boxes of various kinds, click OK in each.**

    When all the dialog boxes go away, Report Designer displays your report. Field Explorer has a new table named Command. Crystal Reports has saved your query as a database table and given it the name Command. You can change the name if you want.

Adding an SQL Command to a Repository

If you create an SQL command that can be used in more than one report, you may want to save it in the Repository. Doing so saves you the effort of recreating it from scratch. You would need only to drag it from the Repository to your new report.

When you're creating an SQL command that may be used in another report, be sure that the Add to Repository check box is checked before you click OK to exit the Add Command to Report dialog box. This saves the command to the Repository, making it available for later use in a different report.

When you add a command to the Repository, a dialog box asks you to supply a name for the new Repository object. Simply name the object and then click OK.

Modifying an SQL Command

Modifying an SQL command is similar to creating one. Here are the steps:

1. **In the Selected Tables pane of the Database Expert dialog box, find the command that you want to edit.**

2. **Right-click the command and choose Edit Command.**

   The Modify Command dialog box appears, as shown in Figure 20-4. The existing command appears in the left pane, although its appearance may vary from one implementation to another.

Figure 20-4:
Modify
Command
dialog box.

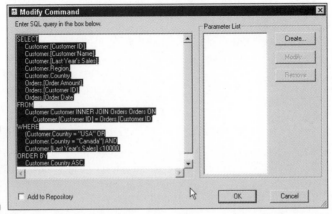

If the SQL command that you want to edit is in the Repository, the Edit Command menu option appears dimmed. As I mention in Chapter 9, you can't edit a Repository object. Instead, you must disconnect the command from the Repository before you can edit it. If this is the case, right-click the command and choose Disconnect from Repository, before you right-click the command again and choose Edit Command.

3. **Make whatever changes to the command that you want.**

4. **If you want to put the revised command in the Repository, click to add a check mark to the Add to Repository option. Otherwise, leave the option unchecked.**

5. **Click the OK button to execute the change.**

The revised command appears in Field Explorer under Database Fields. If you select any of the fields under the command, and then click the Field Explorer's browse button, a browse dialog box appears, displaying all the data that the report retrieved from that field. Figure 20-5 shows the result of browsing the command's Customer Name field.

Figure 20-5:
The new command returns the data in the Customer Name field.

Chapter 21

Programming with Crystal Reports .NET

. . . .

. . . .

*N*ET Framework is Microsoft's new application development architecture. .NET (pronounced "dot net") is designed to facilitate the development of Web applications, but it's also appropriate for applications that don't involve the Web.

Visual Studio .NET is Microsoft's integrated development environment (IDE) for .NET applications. It's a robust IDE that you can use to develop any application, from the smallest single-user application to the largest enterprise-wide multiuser application or Web-based e-commerce application. Crystal Reports .NET is an integral component of Visual Studio .NET. It has the distinction of being the only component of Visual Studio .NET that was not developed by Microsoft.

Using Microsoft's Visual Studio .NET

Visual Studio .NET is a tool intended for professional programmers. Casual code jockeys need not apply. VS .NET is massive and complex. It assumes that the programmers who use it are comfortable with object-oriented programming and Visual Basic, Visual C++, or Visual C#. For developing Web Services applications, they should also be fluent in XML.

Microsoft delivers Visual Studio .NET with three included development languages: Visual Basic .NET, Visual C++ .NET, and Visual C# .NET. Visual Basic .NET is different enough from the previous generation product (Visual Basic 6) to require a significant amount of new learning. Programmers are free to develop .NET applications in whichever of these languages they prefer or any other language, as long as it is .NET-compliant.

Most serious applications include a database of some sort. This is where Crystal Reports .NET comes in. Any application that includes a database needs a way of delivering query results and reports to users. Microsoft elected to bundle Crystal Reports .NET into Visual Studio .NET rather than develop a report writer of their own. Thus, most database-driven .NET applications, whether on the Web, a LAN, or a stand-alone computer, are likely to pass results to their users through reports generated by Crystal Reports .NET.

Crystal Reports in Visual Studio .NET

Crystal Reports .NET is designed to integrate seamlessly with the other components of Visual Studio .NET. After you open a project and make a connection to a database, you can create a report in much the same way that you do in stand-alone Crystal Reports 9.

Here's the procedure for accessing Crystal Reports .NET and producing a report, after your project is open and your database is connected:

1. **On the Visual Studio .NET View menu, choose Visual Studio .NET Solution Explorer.**

   Your project's name is displayed.

2. **In Visual Studio .NET Solution Explorer, right-click your project and choose Add. On the submenu that appears, choose Add New Item.**

   The Add New Item dialog box appears.

3. **In the Templates pane, double-click Crystal Report.**

4. **In Crystal Reports Gallery, select Using the Report Expert, As a Blank Report, or From an Existing Report.**

5. **Click OK.**

   You're now in the familiar Crystal Reports environment.

6. **Use your new skills to build your report.**

7. **Choose File⇨Save to save your finished report.**

Because Crystal Reports .NET is embedded in Visual Studio .NET, the appearance of your report on the screen looks a little different, but all the essential elements are there. Figure 21-1 shows Crystal Reports .NET in Design mode, with a report based on the Xtreme database in the workspace.

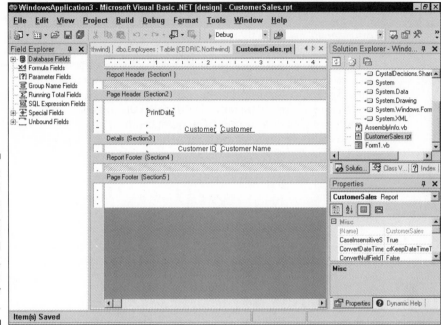

Figure 21-1:
Crystal
Reports
.NET,
embedded
in Visual
Studio .NET,
with a
partially
built report.

Because Crystal Reports .NET is built upon the Crystal Reports 8.5 code base, it doesn't include any of the features that I have identified as being new in Crystal Reports 9. Among other things, this means Crystal Reports .NET doesn't support XML or OLAP connectivity or SQL commands. It doesn't include the repository. It does, however include a runtime license and report viewing APIs that the Professional and Standard Editions lack.

Application Development in Visual Studio .NET

When developing an application with Visual Studio .NET, you must select a language that the application code will be written in. One of the most widely used languages for application development is Visual Basic 6. Visual Basic .NET represents a major upgrade to Visual Basic 6. Features have been added to make the language fully object-oriented. Some people perceive this as a mixed blessing. On one hand, the upgrade greatly increases the power of VB, putting it in the same class as Visual C++. On the other hand, it requires the programmer to adopt a new and probably alien way of thinking and working.

Because this book is about using Crystal Reports to create reports based on database data, and not about programming in Visual Basic, C++, C#, or any other language, I don't go into detail about how to write an application using the Visual Studio .NET IDE. I will state that after you have written your application, you can give it reporting functionality by calling up Crystal Reports .NET as outlined in the preceding section, creating a report, and then embedding the report at the appropriate spot in your application. The report becomes an integral part of the application. With program code, you can create an environment in which users can view the report with a simple menu selection or button click — without knowing anything about Crystal Reports.

Part VI
The Part of Tens

The 5th Wave

By Rich Tennant

"I appreciate that your computer has 256 colors. I just don't think that they all had to be used in one book report."

In this part . . .

The Part of Tens distills information found in various places throughout the book into lists of ten pithy pointers to better reports. It's a good idea to reread Chapter 22 before you start each new report-generation project and to reread Chapter 23 as you are wrapping up each project. These guidelines may help you to remember something that you could do to improve your report.

Chapter 22

Ten Things to Do Before You Create a Report

*W*ith a great report-writing tool such as Crystal Reports, you might reasonably assume that creating a report will be an easy task that will not require much thought or effort. That would be a bad assumption. Creating a high-quality report that truly meets users' needs requires considerable thought and effort even before you fire up Crystal Reports for the first time. You should put thought and effort into at least ten things before you apply fingers to keyboard.

Identify the Users

Identifying the users might seem obvious, but it's not as obvious as you might think. Sure, the person who asked you to create the report is probably someone who will use the report and is easily identified. But who else will benefit from using this report? Other people in your client's workgroup? Your client's manager? People in other workgroups or even other departments? Perhaps even people in other companies? It's important to find out who *all* the probable users are.

Interview the Users

After you identify all the people who could benefit from your report, it's important to find out what they need the report to tell them. What information should the report contain? How should the information be presented? The only way to get the full answer is to interview at least a representative of each different class of user. It's best to interview them all. What's unimportant to one class of users might be vital to another.

Arbitrate Conflicting Demands

It's almost certain that when you have a diverse user community, the needs of one group or individual will conflict with the needs of another. One group may want the information presented in one format, but a second group may absolutely insist on receiving the information in a different format. Someone has to find a compromise that's acceptable to all. As a neutral outside party, this arbitrator often turns out to be you.

Nail Down the Project's Scope

After everyone agrees on what they want, it's important to get agreement on *exactly* what will be included in the project. To make sure that the project doesn't keep expanding as you go along, get a signed agreement from the client on the scope of the project. This protects both the developer and the client. From the beginning, everyone knows what will be delivered.

Nail Down the Project's Schedule

After you know the project's scope, you can estimate how long it will take you to complete the project. Make sure you plan for adequate time to do a good job. If the schedule is agreed to in advance, you have a solid defense against the clients who want you to speed up development so that they can have the report sooner. Quality generally suffers when a reasonable schedule is accelerated.

Verify That the Necessary Data Is in the Database

If you're going to build a report based on data in a database, it helps if the data you need is actually in the database. Sometimes clients will ask for a report that their database can't support because the data just isn't there. You need to verify with a database query that the data you need is indeed present.

Determine How the Report Will Be Viewed

You can view a Crystal report in several ways. What is the primary way that your user community will view it? Will they view it on a computer that's connected to the database that the report is based on? If so, they'll be able to refresh the data to get up-to-the-minute reports. They will also be able to drill down for detail and view the report, including charts and maps, in color.

If the users will be looking primarily at printed reports, they'll not be able to drill down. The data in the reports will be a snapshot of the data when the report was printed, so it may not be up-to-date. Furthermore, if your report is printed on a black-and-white laser printer, color will not show up.

Design your report with your users in mind and optimize the report for best viewing.

Determine the Best Report Type for the Users' Needs

What's the best way to present your client's data? A standard report? A cross-tab report? An OLAP report? Based on the underlying data and how the users want it to be presented, choose the most appropriate report type and then build the report based on that type.

Get Agreement on the Report's Appearance

Users may have strong preferences on how they want the information presented. Their ideas of the ideal presentation may differ from what makes the most sense to you. Make sure you develop a report that clearly presents information that's of interest to all the user communities. This may require meetings of all concerned as well as some negotiation among various user groups. Make sure everyone will support the report's user interface before you put effort into developing it.

Decide Whether to Include Charts or Maps

Some types of reports can be immeasurably enhanced by the inclusion of appropriate charts or maps. Charts present the data in a way that goes directly to the viewer's brain. Sometimes columns of numbers just don't have the same effect. In those cases, adding charts or maps can be a good idea. In other cases, a chart would not add to an understanding of the data and might actually obscure it. Evaluate each case individually and decide whether charts or maps are appropriate.

Chapter 23

Ten Ways to Give Your Reports More Pizzazz

You say you want to make your reports more visually appealing? Crystal Reports can help you with that. In this chapter, I mention ten simple ways to help you lift your reports out of the category of ordinary into the rarified atmosphere of truly extraordinary. You can give your reports maximum impact by tastefully combining several of the techniques in this chapter.

Use the Correct Fonts

Beyond the bare facts presented in a report, you may also want it to convey a feeling or emotion. Perhaps you want the report to put the reader in a sober, strictly business frame of mind. Or you might want the report to playfully remind reader of things that are fun. You might want to call particular attention to certain parts of the report, while burying other parts in a way that makes them easy to overlook. You can accomplish much of this with a judicious choice of fonts.

A wide variety of font styles are available, and you can use several in the same report, although it's wise to not go overboard using different font styles. Three different styles are usually plenty. You can also vary the size of the font, and whether it is bold, italic, or underlined. By combining all these options, you can have your report project an image that enhances what the bare words and numbers in the report have to say.

Make Tasteful Use of Color

Reports that are meant to be viewed on a computer screen can make use of a full palette of color. So can reports that will be printed on a color printer. Color capability makes it feasible to incorporate charts and maps in your report, as well as graphical images. You can use color also to emphasize text elements or to set off drawing elements such as lines and boxes. You can even give different sections of the report their own unique background color.

Use your imagination to think of ways to use color to add impact to your reports. Remember, however, to not overuse color effects. Make sure that any color effects that you do use are appropriate to the material and what you are trying to communicate. Don't use multiple colors just because you can.

Enclose Text in Boxes

One way to make titles and important areas of text stand out is to enclose them in boxes. Crystal Reports makes it easy to enclose text in a box; simply drag the cursor over the text. You can give the box sharp or rounded corners, and you can give it any color available on you palette. Boxes are a good way to call attention to text.

Emphasize Objects with Drop Shadows

You can give a box, such as the one described in the preceding section, even more emphasis by giving it a drop shadow. The drop shadow makes the box appear to come out of the page in a 3-D effect. To get a drop shadow, just right-click the box and choose Format Box. In the Format Editor dialog box that appears, select the Drop Shadow option. When you click OK, the drop shadow appears on your box. The drop shadow feature is available only with rectangular boxes. If you round the corners of your box, the drop shadow feature becomes unavailable.

Produce a Consistent Appearance with Templates

You can determine many of the formatting details of a report with a template. Using a template also helps to maintain consistency from one report to the next. You could have one template for one type of report and another template for another type. Readers will become accustomed to seeing information presented in a consistent way from one report to the next.

Add an Image

An old bromide says that a picture is worth a thousand words. Sometimes that's true and sometimes it's not. When a picture can help to get a point across, use one. Crystal Reports makes it easy to insert graphical images into your reports wherever you want them. You can use this capability for corporate logos, photographs, drawings, or images of any kind.

Add a Chart

Numeric data presented in tabular form conveys the facts but often doesn't clearly show trends or relationships between data items. Charts, whether they are line charts, bar charts, pie charts, or some other kind, can show trends and relationships clearly. When trends or relationships in data are important, by all means use a chart to bring that point out and hammer it home.

Add a Map

For some kinds of reports, it's important to show readers where things are. If your data has anything to do with geographical locations, such as sales territories or political boundaries, Crystal Reports' mapping facility can make your report much more valuable. Maps cover the entire globe, showing countries as well as individual states and provinces.

Combine Two Objects with an Underlay

You can give your report a watermark effect by underlaying words or symbols in a light font beneath the main text of your report. You can also use this facility to position a chart or map beside the text that it refers to rather than above or below it. For example, with an underlay, you might line up a chart with the detail section that contains the data that the chart is drawn from.

Separate the Summary from the Details with Drilldown

The drill-down facility in Crystal Reports makes use of the fact that more and more people are viewing reports on their computer screens rather than reading them from pieces of paper. Drill-down capability allows viewers to interact with the report, viewing detail when they want to see it and skimming past it when they don't. A person can quickly get the gist of what they want from the report, and then move on to make decisions based on what they've learned.

Index

● *G* ●

Notes

Notes

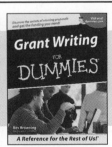

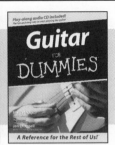

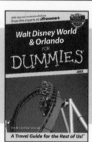

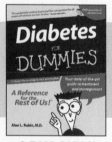

FOR DUMMIES®

Helping you expand your horizons and realize your potential

GRAPHICS & WEB SITE DEVELOPMENT

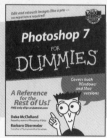
0-7645-1651-5

0-7645-1643-4

0-7645-0895-4

Also available:

Adobe Acrobat 5 PDF
For Dummies
(0-7645-1652-3)
ASP.NET For Dummies
(0-7645-0866-0)
ColdFusion MX for Dummies
(0-7645-1672-8)
Dreamweaver MX For
Dummies
(0-7645-1630-2)
FrontPage 2002 For Dummies
(0-7645-0821-0)

HTML 4 For Dummies
(0-7645-0723-0)
Illustrator 10 For Dummies
(0-7645-3636-2)
PowerPoint 2002 For
Dummies
(0-7645-0817-2)
Web Design For Dummies
(0-7645-0823-7)

PROGRAMMING & DATABASES

0-7645-0746-X

0-7645-1626-4

0-7645-1657-4

Also available:

Access 2002 For Dummies
(0-7645-0818-0)
Beginning Programming
For Dummies
(0-7645-0835-0)
Crystal Reports 9 For
Dummies
(0-7645-1641-8)
Java & XML For Dummies
(0-7645-1658-2)
Java 2 For Dummies
(0-7645-0765-6)

JavaScript For Dummies
(0-7645-0633-1)
Oracle9i For Dummies
(0-7645-0880-6)
Perl For Dummies
(0-7645-0776-1)
PHP and MySQL For
Dummies
(0-7645-1650-7)
SQL For Dummies
(0-7645-0737-0)
Visual Basic .NET For
Dummies
(0-7645-0867-9)

LINUX, NETWORKING & CERTIFICATION

0-7645-1545-4

0-7645-1760-0

0-7645-0772-9

Also available:

A+ Certification For Dummies
(0-7645-0812-1)
CCNP All-in-One Certification
For Dummies
(0-7645-1648-5)
Cisco Networking For
Dummies
(0-7645-1668-X)
CISSP For Dummies
(0-7645-1670-1)
CIW Foundations For
Dummies
(0-7645-1635-3)

Firewalls For Dummies
(0-7645-0884-9)
Home Networking For
Dummies
(0-7645-0857-1)
Red Hat Linux All-in-One
Desk Reference For Dummies
(0-7645-2442-9)
UNIX For Dummies
(0-7645-0419-3)

Available wherever books are sold.
Go to www.dummies.com or call 1-877-762-2974 to order direct